INTERKNOT

INTERKNOT

✦

Adventures in Internet dating

David Osterczy

iUniverse, Inc.

New York Lincoln Shanghai

INTERKNOT
Adventures in Internet dating

iUniverse, Inc.

For information address:
iUniverse, Inc.
2021 Pine Lake Road, Suite 100
Lincoln, NE 68512
www.iuniverse.com

ISBN: 0-595-32524-6 (pbk)
ISBN: 0-595-66629-9 (cloth)

Printed in the United States of America

Foreword

I am a storyteller.

First and foremost and above everything else in my life, I am a storyteller. I have always been this way. I will never change. It is who I am.

I can remember being nine or ten years old and playing with matches on the window of my bedroom in the Bronx. There were these cute red fuzzy ball thingies on long red strands of yarn that my mother had constructed as a sort of window shade. Well I can tell you my surprise when they all came screaming down around me, ablaze, as I must have been a bit careless in my pyrotechnic youthful exuberance.

So I scooped up the charred remains and attempted to re-construct the shades, to no avail. When my mother returned home she was inundated with stories of space aliens with ray guns and green helmets that made funny noises. The aliens in their haste had used up all the fuel in their ship and were seeking alternate means to power their vessel. The fuzzy red balls seemed like a good possibility but they needed to test this theory by first burning a few. Unfortunately they burned too well, leaving nothing behind. The aliens then beat a hasty retreat, leaving me to hold the bag.

She would normally have killed me for nearly burning down the entire house. However, she was too busy laughing her ass off at my sheer audacity for even attempting to explain away my actions.

I had the most amazingly creative imagination as a child. I would weave tall tales of fabulous adventures on alien worlds or far off lands with wonderful creatures. I once imagined that my cousin Michael was eaten by a herd of wild giraffes while standing in the lobby of my building as I watched from the elevator window. I was very young and truly believed that this event occurred. I was so distraught over these events that it prompted my cousin to have his dad drive him to my house to prove to me that he didn't live in the belly of a beast. He still laughs heartily about that until this day.

Storytelling has been both a gift and a burden to me. In relationships with friends, when you can weave tall tales for their enjoyment or put a humorous spin on a real event that occurred, they tend to stick around a while. In the business world however, telling stories can get you fired from a job in a hurry. I'm not talking about lying here. I'm talking about *talking*. Telling tales to others when the only thing the boss wants is the job done, like, yesterday, with your mouth closed and the operation running smoothly. My mouth has gotten me into more trouble in the business world than I could fit in this book! In relationships however, it has won me many friends and keeps me in good standing with most of my ex-girlfriends. I said *most*; nothing in life is one hundred percent!

So, where do you begin with so many stories and so many opinions? He said, she said, who's right, who's wrong? It can be maddening and the very mention of the word "dating" elicits such passionate feelings in so many people that this book could not contain enough words to describe it. Throw the Internet into the mix and, well, you've put an entirely new spin on a very old game. The very mention of the word "game" presupposes a rulebook. Rules of Internet Dating? Heaven forbid! Why you ask? Simply put, the very rules you follow to open the door for some may close the door to others permanently! You see, the Internet dating scene is non-forgiving, so when you e-mail your "love," your first mistake is usually your last. No second chances, no explanations, you're just toast. They're on to the next profile and you don't even exist!

This book, for what it's worth, is the culmination and continuation of two years of back-breaking, gut-wrenching, emotional research into the human condition and examines it under the microscope from many different perspectives. Those perspectives being male-based and female-based and the totally different ways that we handle relationships, rejection, emotion, sex, communication, love, longing, loneliness, and perhaps even some insight into why we react the way we do. You're going to read stories that will make you laugh, cry, cringe, think and wonder, and perhaps some that you will simply not believe. But judge not the characters herein, as you indeed may be looking into a proverbial mirror.

I do not profess to be a professional anything in giving you my perspectives on this phenomenon called online dating that is sweeping the globe. I am only here as the narrator with some amazing stories to share myself, take it or leave it!

The characters running through this book come from many walks of life. Some are wealthy and some are poor. Some have open hearts and some are so beaten down that they shouldn't be dating a rock, but they all have one thing in common, that being a passionate desire to meet the person of their dreams and end forever their online persona that may mask the true person within.

Every person, every story, every word written in this context is real and happened in real life, even if much of it was "cyber-life." All the names have been changed to protect the anonymity of the people who volunteered to bare their souls for me, as are any e-mail addresses, telephone number and others things of that nature, for disclosure reasons, but the stories are word for word as received, including the multitude of e-mails contained in the text of this manuscript.

"Why are you boring us with all these stupid details, dude?" Well…. because I can!…And also because you need to know that this is a work of non-fiction and as real as it gets.

So for all the millions of loving people who search for their soul mate online, who shell out their hard earned bucks to buy this book, I thank you. It is my sincere hope that after reading these words you realize once and for all that you are not alone. That's right, you're not the only one who "THAT" happened to!

Enjoy my silliness,

…me…just me…

David

Foreword and a half: Cast of Characters

Yours Truly, David

So I was 21 years old and battered from playing a particularly grueling hockey game that afternoon. I decided to entertain myself in a local watering hole on Kingsbridge Road in the Bronx. I sat down at the bar and ordered a beer from Teddy the Red. After a few minutes, in walks my friend Patrick. Patrick is stewed to the gills. Patrick is 6 feet 5 inches, 250 pounds and as Irish as they come. He spots me immediately and proceeds to give me the sort of hug reserved for male friends only when you are extremely drunk. I was then 6 foot 1 and 150 pounds dripping wet. Patrick ordered a beer.

After much conversation and bragging, he decided that we *both* needed to go to the bathroom and attempt to see who could break the most bathroom wall tiles with their bare fists. After my fourth beer and an equal number of shots of Jack Daniels, this seemed reasonable to me. The loser would pay for the next round of drinks. I lost. He drank. I bled profusely. I was a man. Men do not complain.

Shortly before passing out from loss of blood, a vision of beauty the likes of which I had never seen before walks over to me. Her name was Debbie. She was all of 17 years old. Her face shone like Joan of Arc. Her eyes were deep pools of dark chocolate. Her hair was like caramel colored silk.

This angel of mercy proceeded to swab the blood off of my right fist with a clean bar rag, removing chunks of porcelain as she went, and finally wrapping the hand in paper towels, no doubt saving me from a very messy evening as well as a trip to the emergency room. I was smitten. After several drinks she left for the ladies room. As soon as she departed, Harry decided to sit in her chair. He needed to save me from this girl who he said was "bad news." That was the nicest thing he said. Harry was not anyone I really knew, he was just a guy from an adjacent neighborhood who hung out with guys that I did not like. He was white trash in every sense of the word.

Upon her return, Debbie was not pleased that Harry had stolen her chair. Not pleased at all. She began to discuss this predicament with Harry as he stood up and became very obnoxious and threatening. Everyone in the bar was watching at this point to see what would transpire between the jerk and this seemingly innocent creature. Did she back down? Did she start to cry? Did she run for fear of her life? Not my Deb. She balled up her fist, swung with all she had, and knocked Harry over his barstool tipping over the stool, as well as several other inebriated patrons who were oblivious to the proceedings.

I was so in love with this girl! Teddy threw her out of the bar for starting a brawl. I followed her out and gave her the hug that she needed. Four weeks later we got our first apartment together. She was 17. I was 22. We had a very stormy relationship together due in no small part to our inexperience and the fact that we were basically still children. Our fights were legendary. Our sex together was even better. One night while going through our dresser, Deb discovered a purple BB. It was not originally purple. This was a brass BB used in pellet guns. I had several of them when I was a kid and some of the shot still survived. I guess over time the oxidation of the brass pellet turned it to purple.

Deb asked me what it was and I proceeded to tell her the story of the kingdom of the purple bee bees. Every time I would tell her one of these make believe fairy tales she would look on in wide-eyed wonderment and laugh heartily, totally adoring these stories. The stories have grown to include many characters over the last 20 years or so, and excite and thrill my children to this day. No, I will not share them with you here; this is not a children's book after all. Perhaps in volume two!

Brando

During my seven-year relationship/marriage to Debbie, I played in an amazing band. The lead singer and guitarist was named Doug. He looked like David Bowie, played a mean guitar and had a voice that blended very well with my harmonious meanderings. Our drummer was named Brando and is one of my best friends to this day.

Brando is a talented photographer, a health food junkie, killer drummer, and a handsome devil. A few years after the band broke up, Brando met Nina. They seemed to be meant for each other. I never liked her though as I thought her nose was placed a bit too high in the air for my liking. They married several years later in San Francisco, moved to a beautiful home in Connecticut near the Long

Island Sound and seemed to have it all, money, home, business, and a gorgeous new son.

Several months after their son was born, Nina disappeared with him to parts unknown to Brando. After frantically searching, he located her in Maine and eventually convinced her to return home with their new baby. She did, but not in quite the way he had intended, as when she returned it was with her lesbian lover. They moved into his bedroom as a couple and informed him that if indeed he did want to remain, it would be as a resident of his son's bedroom. He tried every way of reasoning, including calling the authorities, but to no avail.

By the end of the divorce proceedings, he was left near destitute, very bitter, very backstabbed, and very, very alone. This was the frame of mind he was in upon his early baby steps into online dating almost five years ago.

Brando brings a very different perspective to this book than I, yet his voice needs to be heard as he has much to say, albeit in a slightly different style than my own.

Anna

After Debbie and I ended our marriage I received custody of our three-year-old daughter. Well, let me tell you, with a full time management position on Wall Street and a teeny tot at home, I was scared to death. So I discussed this with one of the senior partners of the firm and they gave me a pink slip with a very nice severance package after only 2 years with them. I started my own photography company, affording me both the time as well as the income to raise my daughter. Dating was the last thing on my mind, but it's amazing how many women come out of the woodwork when you're a 29 year old guy and a single dad with a nice car, decent income, and kinda cute to boot (if I do say so myself)! I dated on and off; nothing serious for almost five years, until I entered the home of a single mom with the most adorable big brown-eyed, curly-haired, three-year-old angel I'd ever seen. This little pistol sat in my lap as I loaded the camera after the shoot was finished, looked up at me with her puppy dog eyes and said, "You're not gonna leave my mommy are you?" before burying her head under my chin.

I was done. This little weenie had my heart in her hands immediately, although I would probably never have seen her again if not for the fact that her mother bounced her check to me (a sign I should have heeded). We started to date, lived together for ten years, had two amazing, smart, wonderful kids together, but in the end grew too far apart.

I entered the Internet dating scene about nine months later, with a deep hope that I would not embarrass myself too much as I hadn't had a date in over eleven years. One of the first girls I met was Anna. She is a senior level executive at a major New York corporation possessing a great job, great income, lots of responsibility, and lots of stress. Anna had little time to date. She worked, she took care of her home, and she worked some more. She was content with her life and didn't really need a man. Her children were grown and both on their own and in relationships. She was content that is, until two planes took out the World Trade Center on that horrible day we will never forget in 2001. She suddenly realized after the dust had settled how very alone she was. She decided then and there to make every effort to never be alone again.

She put a very sketchy profile on an Internet dating site containing no photo, as she is in a very public position and didn't want to feel embarrassed if any of her co-workers saw her there. She would cruise the profiles every now and again, but never contacted anyone. Then she saw my profile. She was floored. She sent me a very nice note and we chatted for several days until we decided to meet at a coffee house in Nyack, New York.

So there I am waiting and she's late. My cell phone rings. She is lost. She got off the wrong exit on the New York State Thruway and drove south into New Jersey. I give her directions on how to alleviate the situation. She calls me back in fifteen minutes more lost than ever on a dark road with no signs and unable to tell me where she is.

This situation continued for another thirty minutes with everyone at the coffee house being quite amused with the scenario (I can only ascertain from the attention of the other patrons that I speak a bit *loudly* when conversing on my cell). When she finally arrived an hour late, she received a standing ovation from everyone who had been listening to our conversation. She was cute with wavy blonde hair, amber colored eyes and perfectly polished nails. She was classy yet down to earth. She had a personality that would put anyone at ease, no doubt the reason why she rose to such a prestigious position at her job.

The date was all that you could ask for and ended with a smooching session in my pickup truck that left all the windows fogged.

We dated exclusively for nine months. She became a fixture at my apartment. My ferrets, Flash and Snowball, loved to terrorize her. She grew with me in ways that had eluded her in all past relationships. She fell head over heels in love with me and I got close. "Close" is *close*, but not all the way there. I wasn't ready for a woman of her substance and hurt her deeply.

Understand the difference in where our mindsets were when Anna and I met. She had all her ducks in a row and was ready to find her lifetime partner. I was still looking for my ducks, having misplaced them in a recent divorce, and just wanted to feel cared for by someone, hell by anyone!

Our timing was off. Timing is everything in relationships, as many of the stories in this book will convey. Sexual attraction, chemistry, laughter and compatibility are crucial for a good relationship, but if the timing is not there, you can throw the rest out the window as the relationship is doomed from the start.

She hated me for several months, but eventually we began to speak and met for coffee. Our friendship survived her broken heart because I refused to let it end. I thank God that I count her as one of my closest friends to this day. Anna is a gem.

Linda

After Anna and I parted company, I entertained two back-to-back passionate five week-long relationships. One with my friend to this day, Seebee, and one with a young lady who I pray is in deep therapy so as to not kill anyone with her foul temper tantrums, Blue. (Yes, those are nicknames. Live with it!)

These two young ladies left me shaken and battered. Seebee broke my heart, but in a way so gentle that I still adore her to this day. I can't even view a photo of her now, two years hence, without releasing a heavy sigh. Blue broke my trust of women. She had deep issues that I could not begin to understand or deal with. Common misunderstandings became battles and everything was my fault in her eyes. A shame, as our personalities were in many ways a better match than any woman I had met before or since.

Believe it or not, at this juncture I helped Anna set up her new online profile on another Internet site. And about that same time, while in a shared office with Anna, as we chatted back to back on our computers (we had renewed our friendship and it was stronger than ever, without the…um…benefits), I met Linda.

Linda entered the cyber world of dating after her marriage of nine years ended with her loving husband leaving abruptly. They had the sort of sexual relationship that most only dream of, and for nine years explored their sexuality together with no boundaries, no limits, and total freedom to explore each other's fantasies. I guess he had done all he needed to do with a woman and now decided that perhaps men might be a greater challenge. In so doing, he broke the heart of a wonderful, kind woman, as well as her three children who had grown quite accustomed to his being there. Of course the kids now hated him, yet somehow blamed her. The divorce was typical. She needed to buy out his share of the house, leaving her penniless, heartbroken, and searching for anyone kind enough to just get her through one more day.

Linda was so afraid that I would not be attracted to her on our first date that I decided to try to remove all pressure by bringing along my two youngest kids *and* Anna for support. Although physically she may not have been my type, her stellar personality and beautiful smile made up for any shortcomings. It was an adorable date, with stolen kisses in restaurants and behind trucks. It started a pattern of friendship that I cherish to this day, as we have been there for each other in times of need and heartache. She has become my bouncing post, and I hers. Her stories will be some of the cutest in this book, and a few may even include me!

Freeda

At about the same time that I met Linda, I was in the process of being terminally harassed by a girl on a chat site named Freeda. She had spiky burgundy hair and an attitude that any punk rocker would be proud of. I really thought she was nuts, but she wiggled her way into my heart by being oblivious to the fact that I generally ignored her, as well as having the most interesting stories to tell about her dating misadventures. After a period of time, I just knew she was destined to be a friend, with our very first meeting being when she interviewed with me for her part in this book.

She was as nutty in person as she was online and on the phone! She writes as she speaks, with no pause for breath, commas, periods, exclamation points or anything that would slow the bombardment of information coming your way. She is adorable and will open your eyes with her stories, as well as her insights into the male psyche.

Charley

Several months later I received an e-mail from a young lady named Charley. She was cute and aggressive and seemed to have no problems with going after what-ever she deemed a good fit for her. We chatted promisingly for several weeks and then decided to meet in Pompton Lakes, New Jersey where I lived at the time. She had no problem driving the 40 minutes to meet me.

Charley was divorced several years earlier and has joint custody of her two children with her ex-husband. They have a good relationship with each other, and that's always a good thing when dating a woman. It says a lot about them, but not everything. I call her the cat lady because when we first met she had ten cats. (Ewwwww!) She's down to six now, but believe it or not, you wouldn't know she even had *one* upon entering her home. Clean lady: also a good thing! Long, flowing blonde hair, emerald green eyes and a body to tempt even a saint were nice touches as well.

Our first date was one of those "float going home" kind of dates. Silly, passionate, touchy-feely, friendly and ending on a very nice note. Our second date will take up the better part of a later chapter as it was definitely something to remember!

Swayne

Somewhere along this timeline I began seeking a softball team to practice with. That's where I met Swayne. If we were any more similar we'd have to be in the same body. We have the same look, same height, same build and same nutty sense of humor, but with one glaring difference. He's never been married and has no kids.

Swayne runs a large division of a major pharmaceutical company. He has a busy life and a great career. He has dated on and off for many years and has indeed had a few long-term relationships, but none lasting more than five years.

He decided at 44 years of age that enough was enough. He had accomplished in his career what he had always envisioned, but a family was nowhere to be seen and that hurt him deeply. He is not one of the many "confirmed bachelors" out there. He is a sweet, wonderful lonely guy that just wants to come home to the same girl every night.

So, he placed his first ad on the Internet four years ago in the hopes that the woman he has no time to meet in everyday life might just seek him out in her spare time online. His stories will entertain you as they have entertained me.

These are our players, our characters and our friends who will bare their souls in stories, heartbreaks, wondrous victories, as well as crushing defeats. They are all my friends and are all very human. There will be many others here as well, but these six, along with myself, will be the stream meandering through this book against the backdrop of the cyber world and the many souls that we have all encountered on our journey through life in our earnestness to find the person of our dreams who has eluded us lo these many years.

Dedication

"Where's Sherry?" I asked my son Sammy.

"She's sleeping already Dad. She's a pee-pee head!"

It was 11:45 last night and indeed, Sherry had crawled into the bottom bunk in their room. I kneeled next to her bed and just stared in amazement at this child shining with such beauty in her peaceful slumber...and she didn't even brush her teeth! I moved just close enough to brush her silky brown, curly hair away from her adorable face. I could not stop, as I was just awed by the knowledge that I had been a loving part of the life of this wonderful, spirited child. I caressed my fingers through her hair for a long while as she let out the tiniest, happy little girl sighs reserved only for Daddy. Suddenly, in typical Sherry fashion, she let out an annoyed sounding grumble, the same sound she's made since her birth: a combination of James Brown singing and a 90–year-old annoyed Jewish woman. "Oyyyyyyyyyyyyy HEY!"

I exited her room with an ear-to-ear smile, thinking that the apple doesn't fall too far from the tree. I returned to my bedroom where Sammy had promised he would not fall asleep on my bed if I let him stay up "just a little while to watch you write." He didn't stay up, but instead lay sprawled across my bed like a conquering army, spewing covers and pillows everywhere in his wake.

Again I was kneeling next to a bed. I smelled my only son's hair and leaned back to sit on the floor. I sat there for what seemed like a very long time, tears welling up in my eyes as I realized exactly how much I love him. Once again I was caressing my fingers through the hair of one of my babies. Only a parent could understand the intense love that flowed through me at that moment as I watched my son's chest rise and fall with every breath he took. At nine and eleven, my weenies and I share a bond that warms me like a quilted blanket in moments of deep coldness and loneliness.

At that moment my thoughts turned to my 21-year-old daughter Melanie who is away at school, and how desperately I miss my beautiful, proud, spirited, brilliant daughter. We had some hard times together after the separation with Sam and Sher's mom, and it hurt our relationship. Thankfully, God gives us second chances, and all the mistakes I had made with my eldest I have learned to avoid with my two youngest.

Again, I was caressing Sammy's temples as another thought occurred to me. I realized that the unconditional and indescribable love that I feel for my children is exactly the type of love I desire to feel for a woman, a love which has somehow eluded me my entire life. My son unconsciously moved closer so that I could better rub his sweet face, a face that has never known a frown, a scowl, or anything akin to cruelty as he is perhaps the warmest and most loving human being I have ever had the honor to know.

As I carried him to his bed and he clung to me like bark to a tree, my thoughts again turned to the woman who will someday win my heart with her smile, her kindness, her silliness and intelligence, her attitude and sarcastic wit, and her passionate love for me and the three children it has been my pleasure to have raised.

I do not know where she resides. I do not know what she looks like. But I can feel her seeking me out every minute of every day as she reads through profile after boring profile, and yet somehow misses mine yet again. This book is dedicated to Sammy, Sherry and Melanie, and to the woman that will one day win their hearts and mine.

Yeah, I'm a romantic. So sue me.

Acknowledgements

Many thanks to all who have contributed to the creation of this book:

Editor: Angel C. Kuo
Cover Design: Debbie Dwoskin
Photograph of Author by Sherry Osterczy

Contents

Foreword. v

Foreword and a half: Cast of Characters ix

Dedication xvii

Acknowledgements xix

CHAPTER 1   Your best foot forward. 1

The profile, your online persona, is the first line of attack. This is what you want the rest of the word to see. Mess up here and you're throwing your money away!

CHAPTER 2   First contact. 19

Discusses the many different ways that people say "Hi!" and some initial responses.

CHAPTER 3   "I am the ONE for you! By the way, what was your name again?" 35

Passionate e-mails that never amounted to a date, and often not even a phone conversation.

CHAPTER 4   "Um, like, how old WAS that photo?" 71

Dating horror stories too terrible to be printed anywhere else.

CHAPTER 5   "Why is this bar so empty tonight?". 91

The popularity of Internet dating and why it has become a word-wide phenomenon.

CHAPTER 6   Can I get another hit of that?. 106

The addictive nature of the interactive sites and how online chatting becomes a world unto itself.

CHAPTER 7   The games people play. 132

How the opposite sex hides behind the Internet and why they do.

CHAPTER 8   The hook and bait 143
Online predators and where they live.

CHAPTER 9   "Did I miss something here?" 155
Unexplainable events and what some people do when it happens to them!

CHAPTER 10   "Can you put that back on please?" 172
The X-rated chapter.

CHAPTER 11   Success stories 192
How, when and why it works, and how it feels when it does, even if the success is only temporary.

CHAPTER 12   The writers. 206
The very best e-mails from the most amazing minds with responses from me.

CHAPTER 13   Interknot Knotes 222
The final word: Insights of the denizens on exactly what this all means!

1

Your best foot forward

IZITONLYME???
Photographer seeks brains and style, to match beauty and guile:

<u>Describing myself:</u>

Hmmm, never had to describe myself in a box before! Well, here goes. 45, puppy dog brown eyes, and shortish brown hair that's just the right length to run your fingers through!!! I'm very physical, emotional, affectionate, (with the right lady) and there aren't many things I won't try. I love photography, writing, building things with my hands, laughing 'till it hurts, baseball, hockey, staying in great shape, cooking an awesome meal and sharing it with someone special, snuggling close on the couch, sleeping together like a pretzel, kissing for hours with the right partner and waking up together, smiling, in the morning. I'm tan and fit, love the outdoors, and I've got energy to burn. I've never smoked, always stayed in shape, (except for 2 weeks in 1975, but we'll talk) and plan to continue that, as I like how I feel about ME when I do. Honesty is very important to me. I'm a huge sports fan, but you'll never find me watching a game for hours (playoffs not included) unless of course I'm at the game, hopefully with you! I'm a photographer, writer, musician, sci-fi channel, cartoon network fan and a loving daddy. I love to love, but haven't loved the right woman for so long that I've almost forgotten how amazing it feels. To simply be able to come home again and just KNOW, just totally know that you're loved…To just sit and laugh together until our stomachs hurt, have tickle fights, pillow fights, and then, suddenly catch a spark in each other's eyes and just feel it's right…as I look in your eyes, and KNOW…I'm home. oh and p.s. lest you think I'm just another "nice guy", I assure you there is a bad boy twinkle in my eyes and other venues that has been described as irresistible. Dare you find out?…*grin *

<u>Describing my ideal match:</u>

Everything starts with the first date. If you simply float home afterwards, feet never touching the ground, you KNOW there's going to be more…OKAY!

Ready? Here goes. You are athletic, but all girl. You look equally stunning in a black velvet dress as you do in one of my football jerseys. You live to laugh, to love, to kiss for hours on end, to hold and be held and you take great pride in your ability to please the right man. Honesty is very important to you and petty people turn you totally off. You enjoy sporting events, anything creative, anything outdoors, but mostly the company of one good man (oh, and if you have your own baseball glove, that'd be cool!). Snuggling up close, in my lap watching an old movie on TV with a big bowl of popcorn is preferable to sitting and yelling in a smoky bar. Sipping a great red wine together in front of a roaring fireplace. Acting like you're 13 years old, rolling in the grass, being silly, hitting a baseball, sudden and spontaneous passion, playing Frisbee, sitting at an outdoor coffee house in the Village at 2 in the morning on a Saturday and laughing like life was your personal servant, that's you. Wanting to once in your life feel your stomach do flip-flops when I come into sight, but not so desperately needing it because you're already a happy grounded person. A woman with the strength to bring out the very best in me as I do in her. A woman who understands that someday we may disagree about something and has the capacity to discuss, and not run, as none of us are perfect things, but together we can be so much better than we are alone. Oh yeah, if you also like snowball fights, watching cartoons on Saturday morning, boogie boarding, debating intelligently, and DID I MENTION KISSING? we may be a match......and; finally a woman who wants to come home, look into MY eyes, and know, that she's home. Oh and PULEEEEZE no "winks"!!! SAY SOMETHING!!!

This was the profile that I submitted to Match.com, one of the most popular dating sites on the Internet, way back sometime in July of 2001. The immediate response I received pretty much floored me! I fully expected to get *some* responses, especially since my being a photographer allowed me to take my own photos and I think I looked kinda, sorta cute in them. I had no idea of the sheer volume of e-mail I would receive in the first week alone. It was a daunting task attempting to answer everyone, and while it was pretty easy answering the people that seemed intelligent, nice, and had a cute photo,...then there were "the others."

What do you say to someone you have no interest in meeting, but whose feelings you don't want to hurt? "Geez," you think. "What do I say to this person? I'm not attracted to them and they meet *none* of my criteria. I wonder if they actually even *read* my profile."

The long process of learning how very different the cyber world of dating is from "real life" can take quite a bit of time, and can be a very painful experience if you let it. Rules of etiquette and normalcy do not apply to the cyber world. You soon learn to speak an entirely different online language, especially once you start to "chat live"…Oy vey!

LOL, ROFLMAO, BRB, TTFN, WTF and countless others all have meanings that can leave you totally lost in the sauce and feeling like an ass if you don't get the lingo. Without asking, "What does that mean?" it can be like going to a different country. It takes a wee bit of time to learn about your surroundings, get familiar with the customs and the language, and pick up a few friends who like you enough to teach you the pitfalls to avoid and the tricks of the trade.

For every person you successfully date, you will find that you'll make five friends who you chat with regularly, both online and sometimes over the phone. Friends who will always be there to listen to you as you listen to them. You will likely never meet as there is no physical attraction, but the chemistry for a budding friendship is undeniable, and that is always a welcome thing.

This profile, though relatively unchanged, has been updated by me multiple times due to the fact that situations change in a person's life and as a result, the person also changes. The main reason to keep updating your profile (making small changes to the text) at least on Match.com, is because as you update your profile, you appear higher in the search parameters on the site and therefore your profile can be viewed many more times, especially by new members.

Well, I could go on like this for thirty more pages or so, but I'm even beginning to bore myself! Soooooo…I'm going to re-introduce you to some of my victims…um, I mean, some of my *friends*, who are going to be featured in this book.

First, we've got my buddy Freeda. She is an absolute pisser! Forty years old, looks thirty, acts and dresses sixteen, and we can talk about anything together, and we do! She holds nothing back, is totally in your face, and the guy who eventually ends up with her, will *never* have a dull moment for the rest of his life. The following is some of the text in her online profile, which, like mine, has changed over a period of time, as you'll probably be able to tell.

<u>Where is the best place to go on a Date?</u>

Does not really matter were a person goes as long as they have a good time and get to know one another on the same level.

<u>Where will you be in 3 years from now?</u>

Does not matter where I am but I know this I will still be the same person I am today only older and wiser.

<u>What really makes you happy and what makes you sad?</u>

It makes me sad that there is very little humanatism left in the world and people should be a little nice to one another. Happy life in general for I like who I am and the things I have in life.

<u>I'd just like to Add….</u>

I find that most of the men on this sight do not have pics (pictures) and to be perfectly honest I'm getting tired of getting them and deleting them so please have a pic of yourself on here as it just makes things less complicated and easier for all concerned.
Thank You.

Okay, okay, I know. Not too much info there, but that's because most of the info on that site is in "check-off boxes," and I'm not going to show you those! TUFF! Freeda has been dating online, on and off since September 2000, and has some really interesting subjects to discuss. You are simply not going to believe some of the things that she's done, and especially some of the antics that she's planning!

It totally amazes me and many of the women that I speak to the sheer volume of people who come to the Internet to find love but don't even post a photo. I mean geez! What's the point? If you didn't want to put up a pic, then why not spend a whole lot less money and just put an ad in the local newspaper? YIKES! What's wrong with these folks? I know, I know, there are always extenuating circumstances and a very good reason why some people don't put up a photo. But I figure if you really want to meet someone and you're reasonably attractive, then get some decent shots taken of yourself and post the darn things online!

As a guy who's been a professional photographer for most of his life, it also drives me absolutely batty when there *is* a photo or three on the site, but they're so fuzzy that you can barely even make out if the girl is a blonde, has a mustache, or sideburns, or…WHATEVER!!! AAAGGGHHHHH!!! GET A CAMERA FOR CRIPESAKE!!!

Okay…most of the online community would have read my all caps text as the Internet equivalent of "yelling." And they would have been correct. *Smile* Sorry about that. I get very passionate over the silliest of things!

Oh! Another thing! Why would an attractive woman put a profile online and write *absolutely nothing* about herself or about the type of guy she's looking for? I guess there are those out there who expect that looks alone will win a great guy. The shame of it is that she probably *will* get a tremendous amount of responses to her ad based on a really sexy photograph. It just may not be the sort of responses that she is ultimately looking for. You see, finding the right type of person for *you* online means that you have to be pretty descriptive of who you truly are and the person you are seeking as your soul-mate. This can be a very difficult exercise, as you really have to look in the mirror, take a deep breath, take full stock of your attributes, and ultimately ask yourself, "Why am I really doing this and what is my goal?"

These can be soul searching types of questions and you may indeed need to turn to close friends for help, because it is very tough to write a paragraph or two defining who you really are, who you are looking for, and what you will do when you find them…and be assured they are out there, so you'd *better* be sure you're ready!

And be honest here guys, because the women *truly* can see right through the crap. They truly do have a power. Yes, that's right, they *are* smarter than us! So if you're unemployed, living at home in your mom's basement, and don't even get cable, you may want to wait a wee bit to place that ad online.

All right, that's enough guy bashing for one day. I really could go the other way with this just as easily, but I do believe that the teensy little "lies" that women put into their profiles online, they actually believe. So that makes it okay…I think.

There's a sort of analogy running through my head that I just need to touch on here. As far as the profile viewing is concerned, it's sort of like walking through a crowded mall on a Saturday evening. Every shape and size is walking past you. Some are unattractive, some are kind of attractive, and some make your knees weak and your neck stiff as they walk by while you try desperately not to let them see you notice them. Online it's the same, but much easier and less painful. You scroll down until you see a face that makes you smile and then you click on the face and hope that they have something intelligent to say and that they're looking for someone just like you. There are few things more crushing than finding the face of your dreams and then reading through a profile that has no substance, charm, wit, sense of humor, or anything akin to a spark of human intelligence.

Another of the very yuckiest of feelings is when you do find the profile of your dreams. They're absolutely gorgeous! The profile is descriptive and intelligently written! They're funny, the right height, build, sex, everything! They describe you to a tee! Your heart soars! It's the person you've been looking for your entire life!!! Then, you read the last line…"Don't have kids, don't want any, and don't wanna date anyone who does…" and your heart sinks into the dungeon it was in before you logged online.

Now some of you out there are bobbing your little heads up and down in a frenzy right now, either laughing your tail off because all of these things are common to you, or getting all melancholy because these are not memories that you care to relive. There is a larger group of you however whom none of these things have happened to, because you've never dated online, never intend to, and just bought this book because maybe you liked the cover or perhaps your girlfriend told you to. For those of you in the last category, you're in for the ride of your life, because things happen in online dating that you will just not believe.

Now for those of you in the first category, grab a drink, get out your hankies, and prepare to find much of yourself herein. I can say these things because I have lived through them and came out on the other side of sanity a better person because of it. I have spent multiple hours crying on the phone with friends made online who just needed to cry to someone, anyone, willing to listen. I have made friendships that will last a lifetime, because once you share your heart with someone with absolutely no ulterior motive, you couldn't beat their friendship off with a stick. That's the way it should be. Yes, I do think so indeed.

Now here is my friend Linda. If every woman had her personality, and her open views on sexuality, there would be world peace, like tomorrow! Why? Simple. She is down to earth, smart as a tack, sarcastic as hell, and one of the most talented kissers I've ever had the pleasure to get my lips near.

Linda has a pretty face to go along with a set of, er, attributes, ahem, that could stop a truck…or at least the driver of that truck. She's another girl in her mid-forties who looks closer to 35. Interestingly, this can be a bit of a disadvantage. Because they look so much younger than others their age, the problem that women like Linda tend to run into is that most of the men in their age group often look old enough to be their fathers.

Nevertheless, she's pretty much every man's dream. So why the heck is she still single? Aaahhhh…. The mysteries of the universe are vast in their, um, vastness…

<u>How she describes herself:</u>

People aren't very honest. I am relatively new to being single (anybody got a rule book???) Looking for laughter, a little romance, and someone to spend some time with. I am lighthearted, optimistic, honest, and free spirited. I like music (mostly rock and alternative), comedy, weekend getaways, bike rides, playing pool, long walks, quiet dinners, cuddling on the couch, the ocean, New England, the mountains, pretty much just life in general. Family and friends are very important parts of my life. It's hard to write about yourself and really get across who you are (actually, it's impossible!), so if you want to know more about me, just ask! Please only respond if you have a photo or are prepared to send one, thanks!

How she describes her ideal match:

Hmmm, what to say about "my match." I know you'd have to be honest and sincere, kind and thoughtful, willing to surprise me or be surprised at any given moment. You'd have to like music, laughter, nature, cuddling, kissing, long talks (I'm rambling…) If you are into game playing, keep going. I really can't deal with being dishonest.

Okay, so why is writing from your heart so very important? Why shouldn't I color the truth a little to make me appear more attractive to the opposite sex? What's wrong with saying I make $150,000 a year when I only make $29,000? After all, who am I hurting? What's the problem if I say I'm 6 feet tall when I'm really only 5'5" tall? I like tall women and that's what I want to attract! I really love that photo of myself taken at the beach…So what if it's 15 years old? I look about the same! Hey, what's a few extra pounds and a little less hair? I've got life experience now! That's got to count for something. No one's going to notice anyway! They'll be so blown away with my wit and charm…

Guess what? We noticed!!! There's nothing more offensive than meeting someone you seem to like for a date, and as soon as you set eyes on them you realize that they have totally lied to you. Everything pretty much goes in the toilet from there on out.

Not only is this situation extremely unfair for the person on the receiving end of the lies but what the "liar" doesn't seem to understand is how much they're cheating themselves as well. What I'm trying to get across here by saying, "Put your best foot forward," is put the best of you, *now*. Not someone who will never exist again! If you truly seek someone who will fall desperately in love with *you*, then it's *you* that they'll need to see!

Not every man is seeking a Barbie doll and not every woman is seeking a pro wrestler. In fact, the longer you date online the more you'll understand how far this is from the truth. In the cyber world, if you can convey your feelings in an intelligent, funny, and gentle manner, you may find that you'll get more responses than you ever bargained for.

Sure there are plenty of loony-toons online of both sexes. (That's right ladies, I'm talking to you too!) And you're bound to run into one sooner or later. Of course, there are also folks who are looking for something completely different from what you seek. I have found however, that the vast majority of the people I've dealt with in this "microcosm of the human condition" are just human, nothing more, nothing less.

When I wrote my profile originally, I just let it flow from me and typed until I was done. If you think too hard about what you're going to write to describe yourself or what you're seeking, you may get so analytical that you'll scare everyone away!

One of the biggest mistakes I see women make is a list of all the negative things they didn't like about past lovers. "So gents, if you're not over your wife, or still speak to your ex, or haven't finalized your divorce, or your separation, or eat ketchup, or listen to reggae, or can't string together complete sentences, then move on, okay?" YUCK! Sure, I'm gonna run right over to date *you*. I just can't *wait* to hear all the things that you don't like about *me*!

Lists aren't too popular at all online. So if you're starting your profile with, "My friends tell me I'm attractive, spontaneous, giving, caring, sweet, humble, smart, a great cook, a good friend, an awesome mom..." AAAGGGHHH!!! Who isn't?? What are your friends *going* to say? "She's a total ditz, insufferable, talks too much, wears too much perfume, bothers everyone she gets near, and will you *please* date her, so she'll leave the rest of us in peace?"

Seriously folks, just be real. Throw in a funny or two, act just like you would if you knew someone your entire life *as* you're writing your profile, and you'll be just fine. Relax, have fun, and you may very well meet that person you truly seek and they, you. After all, if you can't have fun while you're dating, what else is left? (Only kidding football fans!)

Oh! Another thing! Be careful how "cute" you get when answering all of the "multiple choice questions" on your chosen site. Those check-off boxes are there to give everyone else a generalized idea of who you are. So, when you check off "do drugs to excess, drink until I throw up on myself and others, wear little to no deodorant, live in a stilt house in the jungle, spit out my car window before opening it, have no children and don't want yours, eat no meat of *any* kind (ouch!), am extremely overweight, am extremely ugly, speekee no Eengleesh, and don't do Dutch treat," don't be too surprised at the lack of responses. If however, a nut like me finds your profile, we'll probably have an awesome date, because I can smell amazing sarcasm a mile away, even though most on the Internet cannot!

Whew. I do get a bit long-winded, don't I? So, where are the guys you ask? I mean, DUDE! There's you, and then these other girls all over the place! Where is the gentle male perspective? Where is the unadulterated truth?

Hmm…How about my friend Brando? What kind of a name is that? Well, silly, I told you earlier that I wasn't using any real names, and he is an amazing character! How do I know that? Simple, we've played professionally together in the past, even recorded together. And we've played recently as well, but just jammin' at a friend's garage.

Brando is another "mid-forties, looks mid-thirties" type person. He's tall, dark, handsome, extremely opinionated, very intelligent, but a wee bit self-destructive. The good thing is he knows it and gets better every day. He has dated over the Internet on and off for about three years and has met a plethora of different women from different cultures and countries. He is taking a bit of a hiatus from it right now, as he is focusing on other things, but one day some amazing woman will come along and tame this wild beast and she will be one very happy lady indeed, because this dude is really *very* deep! He'll be spinning some tales for you as well, but here, as far as he can remember, is the profile he had online, in its latest incarnation:

<u>Where's the best place to go on a date?</u>

Coffee, dinner, museum, music. Outdoors for a walk or roller-blading. Anywhere comfortable, and conducive to conversation and connection.

<u>Where will you be 3 years from now?</u>

Happy, sane, loved and loving. Probably still in this part of the country. I like it here. I sail on the Long Island Sound during the summer, and ski up in Vermont a few times during the winter. I have the best on Manhattan, and the shore, and the woods. I will re-build one of my businesses, computer and/or construction, I'll be living and loving. I'd love to build a wonderful new house in this area. Sold my Weston house during the breakup.

<u>What really makes you happy, and what really makes you sad?</u>

The wonders of the natural world keep me grounded and happy.

Happy: the experience of playing with my son when he is with me. Playing music: hammer, dulcimer, and drums. Exercising. Being in, on, or near water. Sitting in front of a fire. Enjoying the comforts of home. Being successful in my work. Simple pleasures of life. Being healthy, and having access to much.

Sad: the cruel twists of fate, and the reminders of loss. Fighting, environmental destruction, greed, social inequity.

<u>I'd just like to add:</u>

I find this process of self-assessment to be insightful! How about you? Please write me, happily yours, Brando.

Well, sounds like a pretty deep, serious type dude to me. Actually, Brando has a really dry sense of humor, and is funny as hell. It just doesn't come across in his profile. Just for comparisons sake, here's the same section on the same site, but in my little corner of the universe.

<u>Where is the best place to go on a date?</u>

Totally depends on the chemistry (I soooo hate that word! LOL!). After meeting for coffee it s nice to sit by the lake and get to know each other by laughing our brains off! I also like to be real physical so a lady who can throw a mean baseball (and owns her OWN glove!) is a BIG plus. I want a partner not a barbie doll (not that that would be bad, LOL!) When 2 people click it really doesn't matter where or what just how and why!

<u>Where will you be in 3 years from now?</u>

Financially independent due to my internet business with which I help a lot of people make a lot of money from home in their underwear (*tee hee*) while sitting in front of their computer!!! It s TOTALLY AWESOME!! and traveling the world with my kids and hopefully a phenomenal caring awesome woman...After that is I visit EVERY major league ballpark!!!

<u>What really makes you happy and what makes you sad?</u>

Being with my kids, backrubs, kissing, touching, public displays of affection. Knowing the love of a good woman and returning it passionately...Sleeping together like a pretzel and waking up smiling together in the morning. Hiking, baseball, music, really great nookie (!!!) cooking, EATING, staying fit, boogie boarding!! Sad? Me? Nasty people, pollution, not seeing my kids enough...

<u>I'd just like to add:</u>

I m kinda tired of dating. I've met some great ladies and now have some awesome friends. I've had some close calls but no cigar. I seek a woman to walk at my side, not behind, not ahead. An awesome sense of humor with a touch of sarcasm. Passion for life, for love, closeness without a fear of intimacy or commitment. An open heart and a spirit with no taste for defeat. Someone to whom quitting does not compute. Someone who eventually can stare deeply into my eyes and know…she's home…as I stare into hers and feel the same.

Like some *majorly* different writing styles. Yet we're both seeking pretty much the same thing. We just have very different ways of describing it. Brando is one of my oldest friends and I have seen him at totally different phases in his life. I know how insightful and brilliant and wonderful he is. I know what a loving daddy he is. I'm just not too sure that it comes across that way in his profile, though I could be wrong. I often am!

The types of women that I've met, dated, befriended, made love to, fell in love with, had them fall in love with me, hurt, been hurt by, et al., are very different from the sort that Brando has come across. This will become very clear as the book progresses when I begin to describe several conversations with my good friend and his opinions on this whole fiasco. You may form some deep opinions about Brando and me, both as men and as human beings, but judge ye not, as ye are not in our stinky shoes!

Okay, here's a cute story that could only happen online, but I'll be brief, because the jury is still out on this one. I'll call this young lady "Outlaw," because that's one of her online names. A year ago, she sent me the following e-mail and the following link to her profile:

HI I LIKED YOUR AD AND THIS IS MY FIRST TRY AT PERSONAL ADS. IF YOU LIKE MY AD AND LIKE TO CHAT MORE LET ME KNOW.
JACKIE…

<u>How she describes herself:</u>

Have little time but if it's right I'll make the time and hopefully you will too. I'm a certified personal trainer so I have very little personal time and I have a very tight schedule. Since I have to adjust my schedule to fit my clients. I'm looking to change that since it's not what I want to be remembered for and the recent events have made me rethink my priorities. I'd like to make changes in my priorities and work is not in the top five. I'm willing to relocate (just not somewhere that is cold. I've had enough of the cold). I can be described as a dichotomy. I also have a very positive outlook to life but also a realist romantic loyal and I have my own interest some of which you may not like but we don t have to do everything together. I'm secure of who I am and somewhat independent. I'm attractive and very picky. Picky because I know what I want. At least care about your health appearance and be physically fit. (no couch potatoes or muscle heads.) Somewhere in the middle would be fine. More importantly I d like someone who is considerate flexible, fun (takes life at ease) wants to take care of me but also know when to let me take care of myself, likes public displays of affection and likes to be taken care of but also can take care of yourself. You also know your priorities, family oriented, self confident, not too much of a sports freak (prefer to cheer you on in person than watch it on TV) assertive, responsible, affectionate (PDA) romantic, between 37-46 (SLIGHTLY flexible) clean cut, like dogs, loves to travel (somewhere warm and exotic) and there's more but I'll soon run out of room. As you can see I'm clear about what I want. Non-smoker, no drugs and social drinker. Single, Divorced or widowed. If I've got your curiosity going then I'll hear from you. Please only serious response. (not looking for players REALLY NOT KIDDING) I'm looking for a friendship that will lead to a long-term relationship. Willing to get to know each other well.

How she describes her ideal match:

Patient and flexible. Willing to get to know each other and once we see we have similar goals be ready to work on a relationship.

We e-mailed back and forth a few times but nothing really happened. So a year later or so, she e-mails me again from another site saying that I look familiar! Well, she was very cute so when I saw the photo I recognized her immediately. We had several phone conversations after that and on the spur of the moment I invited her over on a Sunday to watch a playoff football game with me and have dinner at halftime. She agreed and we had a really awesome time together. The most amazing part about the entire scenario was when I looked at the date of her very first e-mail to me and realized that our first date was exactly one year to the day from the day she had originally e-mailed me! Weird! You can't make this stuff up folks!

Oh, here is the ad she e-mailed me from last week just before we met. I'm putting it here to show you how very different the content can be on different sites.

<u>Where is the best place to go on a Date?</u>

I GUESS THE BEST PLACE CAN BE SUBJECTIVE. IF YOU'RE WITH A PERSON WHICH YOU ARE HAVING A GREAT TIME WITH THEN THAT'S THE BEST PLACE AND DATE. BUT IT'S USUALLY A PLACE WHERE A CONVERSATION CAN BE HEARD.
I ALSO LIKE SURPRISES BUT EVEN MY FAMILY AND FRIENDS CAN'T SURPRISE ME. SO IF YOU CAN SURPRISE ME THEN IT SHOULD BE PRETTY EXCITING DATE. (AND I DON T MEAN SAYING BOO) ALSO IF YOU PLAN AHEAD TAKE CHARGE BUT ALSO OFFER A CHOICE AS TO WHAT YOU WOULD LIKE TO DO THAT WOULD BE GREAT. I'M OPEN TO NEW EXPERIENCES.

<u>Where will you be in 3 years from now?</u>

HOPEFULLY NOT HERE.

<u>What makes you happy and what makes you sad?</u>

MY FAMILY FRIENDS LIFE AND MY CUTE LITTLE DOG.
THE LAST THING THAT MADE ME SAD WAS 9/11 AND SELFISH MEAN CRUEL INCONSIDERATE PEOPLE.
BUT LET ME USE THIS SPACE TO BE MORE SPECIFIC. I WANT A PARTNER. SOMEONE THAT I CAN RESPECT AND RESPECTS ME. SECURE ENOUGH IN HIMSELF TO LET ME BE INDEPENDANT. WILLING TO SHARE HIS LIFE-GOOD AND BAD. ALSO SHARE INTEREST THAT MAY BE DIFFERENT THAN MINE AND IF I DON T LIKE THEM BE ABLE TO ENJOY THOSE INTEREST ON HIS OWN OR WITH FRIENDS. I'D LIKE A FRIEND AND A LOVER. I'D LIKE TO FIND A FRIEND IN MY PARTNER AND THEN SEE IF THAT FRIENDSHIP BECOMES A LOVING RELATIONSHIP. NOT TO JUDGE OR CARRY BAGGAGE FROM PAST RELATIONSHIPS. EVERYONE IS DIFFERENT. I ADMIRE LOYALITY RELIABLITY ROMANTIC HONESTY SENSE OF HUMOR INDEPENDANCE AND I GUESS I CAN DISCOVER THE REST MYSELF. ALSO I AM FLEXIABLE BUT PLEASE BE BETWEEN THE 37 and 47 YRS OLD AND TALL. IF YOU DON T HAVE CHILDREN OF YOUR OWN IT S A BIG PLUS BUT IF YOU DO I'M FLEXIBLE. LIKE I SAID I DO KNOW WHAT I WANT.

<u>I'd just like to Add….</u>

I'M VERY PICKY AND I LIKE TO KNOW MORE ABOUT YOU THAN THIS FORUM CAN TELL ME. SO IF YOU CAN'T TALK ABOUT YOURSELF AND HAVE A CONVERSATION PLEASE PASS ME BY.

I'M A COMBINATION OF A LOT OF THINGS. I CAN BE VERY
MODERN ABOUT SOMETHING AND OLD FASHION TOO. I LIKE
TO HAVE FUN AND TRY NEW THINGS. I LOVE TO TRAVEL AND
STILL HAVE A FEW PLACES THAT ARE ON MY WISH LIST THAT
I'D LIKE TO GET TO.
I HAVE A GREAT RELATIONSHIP WITH MY MOM AND FRIENDS.
I HAVE A CAREER THAT REALLY GIVES ME A SENSE OF SATIS-
FACTION. I KEEP FAIRLY BUSY BUT I'D LIKE TO SHARE IT WITH
A SPECIAL SOMEONE. YOU'LL HAVE TO BE A BIT SPONTANIOUS
SINCE I DON'T HAVE A STEADY SCHEDULE.
IF YOU'D LIKE TO KNOW MORE THAN YOU'LL HAVE TO FIND
THAT OUT FOR YOURSELF. IF NOT GOOD LUCK IN YOUR
SEARCH.

Well, I've put in my two cents on the importance of the content in your profile, so it's time to give the girls their fair share of opinions.

Here is Linda's perspective on the initial ad:

Let's see, again, like you said, writing about the negative things is a turnoff.
There's not much that you can get from that except anger. Y'know, when ya
see negative stuff it just breeds more negativity, and that's somebody that you
just don't wanna talk to. So it's nice to see the profiles when they tell you what
they like, what their interests are, so that you can compare with them what
you're interested in.

I can't begin to tell you how much I agree with Linda. Anger, frustration, and
bitterness can come across as clear as day in a profile that lists all of the things that
you don't want in a partner. What you're telling everyone who reads your profile
is, "All these horrible things happened to me in past relationships, and as soon as
you do something that vaguely resembles any of it, I will run like hell away from
you, never to be seen or heard from again."

Folks, there is not a one of us that's perfect. There's not a one of us that isn't
going to screw up royally sooner or later in a boy/girl relationship. Why? Because
men and women are wired quite differently. We all know that, and the sooner
you understand it and learn to forgive most of the inevitable tiffs that are bound
to happen, the happier and more productive your relationships will be.

Now, here's Freeda's take on the same subject:

One of the first things I dislike about a person's profile is that they don't have a picture. It's livable, it's acceptable, 'cause you can always get one, but then I hate getting them and having people have my e-mail address, or sending photos and they're nothing about what they appear to be. The second most important thing is, men on these sites hardly ever say anything about themselves! Especially if they're extremely good looking, like they don't have to or they don't know what to say about themselves. Or they put something in there like, "Ask me and I'll tell you." First of all, that's not what it was put there for. I don't mean the silly little questions like, "Where will you be in three years?" or, "What your goal is," yada, yada. I'm talking about just general stuff about yourself. Who you are and what you do, but they put absolutely nothing there, 90 percent of them I'll say. I can't start a conversation with you if I have very little information about you. It, it, it's just wrong! I mean, these people want you to bare your soul to them, have a picture of yourself, talk about you, but they don't wanna tell you anything about them. That is, until the time they think they can, or should, or whatever it is. Y'know, it's just not right!

Well that's two very different ways of saying almost the same thing. Just talk about yourself. Tell the people you want to meet what you do, what you like, what you love, but *not* what you hate! After all, who wants to come home after a tough day at work, open up the profile of a cute stranger and read negative stuff, or even worse, nothing at all? To be honest with you, I move on very quickly when a woman cannot take a few moments to tell me who she is, and what she seeks.

Well on to the guys now, and their perspectives on the initial ad. First Brando:

Well, honestly, I don't believe anything that a woman writes. They all have an agenda and will tell you exactly what they think you want to hear. It's like the ones with a brain are all reading from the same book on how to write a perfect profile. I reserve all judgment until I actually meet a woman and see that she's all that she stated in her perfect ad. If you cannot be honest, then how do you expect to capture the interest of anyone with half a brain?

Swayne says:

If a woman writes from the heart, it usually comes through very plainly in her profile. If I am touched by the beauty of her words, then I'll no doubt shoot her a quick note to show interest. I am usually most drawn in by a sense of humor, as well as a very descriptive ad on what they're seeking along with a truly cute description of the person they are.

What really does bother me is when I see negativity in the ad. My parents taught me, "If you can't say anything nice, then say nothing at all." Do I really need to know about your ex-boyfriend and all his failings? How soon after you meet me will the same type of judging and negativity begin to surface? I can't run away from that type of woman fast enough! Just tell me who you are, and what you like in an open and happy manner. That'll get my attention every time (assuming the pics are cute too!).

Oh, and about the photos! It really is true that as guys we are *very* visual! So if your pics are crappy, don't be surprised at the lack of quality men that e-mail you. Sure, you'll get responses from dungeon dwellers, but never from someone like me who is successful and gorgeous!

Okay, Swayne is very modest, obviously! Knowing him though, I'm sure it was said "tongue in cheek" as he was smiling and winking when he uttered those words. Brando comes from a place of deeper pain however, and his mistrust of women will become more apparent as the story progresses.

I can say that I agree with all four to differing degrees. I agree with Brando to the extent that some people indeed do write based on attracting the most people of the opposite sex, although I do not believe for the most part that it is meant in a controlling or vindictive way as Brando does. I agree mostly however with the other three, who state that openness, with a positive and friendly attitude, will garner the most responses of the sort that will do you the most good. Those being the sort that will be attracted to the real person that resides inside of you. After all, isn't that what we really seek?

The next girl is one of my dearest friends, and perhaps the deepest human being I have ever had the good fortune to meet. She has enriched my life in ways that are unspeakable, and will be held in my heart forever no matter where our paths take us. Doreen is a mom, mid-forties and, as described by my 86-year-old aunt whom she met in the hospital several months ago, is "sooooo beautiful." Her eyes are as blue as twilight and hair as golden as the sun, with the warmth of spirit to match. If it weren't for the distance between us and the situations in our lives right now, she would no doubt be my girlfriend. Fate really sucks!

The following profile is one that she sent to me, as the one on the site she e-mailed me from was not very descriptive of the person she truly is. Read this guys, and see if you wouldn't want to spend the rest of your life in the arms of this incredible woman:

I find enjoyment in the simple things in life. I am not high-maintenance, not demanding. I like a little bit of space to breath and can offer the same. I enjoy an occasional night out, dinner, maybe some cultural indulgences. I have always found that a long walk in the woods, regardless of the season, refreshes my sense of self and reminds me of the magic and little miracles that happen every day. In the big picture, some things just aren't that important. This puts life in perspective for me. I love deep conversations (can you tell?), passionate kisses, back rubs (give and receive), winter sunrises at the beach (blankets included), dancing, dancing, dancing!, sleeping in on Sunday followed by coffee, the paper and "what time is it?!", looking for sea glass, star gazing, people watching, road trips without a destination, new foods, old sea stories, Vivaldi, John Lee Hooker, Billy Holiday, Etta James, Classic rock from the 60's and 70's, a good Hitchcock mystery…yet I am always open to new experiences. I have the capacity to love deeply but I am not willing to settle for someone who treats me with any less adoration than I myself have to offer. I believe in love and yet I understand that healthy relationships are not a magical event. The chemistry that brings two people together may have elements of star-dust, but a relationship of any substance takes a conscious effort of communication, exploration, adjustment and trust. I believe in that kind of love as well as romantic love.

I would like to meet an attractive, honest gentleman who has a clear sense of himself—who understands that there is a tremendous strength in vulnerability, that when one gives of oneself, self multiplies and loses nothing. I would enjoy a friendship with someone who holds women in high regard and treats them with respect. I would like a companion, true friend, partner, buddy, and ultimately, a passionate, caring lover. My perception of an ideal relationship is honest communication, mutual respect, mutual trust, similar interests, values, belief systems yet the ability to honor our differences. Enough closeness to stay connected but enough space to keep our individuality.

Was I kidding? There are too many things I know about this woman to share here. Suffice it to say that her beauty goes *wayyy* beyond skin deep, and the man who someday ends up capturing the heart of this precious creature will be a lucky man indeed. I just hope he likes to shovel snow, because where she's from they get a whole *lot* of it! Of course, the up side is that they'll probably be spending all their time snuggling together for warmth, and you know where *that* leads. By the way, hers was also an excellent example of a wonderfully written profile and one that most should emulate if there is a true desire to meet the person of your dreams.

We'll close here with Swayne's short but very effective profile.

<u>Where is the best place to go on a date?</u>

Anywhere I can stare deeply into your beautiful eyes! Do I have your attention? GOOD! I love to dine out in a small, quiet ethnic restaurant where we can get to know each other slowly over a nice meal. If the conversation progresses sweetly, and if we get through desert, then I LOOOOVE to go dancing! YAYYY!

<u>Where will you be three years from now?</u>

Oh God ANYWHERE BUT HERE! Hopefully in a loving, tender EXCITING relationship (um, with a WOMAN!!!)

<u>What really makes you happy and what really makes you sad?</u>

I love fishing. I adore being in the fresh air with no sound at all but the movement of an upstate stream. I love the mountains. I can't get enough of the water in the summer. I need to play baseball A LOT! I am happy when my sports teams win! (Yankees, Rangers, Knicks, Giants!) I am sad when they do not. I cannot stand prejudice or stupidity ever! I am sad when I see cruelty or pollution. 9/11 affected me very deeply as I lost many friends. I will NEVER forget....

<u>I'd just like to add:</u>

I have pretty much had it with the life of a bachelor. I am successful in my career and seeking the ONE who can sweep me off my feet with the merest of gazes. I am so NOT seeking a booty call so if you're just feeling the waters do NOT contact me. I want an adult who knows what she wants and is not fearful of showing affection if and when she feels it. Can you say "public displays of affection?" I assuredly can. Ta-ta!

2

First contact

So you're cruising the multitude of reasonably decent human beings and you've found one who is not only easy on the eyes, but also stirs your drink with the content of their profile. *Now* what do you do? What do you say? How do you break the ice? After all, we're not all writers. Everyone is skilled at different things and some of us just don't *do* writing very well. The best advice I can give you, besides totally being yourself, (the only person you know how to *be* very well) is to read the contents of this chapter carefully and make your own judgments as to what works and what doesn't.

Of course, the only challenge with this line of reasoning is that what works to impress one person, will do exactly the opposite for another person. That's human nature, so GET OVER YOURSELF! Not everyone is going to answer you, not everyone is going to like you, and even those who do like you may change their minds for absolutely no intelligible reason! Scared yet? I know, you wonder how anyone ever actually finds anyone else online. Well, millions of nice people find each other every day all over the world, and they wouldn't have been able to if not for this silly box of lights sitting on their desk!

Oh, and guys, it's only okay for the ladies to engage in sexual innuendo on a first contact, not us! Not fair, you say? Really? Who gets to walk around topless at any location we desire and not get arrested for public indecency? There's a tradeoff in everything in life and this is just one of those times.

Oh, and ladies? If you don't want to be treated like a piece of meat by the men, then don't start your contact by saying, "Oh, you're just so hot I could eat you up!" followed by the old standard that "Looks aren't important. It's what in your heart that counts." You can't have it both ways!

And here's something both men and women should understand about the way most people do "business" here: no photo, no answer. Simple. So grab your camera, grab a roll of film (or your digital), stand in front of the mirror and make silly faces! Then, after you develop the film, get a friend or two of the *opposite* sex (if you have any, *grin*) to pick the best two or three shots that will go up on the site and try to save the photos online in JPEG format, as almost every site accepts those. In fact, some sites *only* accept JPEGs.

The other thing you should be aware of (especially the ladies!) is that when you bare your soul in a letter to a new person for sixteen paragraphs, the very first thing that person is most likely going to do is link to your profile and look at your photos. Speaking for the men here, if he doesn't like your photos he isn't going to spend the better part of an evening missing the playoffs to read your heartfelt letter to him. So keep it light, keep it brief, and be aware that we all have deep feelings and we all like different things.

What you always *do* want to tell someone is the reason you're e-mailing them in the first place. What is it you liked about their profile? If they didn't happen to write a darn thing, then what was it you liked about, um, other things? Talk a wee bit about what *you* would like as well, but don't write a book to someone new. Keep it short, cute, and to the point. There's nothing worse than getting an e-mail and not being even sure why it was sent to you. I mean, why bother writing to someone if you're not going to give any hint or suggestion whatsoever that you'd like to actually *meet* at some future time?

So what *are* some of the ways people say hello to you for the first time? Surely, you think, they must want to impress you with their wit, charm and intelligence, right? Well, the following lines are the *entire* letters received by my friends and I upon a first contact. Most, if not all, came with a link directly to their profile…Enjoy!

> Are you Italian?

> HI!

> Hello…

> OMG! Marry me!!!!

> Cute!

> I thought you were in the witness protection program, what happened? LOL…

> I wanna bam bam you!

> Nice cleavage…

Where are you from?

Lets spend the weekend together!!!

Liked your profile…. If interested please respond….

Call me, 908-000-0000

How old IS your photo anyway?

Que pasa?

Have we spoken before…

You're absolutely gorgeous!

You're quite beautiful…

You have GOT to be kidding…

What? Because I don't have a picture you won't talk to me?

Those CANNOT be real!!!!

You are quite handsome, perhaps we have something in common….call me….

HELLLOOOOOOOOOO!!!!!!

Are you still there?

Thank you for the letter, but I didn't get it…

??????????????????????????????????????!!!!!!!!!!!!!!!

I would love to run my tongue along your thighs….

What are you doing for the next 30 or 40 years???

Baby, your feet must be killing you, because you've been running around in my head all day long!!!

You are SOOO cute, and you sound like a blast! Have a good one!

You send me!

Baby, I would love to rub something all over you, ME!

Wwwwhere have you BBBEEN? GET OVER HERE!!!

Where in Yonkers are you hiding??!!!

Very cute, check out my profile…

I think I'm in love, lets find out…

Well, I think we'd get along, read my profile and tell me what you think…

Some pair!!! Wanna exchange nude photos?

Have I got something for you…

And my personal favorite…

I can almost feel your balls bouncing against my chin!!!!

Okay, so those are examples of some that were a little bit *too* brief. What, you may ask, are some *really* good examples of an awesome first contact? Ahhh, I thought you'd never ask! Understand once again that the following content is "as received" and not altered in any way. It's generally understood that spelling and grammatical errors are acceptable online since most folks are just rattling off a quick note to someone they may never hear back from. They may also be typing as fast as humanly possible before their boss comes back into the room! Bear these facts in mind lest you become what is commonly referred to online as a "Grammar Nazi," one who judges every error of grammar, spelling and syntax that comes your way.

◆   ◆   ◆

AMAZING!!!
Hello,
    I just joined match.com today so this is my first time e-mailing someone I don't know..I just have to say your narrative was amazing!!lets see I guess you would want to know a few things about me I'm 5'3" long dark brown hair and

green eyes I am slender (I love to stay active) i'm legally seperated with 2 very special people in my life.I love beach,music cooking among other things..

I love to dance I danced in the ballet the nutcracker with my daughter and I ride bikes,do karate with my son.I sailed my first boat this summer to the hamptons and loved it.I live in long island on the north shore near port jones.I love to laugh thats so…. important. I am half spanish so I tend to be on the sensual side. my family is very important to me.I teach handicapped children so I guess I have a lot of patience.I would really like to hear from you. like I said this is my first time doing this so its difficult I really need to look in some-ones eyes to really see who they are and they can see who I am.take care…

gerry

◆   ◆   ◆

Hi…I thought I'd give this a shot…this is my first weekend off since Feb. so I thought I'd do something for myself today…And I found YOU.So I joined…no pressure…lol…Sorry no photo but I certainly can e-mail you some…As I was reading all you had written. You almost made me cry.You said you had almost forgotten how nice it was to come home to someone.I was just telling a friend the other day that I think the reason I don't and haven't minded being alone is because I'm not in love. I do remember how it feels but because I refuse to settle that feeling has not hit me for some time.and Kiss-ing.well this may sound a bit forward but I will share this with you…I can have an orgasm kissing…it's so unbelievably intimate…I don't even like thinking about it I really do miss kissing. You seem like a great guy…and hope to connect…take care…Sasha

Wow! An orgasm while kissing! SEE? We *men* can't say that yet!!!

◆   ◆   ◆

WOW, where to begin….?!?!??!?

I absolutely enjoyed reading your profile, and found alot of ME in it, as well as alot of 'who i'm looking to find' someday (hopefully)….!!

It made me smile that you're very physical, emotional, and affectionate with the right woman, as I am all indeed the same…..WITH the right man.

I don't want to sound redundant in this note, or harp on every (poetic, and encouraging) word you wrote in your narratives, therefore, I will bid you the task of reading my entire profile (not just the excerpt included below), and if you as are intrigued with getting to know more about me as I am you, then I will be glad to forward you some recent pics of me, as this double-blind e-mail system doesnt allow you to attach pics until we've communicated once each with each other.... :(

 I would greatly appreciate a response either way.......THANKS!! ....D

◆   ◆   ◆

After reading your profile I had to write. Are you really a man who loves to kiss? Really loves to kiss? You need to e-mail me ;)

 In all seriousness (not that I'm serious very often) I do share a lot of the things you like. I love life, and would like to find a man who can find happiness in its simple pleasures and honesty. No game playing, no long conversations about how the "ex" was this or that, just getting to know each other one day at a time and seeing if there's anything there to expand on.

 Sound interesting?

 Linda

This was the first contact between me and my amazingly good friend Linda. She is indeed one of the best kissers I've ever laid my lips upon!

◆   ◆   ◆

Can you write my profile for me?

Francey

I know, too short. But what a MAJOR compliment! Not a bad way to start, and isn't that kind of the point? By the way, I met her too and she's a sweetie!

◆   ◆   ◆

I just loved your profile. what a great guy you sound like! I'm 39,blonde blue eyed professional who is divorced with no children but would like to have them. I love the beach and ocean and the outdoors. I look forward to hearing from you soon!

Short, but sweet. That's what I'm talkin' about!

◆   ◆   ◆

hey you!!!!!!
and no—"it's not only you"!!!!!
it's me too!!!!!!! (-;

    and boy, can i talk—and tell you all about me—and why you're oh-so-"seemingly"-sincere and extremely "fetching" and engaging ad has caught my eye…(and that is not an easy thing to do….. i could search through dozens and dozens and dozens before someone jumps out at me and makes me want to share a piece of "me")………….

    please don't be offended at the reference to "seemingly"…. it's only that i've experienced a few rather mis-representing fellows out there—yet i will always and forever remain optimistic—with complete faith that "it only takes one"—the right one—to eventually come along……. especially when i'm being and living the life of the complete and happy soul that i am—i can't help but attract the right man for me into my life (-;

    i would love to share some details about who i am "inside the skin" with you—should you be interested……. my ad is no longer posted on match……. so i'll forward a pix in an e-mail to immediately follow this one……. hope you enjoy!!!

    should you like to respond—and pick up the ball from here—i'll glady follow……..
you can reach me at blahblah@blah.net
have a beautiful evening…..(-;
    Donna….

What an adorable personality! But no, we didn't meet. No reason, just didn't!

◆   ◆   ◆

This next e-mail is the kind *every* guy hopes to get at least once during his lifetime:

YO! YOU are adorable! I can tell you're just as much of a ham as I am. But I'm a southern one who is one hell of a kisser who you could wake up in bed with, and then be served, in bed, banana-bourbon french toast, southern style. !!!!!!!!!!!@@@@!!!!!!!!!!!!

    as far as my body, it's anything BUT average. i'm a smack-dab in the middle medium. and i love it! i work out as much as i can, and i'm starting a yoga class in a couple of weeks.

have a great day over there in yonkers!
josie…

Like, WOW! Breakfast in bed and we haven't even spoken yet! Are you beginning to see the advantages of a well written, well thought out profile?

◆   ◆   ◆

We could be a match!!!
Your photo caught my eye, however your expressive ad, ability to convey your thoughts and feelings compelled me to write….
As I read your profile, I found myself thinking how I couldn't have described the relationship I would like to be in any better…we definitely need to chat and get to know each other…
You sound like a caring, thoughtful, giving and playful guy who knows what you want and is ready to meet the right lady…
Where have you been….lol
I think you may have met your match….
So looking for to hearing from you…
Take care,
Kristen

Loved her writing, didn't love her photos…Oh well…

◆   ◆   ◆

I read your profile and you sound delightful. I love your sense of humor, already!! I have been to 49 of the 50 states and I have to say I haven't yet been to Yonkers!!!
I love photography. too. Have you traveled to Europe? I found soooooo much there to take pictures of. It is just great shot after great shot. I think I really just wanted to bring it all home with me. My favorite place is Paris I think it so beautiful, as cities go. I particularily like Montmartre on the outskirts of the city. I found it a good place for the soul as well to be where the French Impressionists gathered.
Well, you sound like a lot of fun and I look forward to your reply.
Marla

◆   ◆   ◆

Hi there…

Wow…I like so much of what you said about yourself….and what you are looking for, too…

I am an artist, writer, entreprenuer with big visions…and also love music, photography, and so much else of what you mentioned….

I am also someone who can be deeply reflective, and LOVES deep, constant communication…always done in a totally gentle and compassionate way…but I am also very playful, and Love to just have fun, in every possible way….

And…my top priority of the moment is connecting with a fabulous man who really wants to co-create a spectacular romance, and ultimately life, based on compatibility in every way, emotional intellectual, physical, and spiritual…

And…I happen to have a fabulous website, and am deeply intrigued by what you say you do for a living…because I am looking for someone to help me make this great web site of mine make money…

AS is now, it sells my product line, my books, and such, but I have barely begun to scratch the surface of it's moneymaking potential…

SO..take a look at my site, it is called www.Theooo.com….you can also see a photo of me there on the page that says "About Brandee Julie Abraxas…. (Yes, that's my real name…) and who knows…even if ultimate romance isn't in the wings, maybe you can do some internet consulting for me…anything is possible…

And oh…I am FROM NY, love my hometown, but currently live in New England, 3 hours north, in Western Mass. But I think searching for your soul mate is something you shouldn't put limitations on…so, I am willing to look far afield, and trust that if it is meant to be, even a long-distance relationship may be worth pursuing on the one in a million chance that it can lead to the ultimate everyday romance that I know we are all seeking…

SO, big brown bedroom eyes, PLEASE write back….and maybe we can see what's possible…

Till then, take care…

Brandee

Nice, verrrrry nice! She just lived way too far away. I need someone who can drive to me when I don't feel well, or vice versa. Not take a plane. Someone I can grab a burger and a beer with on 30 minutes notice. Yeah, I know that's a limiting mentality, but it is what it is, and that's all it is!

◆   ◆   ◆

I could be the one........

All I have to say is that your words kept my attention from the first to the last.....

You are Perfect.......Everything I have ever been looking for and more. You are so passionate about what it is that you are looking for and it made me have chills....as I continued to read on....

I'm here in Indy and you are in New York.....Please dont let that be an issue.....

It would always be the Question What if....

I am very open to travel as I am in New York often for Business. I actually would like to call NY my home....

You are simply amazing....I am so very serious! I am a professional Photographer and own my Business so that gives me the freedom to set my schedule....I love what I do and although I work like a dog I am ready to slow down and focus finally on my personal life.

Well Hun its so late as I just finished doing some proofing and I am off to bed. I will keep my fingers crossed!

Lucie Ann

Indianapolis, Indiana? *Waaay* too far! But what an awesome first letter! We did indeed speak on the phone, but the woman seemed a bit crazed so there never was a second conversation.

Okay, so let's move on to the women's perspective on first contacts. I asked Linda and Charley what would get them to respond to a guy just about every time, assuming they liked the prospective man's photos first.

Linda: If he's genuine. Somebody who doesn't boast about himself. I can't stand that! If you gotta tell me then you ain't that good!

Charley: Someone who's complimentary, who says they like my picture, who has the same interests. It's better when there's a guy who's had kids, who's been married with kids as opposed to single guys without kids. When they like kids that's definitely a plus.

Will you answer a letter from a guy if there's no physical attraction?

Linda: No. It's definitely not even close to the most important thing, but if there's totally nothing there to build on? I mean what the hell?

Charley:	Initially, I used to answer everyone, but I realized how counter-productive that was. I don't anymore.
	So we're probably all on the same page here. If there's no physical attraction you won't even answer them?
Linda:	Initially…I found that most people don't even look like their pictures.
Both:	Some look better but most look worse!!! *laughing*

I'm right there with the ladies. I also used to answer everyone. That lasted about a week and my fingers were ready to fall off from typing! It's understood by most everyone online that it's just a numbers game. E-mail enough people of the opposite sex and sooner or later you will get responses. That is, of course, unless you're pitifully ugly, boring, ill-mannered, unable to write a complete sentence or spell at all…Actually that's wrong…There will *always* be people out there who would settle for less than what they should. Just make sure *you're* not one of them!

So, once again, like the girls said (for men and ladies alike), just be genuine and honest. Talk about what you *do* like, *do* want and *can* offer someone, and you just might get lucky!

Now changing gears a bit here's an excerpt of an interview I did with my sweet ex-girlfriend Anna. Her perspectives are clearer and really on the ball.

> I don't think you can be as honest and up front with people as David and I are. I think you have to have that air of mystery about you. You cannot give away too much too soon. It's almost like giving sex too soon. Okay? The same thing of what you're all about, your life experiences…there has to be this allure in order to keep them interested. David and I have a tendency to be too upfront, too honest, um, answer questions…. There's no other option open to us but to BE forthright and honest. I think what this is teaching David and I both is that we must learn how to play the "dating game" and not always answer the questions. I've gotten very aggressive in my display of sarcasm and wit online and if he takes it the wrong way then so be it. He's not for me anyway!

And you know, it's not just because you want to be completely honest with somebody, but there are so many women online who will type out exactly the man they're looking for in every single capacity, yet when they find him they're not ready for him. I also believe that some people go into this with a list, a mental list where they need to check off everything and if you don't meet all their criteria they're on to the next person but they're never going to find that person because they don't exist. Yeah, a bit of mystery is definitely a good idea Anna!

So have you ever been so close to a situation that you just don't realize what's missing? I've been there for a long time. Well, up until about five minutes ago! I realized that I had placed a plethora of received first contacts, but none that I had sent to women. The main reason for this is that on most sites, unless you save the message, it just sort of goes off into the ether. Well, I was researching myself (yes, you can do that), and actually found a handful that I had sent. You may judge for yourself why most of them were never responded to. If you find some of these a bit confusing, remember that the messages are responding to the content posted in their profile online. They follow:

> Grey eyes???? Hmmmmm. BIG dogs? Imagine all the depressed looks on all the tiny dogs out there who discover that size matters to you? hehehe..... Wacky? Yer talkin' to him!
>
> Anyhoooo.... judging from the adorable photo that Match deigned sending to me in todays "meet" market, I assume you'll be getting a plethora of responses from male suitors, or suits, or just guys that don't even know the difference, or care, or be able to string intelligible sentences together, or care to, because the only thing they see is a pretty face and wide age parameters (did you get any of that? I'm too pooped to re-read it!).
>
> So, since I may or may not still be a member of this silly site, I'll just take a shot in the dark that you'll actually receive my silly note, read my not very brief profile, and perhaps decide to answer back a guy who posesses most of the attribes you so honestly seek.........................and NOT just in a dog!
>
> *grin*........ ttfn.... David...

◆   ◆   ◆

> What do you say to the girl next door? You sorta have that "take me home to your mom" look. Is that good? Guess so. Well, I live here in the wonderful borough of Riverdale (don't dare call it the Bronx. The rents are too high and people get offended! *grin*) I can be in the city in about a minute, and into "Joisey" in 6 or 7......why am I going on about such boring details....well, because it's late and I'm semi comatose! So before I go I'll just say, I liked your profile, I think you're cute, and I'd love to cross the bridge for coffee..... maybe a danish..... okee doke? *smile*......toodles!......David...

◆   ◆   ◆

Hi Suz!!! So, d'ya think a photographer and Fashion exec could have anything to talk about???? Gee, I dunno! *grin* The fact that you're a hockey fan is HUGE to me! I won't tell you which team I bleed for, I'll just let you guess! So take a gander at my silly lil profile, and hit me back!.... toodles!.... David..

◆   ◆   ◆

Okay, you got me with the Jets, Rangers and the Knicks...The Yankees.....well, we can't agree on EVERYTHING!!!!! I also can't resist a woman who wears odd things on their head. I'll just totally stop someone in the street for that (very embarrassing if you're my date, or very endearing if you're a people person!) Well, I've gotta scoot now, but I hope to hear back from ya, as I can't wait to see you new taste in "headwear"........ *grin*.......... *hugs*........ David...

◆   ◆   ◆

Oopsie! pressed the wrong button!!!! No doubt you think I'm nuts by now or perhaps a stalker given this is my second (sorta) message to you.

Okay, as I said in my first failed effort I never do this! I'm normally the one receiving the e-mail......but your face was zapped to me by the Gods of Match and in it's shining brilliance I just HAD to respond! *grin*..... um, seriously, your pics were cute but it was the written word that convinced me. Perhaps it was your rebellious spirit, or that you're a mom like me (yeah I KNOW I'm a guy but I raised one of my daughters sans a mom.... so there!!!!) More likely it was the writer part as I'm about a stones throw away from finishing my first lengthy novel (no,,,, I will NOT blab about it here! That's what first dates are for silly!)

I trust that I can match you "energy erg" for "energy erg" and I DO hope you can catch a softball and LOVE to hike in the most AMAZINGLY beautiful places that I've discovered with my little weenies (that would be Sammy and Sherry).

Well, before this becomes a chapter I'm gonna scoot, but I've just gotta share that you are VERY cute, it is NOT a line as it comes from the heart you'll see, get to know me, I am pretty smart!!!

hehehe......not too bad..... I've done better!

Later gator!......David...=)

◆   ◆   ◆

First things first............You need to know that my daughter Sherry (11 yrs. old and VERRRRY precocious!) found your profile. It came in one of those wonderful match e-mails that we all get and I usually delete. She was attempting to access cartoonnetwork.com and simply pressed the wrong button (so she says!) She called in my son, Sammy (9 yrs. old and already all the girls are chasing him, but I think it's for his heart as much as his looks!) and he fell over from your photo (I worry about him! *grin*).However when Sherry saw that you had FOUR daughters my son X-ed out of the program immediately! Soooooooo........ Sherry yelled for me to come into the room and find you again, so I did. Just a wee few points before I go nitey night (I promised my son that I wouldn't contact you, but he's asleep and I'm sure you won't snitch on me!)

Okay, first ya need to know that I'm also a writer. My first LOOOONG novel is nearing completion and everyone who has read drafts swears that it's gonna be a bestseller. Big whoop. I do love my writing but it's to be ascertained whether the buying public agrees with their money! *smile*

I am a professional photographer specializing in portraits. I photograph beautiful women on a regular basis......but rarely have I seen a face that shines as brightly as yours....... (you can blush now..... it's kewl!)

Your work is adorable. My daughter says that #15 reminds her of me because my kids adore me with a passion and think I'm Superdad. I'm not. I'm just a loving guy who is never happier than when I'm buried under kids, with my gilfriend rolling her eyes and smiling as she realizes that there's ONE MORE in the house to deal with (in a good way, as I do dishes and cook REALLY well!!!)

So, between my lengthy profile, as well as the short novelette I just typed to you, I assume I'll hear back from you in a week or so when you're done reading it all!

Gotta scoot now!

Later gator!...........David

◆   ◆   ◆

OK...challenge! Does being a gourmet cook mean that we'll be battling for kitchen time!? Cooking is way up on my list of loves, and there's few things I enjoy more than preparing an excellent meal with someone special. Of course eating the meal is just as great! I don't send very many e-mails on this site, for a variety of reasons, not the least being time restraints...;.. yet there was just something about your photo that struck me. You have a very self aware look to you, as well as seeming very self confident. That's pretty much the only type of woman I will date, those having a high self esteem and an awareness of the world around them.... after all. we DO need something to talk about between kisses........ *grin*......toodles!.... David...

◆   ◆   ◆

I do hope I've made my point. What point is that you might ask? Simple. All the preceding messages were cute, to the point, a bit silly, and most women would answer a similar intelligently written note..... if there was any attraction. I can only assume that for these women there was none for me! Personal preference I guess. The funny thing is that Match.com sent these to me as 90 percentile or more matches, based both on the physical as well as the personality. Ahh, what does a computer know anyway?

When I asked Linda and Charley how they felt about a "no answer," this was their response:

Linda: Screw 'em! They do NOT know what they're miss-
                         ing.

Charley: They all answer me because I'm sooo gorgeous.
                         laughter

We all agreed however on my earlier points. If you throw enough mud up on the wall, eventually some will stick. There really isn't one perfect formula for this folks! Send out enough messages and sooner or later you'll meet someone wonderful. 'Nuff said.

As a final parting gift for this chapter, this next message will either make you laugh yourself to death, or just cry that there are people living here who write this way, and perhaps even communicate this way on a regular basis. I know, I know. I'm a writer, so I express myself a wee bit better than some, but you've just got to see this next one and judge for yourself. Besides mercifully changing her name in the text of her e-mail to me, I left *every single letter intact*. I swear I didn't change a thing! It would just figure if she were someone's secretary! I could not possibly make up a better representation of both the wrong way to contact someone for the first time, as well as a tremendous case for running your e-mail through a spell-check. Here goes:

Hello! the name is bernadette, and i'am 39 white itlaian irish women who love's to read people profile and when i saw your's you hited it right on the head.And i feel so dump telling you this see i'am divorced and i'am looking for some one who like to have a good times and i saw your ad and i said to myself why not answer this guy ad what could happen if he answer it great and if he dids't well that's okay to no big deal....

Yeah, me too! I just looked at this note with a glaze over my eyes and wondered if her ex-husband killed himself, or just moved *very* far away. Okay, okay...I can feel some of you getting ready to start yelling at me for bashing this poor woman. I'm just being silly! Yikes!

3

"I am the ONE for you! By the way, what was your name again?"

Everyone has a fantasy of what their perfect mate would be like. The way they would smell in bed. The color of their hair as the sun glistens off of it. The way their mouth will taste ever so sweet. The way they will touch you, caressing the hair away from your face and kissing you gently on your neck sending goose bumps up and down your spine. Their capacity to listen when you need them to. An exciting personality, someone who's not boring. A funny person who makes you laugh, even when you're down. Someone whose clothes you can't wait to rip off because they are *so* damn sexy to you. The way they'll make passionate love to you, as if you were both in a romance novel, gazing deeply into each others loving eyes. Mostly though, we fantasize about the way they will look at us, and we at them, when we're deeply in love. The kind of look that can come from across a crowded room and still make your knees weak…

One would think that it takes a considerable amount of time to *get* to this point. One would think that a first or second contact, especially in a blind situation as online dating most certainly is, would be a bit, um, sedate? THINK AGAIN!

So, you're home. Alone. Once again. You've just had another terrible date. It's a Friday night at 9 o'clock, and you're back online in a very melancholy mood. You'd hoped you would be out all night! This last one had so much potential…and then they opened their mouth. Ugh!

What *were* they thinking? What were *you* thinking? Did they really have a turtle shell collection at home that they wax every day? Did they really need to describe in graphic detail exactly the proper way *to* wax a turtle, and for 2 hours?

Then when you finally got a word in and convinced them to change the subject to something of a more personal nature, what did they decide to talk about? What else? Their ex!

AAAGGGGHHHH!!! PLEASE KILL ME NOW!!!

So you hit that button on your cell phone. You know the one. The emergency escape button that makes it ring.

"Hello? Oh my God! Really? Okay, I'm on the way now!"

You apologize to your date and beat a hasty retreat home to the safety of your computer and a full glass of ginger ale!

You log on to your dating site with little enthusiasm, but lo, who is this gentle creature? This one is different. The face, the body, amazing! You begin to read her profile and a warm glow spreads through your body as if angels had touched you on the shoulder and whispered, "Pssst! That's the *one*." What do you say? It better be good, you think, since you know that you only get one chance in this cyber-reality to make an awesome first impression.

The following letters represent some of the very best of these passionate responses to an online profile, with only one difference from the other chapters. None of these people ever actually met for some unexplainable reason. Only the original sender of the letter could give you an answer to the age-old question, "Why?" or rather, "Why not?"

> You're a cutie pie, and sound like tons of fun!
> Have a good one.............Samantha

Short and sweet. So I went to read her profile, and was blown away with a great personality, and a very sexy photo to boot. Here's my response.

> Okay Sammie, you're REALLY in trouble now.....ya put up an AWESOME profile, adorable photo, e-mail ME first..... and then you have the NERVE to live in Podunk!!!!! Welllllllllll......I guess you're not TOO far..... If we both drive really fast, we could meet in the middle in roughly an hour each.... and I am SOOOO worth it too! That's for you to find out however. Just so you know, EVERY woman with blonde hair and green eyes that I've ever dated, has attacked me on the first date!! *smile*, and Scorpios find me TOTALLY irresistible, must be an Aries thing!!! *grin*. You do seem, on paper to have the type of personality that would "click" totally with mine, sooooooooooo.... since you buzzed me first, tell me in 16 paragraphs or less, why you're the one girl I want to be holding in my arms for the holidays.... and beyond?......See ya soon kiddo!...*hugs*....David...

All right, now you're not going to *believe* her response to me!

Oh, no, now you've gone and done it, and your name has to be David............god, if I meet one more David, musta been the name back in the day..........I dated a guy from Match who lived in Boonie, NY, David was his name and he was a Aries! Whew, this is scary! We clicked right from the start, we talked on the phone for hours on end and finally he came down for the weekend. Neither one of us had a problem with the distance, that was how amazing it felt! I have a point here, not trying to get you aquanited with my ex,lol. anyway, David, when I tell you it was magical (they were his words), two days after he went back home, he called to tell me he HAD (like those choice of words) to go back with his ex because his son was in a "whirl" because of the separation, so he was separated and not yet divorced! He originally told me he was divorced! So go figure.....................end of that, now what the heck was my point, lol.........So tell you why I should be the girl you're holding in your arms this holiday, well now................this should be good.....................this is why I love Match! lol Well like you said, I am sooooooo worth it, if a man knows how to treat me, I give 100% and then some, but to make this more interesting lets do this.....................

TOP 10 LIST ON WHY DAVID SHOULD BE HOLDING SAMANTHA IN HIS ARMS..THIS HOLIDAY SEASON!................READY!

10. She has a sexy Santa's helper outfit with all the trimmings (or without, whichever you prefer) and hey, they don't call her Sexy Sam for nothing!

9. She is genuine, is good hearted, has values, brings out the best in people, loyal, aggressive (as you can see), adventurous, has multi-skills outside the bedroom, well I mean in the kitchen! lol.......witty, and a whole barrel of fun and laughs!

8. She will do anything, everything for her man! Except, put the toilet seat down, so tired of that task! plus I have to wipe the sides, walls, not my scene anymore!

7. She would travel the ends of the earth for a decent, honest, loyal man!

6. She gives the best BJ's, sorry, just being honest! lol, did I mention that I am brutally honest, ok, maybe I didn't have to there!

5. and hey, who wouldn't like to have a 5'8, blonde, green eyed, skilled, smart, who can do all the above and still look good wrapped on their arm! lol

4. are they getting weaker? lol..............ok, she doesn't spit! lol and I don't mean saliva dude........................

3. and hey, who wouldn't want me to meet their family.............ouch!

2. and to make things easier on ya, she isn't materialistic, material things have no importance on her, it's the richness that comes from within oneself that makes me rich! Wow, did I really say that, ok, I did, but it is me to a T!

1. and the #1 reason why David should be holding Samantha in his arm this holiday season...are you ready for the ride of your life.............................because once you know "me" you'll wonder where I have been all your life, your world will be turned upside down for the better of course and you'll never ever let me go, I promise this...........where do I sign! but the question is David, can YOU handle me, and what would you do to better know me, and now let's see just what kinda man you are in order to start the ball rolling.......................................

Sammie

Oh my God, how can you *possibly* respond to a letter like that? What an awesome girl! Who wouldn't want to spend the rest of their life with an amazing, sexy creature like this? So, for my reply, I responded in kind!

Top 10 reasons Samantha should RUN to NYC to spend the holidays with David...

10: The view of the Hudson River, George Washington Bridge, and amazing sunsets outside my living room windows are breathtaking!

9: I look killer in my tight black boxers!

8: You will NEVER find ANYONE who kisses more passionately than I do...tasting, nibbling, suckling, caressing, probing.... and so much more.....

7: I will keep you laughing so hard your ears will fall off, but fear not, as I can sew!

6: I have the most amazing, friendly, physical, adorable kids in the entire world, who totally accept and love, anyone who makes their daddy happy.

5: I seek a partner, who is my equal in every sense of the word, who will walk beside me, not behind, not in front. When I find her, I will lay the world at her feet, and love her as if every moment were our last....

4: I will make your torso rise to meet me, yours eyes roll back in their sockets, and your body shake with orgasmic passions you didn't know existed, when my mouth is between your thighs….. again, and again, and again……

3: I am one of the best guys around a kitchen stove that you'll ever meet, as is my 19 year old daughter Melanie, who I raised by myself…. she is da BEST! I have gotten marriage proposals for my Lasagna, and my chicken soup could cure Cancer!!! OH! and I have a George Foreman grill!!!!! KEWL!

2: I have an AWESOME voice, and will sing you to sleep every night….. although…I really don't think we'll be GETTING too much sleep…. for a while, at least!!! *tee hee*

1: but can YOU, handle ME? You talk about the ride of your life? I wear my heart on my sleeve, and you will never have to guess where my head is at, as you'll know. It goes from my brain to my mouth, no filter in between. It takes a very rare woman to win even a piece of my heart, but when I give it I give it for life. FYI, my ex is remarried……. just thought I'd put ya at ease! I love with every fiber of my soul, and I'm kinda tired of being alone in this big apartment. I love being surrounded by people I care about, and who love me as well. My love is unconditional, and total. Be very careful, my friend, because you may very well have just stepped in the shit! See ya!….D…just me!

This next message is another response to the same e-mail Sam sent. We were going back and forth so much that it gets a wee bit confusing!

Well, first of all, that other guy was NOT a New Yorker!!! He lives in Boon-ieville for Gods sake!!! That's a good 45 minutes North of here, up in the damn boonies!! I AM a New Yorker, born and bred, and if you give me the chance, I will also give YOU the chance, to make each other the happiest cou-ple alive. Yeah, I know, this goes BEYOND premature, but I've got a feeling about you, and whenever I don't follow my feelings I get burned. I am very spontaneous and do things that most people would NEVER consider doing…mostly in the name of love. You make me smile, something I haven't been doing enough of lately. I look forward to hearing your voice this evening, but I'll be leaving around 7:00 pm to go play with a band in Connecticut and see if we click at all. So call me when you get home, and maybe we can grab a few minutes together B4 I have to go….. I'd really like to get to know you bet-ter, and perhaps meet very soon…. as none of this truly matters, until you're looking into each others eyes, and just know, that it's right……D…

A 20 minute telephone conversation followed this, after we exchanged phone numbers online. And then, a bit more back and forth:

> David-
>
> I just read your top 10 list, wow, you hit me heart and soul! Especially #1, for I too wear my heart on my sleeve, all the time, it's who I am, and we have all been "railroaded", and I keep saying the right guy is gonna come along, but when he does they all turn out to be dicks! Sorry! I would travel the ends of the earth for a decent, honest, loyal human being! We sound very similar! My last encounter with a NYer well, took a lot out of me, but I always come back for more, cuz I know what I have to give to someone! Sam…

◆　　◆　　◆

> I was laying on my futon late last night, dozing, thinking about the many women pursuing me, and how I felt no passion for any of them. I often talk to God, and he looks down and laughs at me. "Silly little man," He says. I wished with all my heart for a woman who not only excites my senses, but entices my soul as well. A woman who can make me feel *alive* again, and I'm not talking about in bed. Someone who "gets me" and is so totally pumped that she finally *found* me. Have we found each other? Are WE for real? I believe we should find out…. and soon…. life is too short….. I await your tender mercies……. D…….

◆　　◆　　◆

> Well David, that other guy doesn't matter anymore now does he………………and hey, I am all about taking risks, that's what it is all about! Now, during the week after work I hit the gym for about a hour or so, so I usually don't get in till 7-7:30, so I don't know if I will have a chance to call you! So, I guess we will talk over the weekend? Let me know…………………………Sam…..

Talk over the weekend? WAITAMINIT! Passionate e-mails back and forth dripping with lustful hints? Made for each other possibilities, and we'll talk over the weekend, *maybe*? The more I pursued this girl, the further back she pulled despite several phone messages and passionate e-mails, including a poem that was one of the most passionate I've ever written to a woman. So I ask you, was she married? Did she have a boyfriend who she was just mad at and then got back together with? Was she just playing with me from the beginning? Did she ever have any intentions whatsoever to meet me? Did the distance between us and the fact that she had dated a guy from this area unsuccessfully, scare the crap out of her? I don't really know. What I do know is that we are all human beings and sometimes we get scared. I really wanted to meet this girl and pushed pretty hard to actually *be* holding her in my arms for the holidays, but no dice. She was in no hurry at all and perhaps my desire to meet her, passionately, scared her away. I regret very much not meeting this incredible woman, but perhaps she wasn't any of the things that she wrote about except in her own mind. I have the feeling though that she was all of those things and the circumstances were just not right for us to meet. DARN!

One of the things that is the most difficult to swallow once you've been doing this cyber thing for a while is that you never know the mental frame of mind of the person you're chatting with. I have spoken to hundreds, if not thousands of men and women who have dated online, and almost every one of them is convinced that almost everybody else online is nuts!

There really isn't too worse of a feeling than sitting across the table from an attractive person, a person you have chatted with for weeks, when you suddenly realize that they are a few cards short of a deck! Perhaps they are droning on and on about their broken marriage and their horrible ex-spouse, always fun to listen to. Perhaps they have totally lost all capacity for human kindness, or closeness, or compassion, because they have been hurt just one time too many. Perhaps they just got out of a very physically or verbally abusive relationship and are so very hungry for human kindness, tenderness, and affection that they scare the hell out of most people of the opposite sex as they seem terribly needy.

Or perhaps they are like the vast majority of us: hard working, friendly, normal people who are just a wee bit lonely. Who just seek a friendly face, a gentle touch, a sweet caress in the morning and a knowing smile? Perhaps they are everyday people who are just sick and tired of waking up hugging their pillow instead of spooning with someone special. Perhaps we are all seeking the same thing. That one person who we can feel at home with, who makes us feel special as they pat us on the butt, on our way to work.

This next woman is not atypical for the Internet. Pay close attention to her wonderful description of me in her first e-mail that follows, and then her description of me in her parting shot after I declined her attention.

Hi!

You look so great! You exude kindness, sincerely, down to earth easiness, thoughtfulness and someone who likes to workout.

I LOVE YOUR PROFILE. THE FIRST TIME I DID MY PROFILE, I WROTE THAT I WANTED TO SIMPLY FEEL LIKE I WAS 'HOME'...IT WAS DELETED SINCE I'M NOT GREAT NAVIGATING YET AND BUMPED MYSELF OUT OF THAT SCREEN. SO I REDID IT QUICKLY SO I COULD SEND YOU THIS E-MAIL.

Do call tonight or soon!!!!!

Lorrie

952 000-0000

My, my...A phone number on a first contact? Very rare, and very foolhardy. How does she know I'm not some raving lunatic who will harass her relentlessly until she travels to New York to tell me to leave her alone? So, my red flag went up immediately, especially since her profile didn't as yet exist, thus no photo either. So did I ignore her and listen to my inner person? Of course not! I called her that night and spent the better part of three hours talking to her. The phone conversation was cute, but uneventful. Since she lives half way across the country from me I didn't really intend on calling her again, until today when the following e-mails arrived with her very well written and passionate profile.

HEY, HANDSOME...JUST SENT MATCH MY PIX...TELL ME IF DISTORTED..

HOPE TO HEAR FROM YOU SOON.

LORRIE

◆   ◆   ◆

You copycat you!!!! ONLY KIDDING!!!! Hi sweetie. Yes, I did love what you wrote, and as we've already discussed, we DO seem to be looking for exactly the same thing...on paper.... I have found that in application however, there may be differences, but I think you might be worth finding out...Soooooooo..... lemme go out on a limb B4 I see your picture (since you think you're soooo amazing!!! *smile*) and give you my phone #, 718-000-0000..... good luck finding me home though, although any night.... um, like NOW..... would be good after 9:00 pm or so......okee dokey Smokey????.... *hugs*....

David...

Okay, now the "copycat" statement was because her profile was very similar to my own in its content. The rest was familiarity. Now here is where it gets weird. I sent her another e-mail saying, "Oopsie, you already have my number," as we had spoken at length before. Here are the 2 responses to the 2 e-mails, sent moments apart.

SO ARE YOU GOING TO CALL?
LORRIE

◆   ◆   ◆

Just found this e-mail in the junk file. Message said it was there because of graphics. Don't get it! Others have sent their profiles. Thanks for the compliment and for your number but I prefer the man calls me. Loved this message. Am going to eat and for a walk…You're welcomed to call after midnight but near if you're up. Even call earlier if you choose.
    Lorrie

Okay now. Please explain something to me, as I'm just a dumb guy here. Doesn't it seem a wee bit strange to you that sometimes she writes her name like the rest of us, yet sometimes all in upper case letters? You know, CAPS? Doesn't it seem strange, since it was *she* pursuing *me* from the get-go, that she "prefers the man call" her? Doesn't it seem strange that when I did call her this evening, per her request, that she didn't know who I was, especially since we had already spent a good deal of time on the phone previously? That she needed to tell me about the 399 e-mails she's received in less than a week, (with no photo posted yet mind you) from possible suitors, like I *needed* to know that? Geez Louise!

Learn a lesson here folks, and learn it well. When you first enter the cyber world of dating, unless you are totally hideous with no personality, you *are* going to get a ton of e-mail from people because you are "new meat" and everyone suddenly wants to know you. Do not make the mistake of ignoring the few for the many. If there is someone who blows you away the first time you see their profile, as I did to this young lady, do not make the mistake of getting sucked in by all the responses from the opposite sex who are seeking *you* out! If you pick someone and send them several passionate e-mails, at least have the manners to remember who they are if and when they do call you, or you'll get laughed at and hung up on, as did this young lady this evening! Yikes! Well, you know something? People do *not* like being giggled at and then hung up on (I did nicely say goodbye, and good luck though). So when I called her back a few minutes later to attempt an explanation, she called me a loser and other less complimentary words, and then slammed the phone down. Hmph! She sure told me! So I sent her what I thought would be a parting shot. (Hey, I'm not perfect!)

> and you wonder why you're single?????? =)

Not too nasty? I think I made my point. Then, she made hers. Be ready to duck now!

> I KNEW YOU'D SEND SOME EGOTISTICAL MESSAGE...
> I DON'T WONDER WHY I'M SINGLE...AND I CERTAINLY KNOW WHY YOU ARE...I'D JUST SAID TO SOMEONE EARLIER THAT THERE HAVE BEEN MEN WHO THOUGHT I SHOULD REMEMBER THEM AFTER ONE CONVERSATION DAYS EAR-LIER...TO TOP IT OFF THEY WOULD NOT GIVE THEIR NAME...BUT THEIR EGOS ARE SO HURT THAT I SHOULD BE ABLE TO KNOW THEM WHEN THEY HAVE CALLED ME OUT OF MANY (399 AS OF YESTERDAY) WHO'VE CONTACTED ME.
> I'M SORRY YOU HAVE A SELF ESTEEM ISSUE BUT I DON'T HAVE TIME FOR YOUR INSULTS, WHINNING, SARCASM OR SHIT.... THAT'S WHAT YOU FIRST CALL WAS, YOUR SECOND CALL AND YOUR E-MAIL....
> HOPEFULLY, YOU WON'T RESPOND...BUT I BET YOUR EGO WON'T LET YOU.... 'LET IT LIE'.
> ALL THE BEST TO YOU, DAVID...SORRY YOU'RE GOING THRU SUCH A ROUGH TIME BUT YOU'RE NOT WHAT I'M LOOKING FOR...BUT YOU ARE ONE HELL OF A GOOD LOOK-ING GUY...JUST NEED TO GET THAT EMOTIONAL SHIT TOGETHER AND FINANCIAL.
> LORRIE

Ay Chihuahua! That would have stung if there were a grain of truth in it. Here is my response, and then the back and forth between us, that actually bordered on niceties.

> My, my, my!!! Don't you and I both have strong personalities!!!!! What a rela-tionship we'd have!!!!! Anyway, I'm not gonna attack you back, as it's really not my way. Sorry ya got the wrong impression, but such is life, I'll live. I am a bit sad today, as a great Minnesota native died needlessly last night in a car accident. Herb Brooks was the coach of the 1980 U.S. Olympic gold medal hockey team, a coach of both the New York Rangers, New Jersey Devils, and

several other teams. He was a winner wherever he went, and exuded a level of class that most people can only dream of. I will miss him, as will the entire hockey world. Once again, It's a shame we didn't see eye to eye, but isn't that just so human?..... toodles......David...=)

◆   ◆   ◆

WE DO...AND I'M WORN FROM KEEPING SOMEONE ALIVE FOR 2 YEARS..
WHAT'S YOUR EXCUSE?...lol NOT LOOKING FOR ANSWER...
HOPE YOU FEEL BETTER..
ALL THE BEST...
     LORRIE

◆   ◆   ◆

Just some words of wisdom: Take 'em or leave 'em......

Now that we've stopped tossing rocks at each other, I just wanted to share something with you from experience, and to save the next poor fool who pisses you off a tongue lashing! *SMILE* It takes time to learn even a little bit about a person, yet it's so easy for us to make value judgments. Let me tell you where I was today from 3:15 until 5:45. I was at the same place that I'm at every Thursday and Tuesday, for as long as I can stay, that being the nursing home with my 86 year old aunt Jeanette. Why? You might ask do I need to see her so often? Because I make her smile. Because I love her desperately. Because I don't know how much longer she'll be around to smile at me when I arrive with KFC and cookies. Because no one else can go on those days. My friend Peggy goes every Wednesday. My cousin Nita goes every Saturday, for the whole day. She would go more often (after all, it IS her mom) but she works like a dog, and just cannot physically do it. She has an aid that keeps her company on Mondays and Fridays, so she's almost never without company, but she REALLY seems to brighten up when her wiseass nephew comes, joking with the entire staff and all the residents who can still function as human beings.

I guess my point is the following. I love what I do (writing and photography) I have the best kids on the planet who love me to death and tell me every chance they get. I have a ton of awesome friends, both male and female, and am NOT in short supply of female companionship. My future is bright, and I'm truly proud of the person I have become.... okay, I'm getting long winded here..... here's the poop.... your words to me left me smiling, because they were so far off base, as to be laughable…. HOWEVER, there are many people out there who, those selfsame words might damage mightily. People who indeed ARE at a very bad place in their life. People who might just get pushed over the edge by nasty words from a person of the opposite sex.

I implore you to please, PLEASE never write such graphically judgmental words to another person, as you might just hurt someone beyond repair……okee dokey Smokey?????….. *hugs*….. David…

Of course there was no response to this heartfelt letter. There rarely is once a person realizes that despite their attacks you have decided to be understanding and take the high ground. It usually works wonders, but on occasion totally infuriates others.

The following is an e-mail exchange of something that could have been, that should have been, but perhaps the timing was just wrong.

No, itznotonlyu…LOL
Hey there,
Well maybe you already found your Valentine, but I thought I'd take a chance anyway. I haven't found mine! This is the first Valentine's Day that I've ever spent alone for as long as I can remember.

I live in Duckwalk, CT for the past 10 years, but I'm originally from The Bronx (Cows Neck). I lived there for 29 years. My family is still there and I visit often.

I read your profile from start to finish and I must say, I liked it and I must say, you're very good looking too. I attached my profile and if you're interested, write back and I'll send you my picture. I don't think you'll be disappointed. And I've got lots of love to give to the right man!

Hope to speak with you soon.
Anna

◆   ◆   ◆

Thanks for the kind words. I normally don't respond to e-mails without photos, but yours was different for many reasons. First, this too is my first ever Valentines day without a girlfriend/wife/significant other…. yada yada. It was not however a day spent alone. One of my dearest friends is named Linda. She's a little self destructive in the dating department (always the wrong guys) but has a heart as big as Texas. Well, she and her most recent boyfriend, one who she truly loved, broke up 2 days ago. She needed company, a shoulder to cry on......guess who spent the day with her? She wanted me to go out with her and her girlfriends tonight but I didn't feel up to it.

Second coincidence, my ex girlfriend is named Anna. She got the closest to winning my heart. Close. Just not close enough. Today was her first wedding anniversary with her new hubby. I hope she's happy as she's a luv.

Third coincidence, my dad and two sisters live in Cows neck. What-EVAH!

Fourth? I just liked what you wrote. You have confidence and I find that irresistible.

So send those photos, and I promise to leave a phone number. I could use a sweet voice and a pretty face to chat with tonight. Sometimes it gets a little hard being there for everyone else, yet still coming home to an empty house........

toodles.....

David.... dosterczy@boogies.com

Oh yeah, I forgot a bunch of other stuff..... I love classic rock, have a ton of home baked candles in my house with scents like English Pound cake, Peach Cobbler, Apple crisp, Cranberry spice, and a ton more, have you beat 3 kids to 2, and would travel to the ends of the earth to gaze lovingly into a pair of huge brown eyes..............=)

◆   ◆   ◆

Hello David,

Thanks for responding so quickly and even responding to someone who didn't send a picture right away. I attached the one to this e-mail and it's the only picture I have of myself on my computer. It's me and my sister-in-law. I'm the one in the picture wearing the necklace and I have the longer darker hair. I do promise that I look even better in person.

Well the fact that you spent the time with a female friend who was hurting shows you have compassion. A very good quality in a man that not too many seem to have. You seem very upbeat and friendly too which is something I appreciate in a person. I'm like that as well. I was supposed to have my family from The Bronx over my house today for my Grandmother, Grandfather, Mother, Sister-in-law and Son's birthdays. Can you believe it...Geeeeez!!! They're all born in February. I was supposed to make this big dinner for all of them and I bought all the food too, but my youngest son got sick so we postponed it until next Sunday. I didn't want my little neice and nephew to catch what he has. It would have been better to have it today, because I don't have to work on Monday. So next week, I'll have to do all that on Sunday then work the next morning...I'll be tired! As a matter of fact, I'm on vacation all this week...so I'm happy about that. I could use the rest. I have two son's one is 19 years old next Monday and he recently moved back to The Bronx. He never liked living in Connecticut since all his friends were in New York. So as soon as he got a job, he moved back. He comes up when he can get off from work and he visits or I see him when I go down there. My other son is 4 years old and he lives with me. He stays with his dad once or twice a week.

So where in the Bronx do you live? I have family in Cows Neck as I mentioned, Maple Park and Freekie Bay.

Well it appears we have some things in common. So I would definitely like to get to know you better. And…I made it through my first Valentine's Day alone…whew!!! LOL I just went to bed early. I couldn't take watching what was on last night, nothing but love stories it seemed…just to rub it in even more! ;-)
Hope to speak to you soon.
Anna

Well, so far so good. It seemed to be going smoothly and uneventfully. The photo that she sent was indeed with her sister, but Anna was behind her as well as in shadow. I mean the photo was dark and you could not really make out her facial features. So we continue:

Truly, I agree. I went to bed early as well. How dumb is it to have all those heart warming love stories on TV on V day? I mean all the lovers are out having fun together and the rest of us who are alone are just annoyed that everyone else (on TV) are so blissfully happy! AAAGGGHHH! So who watches it? *sheesh*

If you'd like to gimme a holler before your little "sickie" wakes up I'm at 718-543-0000. We can talk about my favorite subject, that being my kids! toodles……D……

◆   ◆   ◆

I'll give you a call in about 15 minutes. I have to go make my coffee first. Gotta have it!

And she called. And we talked, and talked and talked. Three and a half hours of blissful, cute, funny conversation followed by two hours with my heartbroken friend Linda, and then another five hours with Anna that evening until nearly 3:00 A.M. I had mentioned on the phone that I would truly like to see a clear photo of what she looked like. She informed me that although she had no more pictures of her face, since she's usually the one behind the camera, (totally understandable being a photographer here) she did indeed have some racy pictures taken by her ex-boyfriend of her very fine body as taken from behind. This at face value did seem a bit strange, but put yourselves in my position here guys! You've just spent the better part of your entire day on the phone laughing and flirting with this woman who now wants to send you semi-naked photos of her body. I don't know about you, but I was excited!

After waiting for her photos but not receiving them fast enough for my hungry eyes, I sent the following note, after which the pics did come..... and *boy* did they ever!

> Well, my eyes are starting to shut as a thought occurred to me. Perhaps, since I didn't receive your photo, you somehow mixed up the letters in my name and sent your sweet tooshie elsewhere. As I type these words at this very moment, some 65 year old man in Czechoslovakia is poking his weenie to a picture of your fine round butt. I am in tears right about now..... too funny!!!!!
> Goodnight my sweet......hehehe........ *grin* D......

◆　　　◆　　　◆

> I sent you the pic...hope you got it...I'm sitting here hysterical...Anna

◆　　　◆　　　◆

> I got it..... I am in deeeep trouble.........*gulp*.... D......

At this point I sent her off several more very sedate photos of myself, my family, and some artsy shots I had taken in Michigan. Understand what was going on here and the very different messages we were sending to each other. I was sending wholesome family shots to her. She was sending borderline porn shots to me. Are you getting the picture here? Are any red flags beginning to develop in your mind? And it continues:

> Your pictures are great...your children are adorable. You're adorable too! Sherry looks great and so does your dad. Well anyway, take care of Sherry, she needs you. I can tell she has a kind heart...you can see it in the picture. (She confused my heartbroken friend Linda for Sherry. S'okay, no prob!)

Talk to you tomorrow. Good night handsome!

◆　　　◆　　　◆

So does that mean you like? Does that look like a fat girl to you or just a sexy one??? Hehehehe
Hey, log off...I need to talk to you for 30 seconds....ok?
D......

So we spoke yet a third time in the same day. Well, sort of, as it was by now the middle of the night. I do not remember this short conversation but I'm sure it was as cute as the previous two, albeit much more brief.

I am so pooped. Someone kept me up WAYYY too late last night. If someone EVER keeps me up THAT late again it best be for a better reason! *grin*
Had a super productive meeting with a future board member of my Coalition (investment banker) then got a call from my cousin Nita who is really down with the flu to ask if I could go visit her mom today. I did. My aunt Jeanette was thrilled! She loves me so much that her eyes just light up when she sees me. But then everyone's eyes light up when they see me! *tee hee*
Shot home to write you a quick note and I'm back on the road until about 10:00 pm......see ya later gator!
...D......=)

So we spoke that night, a conversation that revolved around compatibility and star signs. At this point she informed me that she had shown my photos to her mother who responded that I was simply adorable. She then sent my birth date and hers, which she had asked me for the day before, to an astrologer for a compatibility test. She explained to me that she had done this in several past relationships and that the test always came back very negative. She never listened to the results though and usually ended up getting hurt in yet another failed relationship. Ours however was another story. Ours came back so completely positive that I think it scared the crap out of her! It follows:

You sent us the following question: I met a man online yesterday. We seem to want exactly the same things. We spoke on the phone a total of 8 hours yesterday. We plan to meet this week. How will this turn out?

Wow! I think that sparks are going to fly, Anna. This relationship shows a lot of potential. In astrology, we look to positive connections between the Sun in one person's chart and the Moon in the other to judge basic compatibility. In your Natal Chart, you have the Sun in sensual, passionate, and intuitive Scorpio, a water sign, and he has the Moon in Cancer, also a water sign, which is a very positive connection. Also, he has the Sun in Aries, a fire sign, and you have the Moon in Aries, another water sign—also a very fortuitous connection. A positive Sun-Moon connection is vital to the success of a man-woman relationship—and you and he have a DOUBLE Sun-Moon connection. You can't get much better than that!

Astrologers look to connections between the positions of Mercury, planet of the mind and of communication, in the two charts to judge how well a couple communicates and how well they understand each other. You have Mercury, planet of communication, in Sagittarius, a fire sign, and he has Mercury in Aries, which is also a very positive connection and implies that you think alike, understand each other, share a lot of interests and communicate well.

Your Natal Venus, planet of love, in Libra, an air sign, blends very well with his Natal Venus and Mars, planet of desire, both of which are posited in Aquarius, another air sign. This means that there is a strong physical attraction between you, as well as potential for a very strong and powerful love.

Both of you are probably going to be blown away by each other. You probably already know each other pretty well, but actually being able to see each other is going to make a difference. And if you don't want this flame to burn out quickly, you'll have to keep it on an even keel for awhile, neither trying to rush it yourself, or allowing yourself to get caught up in his attempts to rush it. You and your friend will get off to a great start, and you could find yourselves making lots of plans for the future. When this happens, however, don't take everything he says at face value. He may have a lot of ideas for things that you and he can do in the future—but at this point, he's probably fantasizing. Don't respond too strongly or too enthusiastically or you'll scare him.

All this having been said however, this looks great. Good luck!

Well, I can tell you that at this point my head was spinning a bit. This seemed to feel just right. She was sexy and aggressive and just totally pleased with the idea of getting very cozy and physical with me very soon. Our telephone conversations were getting pretty specific sexually, but in a playful way. It was blatantly obvious to both of us at this juncture that we would be extremely compatible in at least one area, that being the bedroom.

Hi David,
Just wanted to write you a little note to say hello. I hope your day is going well. Mine is okay so far. I spent the morning talking to two of my girlfriends who called one right after the other. Suzanne and Alison. Suzanne is the one

I'm visiting tonight, the one who lives in Brooklyn. Her husband is traveling today, so it will be just the two of us. It's nice, we have dinner and a few drinks and just talk and have lots of laughs. Not sure if we'll go out somewhere or just hang in. I enjoy doing that with her. Alison, I may see on Friday. She lives in Byram, CT and we'll probably meet for lunch at the Galleria mall or I'll just go to her house. I haven't seen either of them in a few weeks. It's hard to while I'm working.

I'm about to run out and do some errands. I also wanted to wash my car, but I hear it may snow tomorrow, so maybe I won't bother for now. My car is blue and shows every bit of dust that hits it. I like my car clean so just imagine how this weather drives me nuts. I am so ready for Spring!

If I don't get to talk to you later, enjoy your evening with your children and your day with them tomorrow.

Talk to you soon.

Anna

◆   ◆   ◆

I'm smiling right now. Thank you so much for the cute note, as well as your itinerary over the next few days! I just ran in for a minute. This has been a stress filled day so far.... and it won't be over for a WHILE! I guess I won't be able to chat with you tonight,,,,,,,, *boo hoo*..... but I concentrate on my kids when they're with me as I don't get to spend nearly enough time with them. That will change, but not for a while.

So I'll give you a holler tomorrow night sometime so that we can firm up our plans for Thursday morning. Okay tooshie?

See ya sooooooooon........ hehehe............

D.... just me..............

◆   ◆   ◆

Glad you liked the note and the fact that I can make you smile makes me happy. Sorry to hear your day was stressful, I know how that can be. I just got back from shopping at Costco. It's one of those huge price club stores incase you didn't know. But always crowded and crazy. Now I know why I don't go there too often.

I'll be leaving here around 6:30 or 7:00pm after my ex picks up my son. It's a free night for me. I love my son, but sometimes I enjoy the night I get to myself. Well have fun with your kids.

Talk to you tomorrow.
Anna

As is apparent in the letters we were both going to be quite busy for the next few days and would not have an opportunity to speak because of our schedules. We set a date to meet for Thursday morning (two days hence), and to speak in confirmation of that date on Wednesday evening. Well I had called her several times anyway to see if we could hear each other's voices, just to be playful. After all, we had practically spent two entire days together on the phone. It was tough going cold turkey from that! I didn't leave any messages and was a bit surprised that she didn't call me, but brought my kids back to their mom's house and upon returning at 10:00 pm gave her a call.

She was very quiet and distant on the phone, not at all the woman I had spoken to previously. She informed me after several minutes that our date was indeed off due to the fact that her eldest son needed to work and she had no one to watch her youngest child. I asked her when she knew about this and she said that it was in the afternoon that she found out. I was very taken aback that this adult female upon realizing that our date was off did not deem it fit to call and tell me about it. Since she had been sleeping when I did call, I asked when she had intended on informing me of the bad news. Her response was horrific. "Sometime tomorrow I guess." Nice. Very, very nice.

Now it was my turn to become quiet. I did not know what to say or how to react. I am just a decent, lonely human being who was becoming very taken by this woman who had sent me, to date, a total of six very sexy photos of herself, spent countless hours laughing on the phone, and who was telling me with every gesture that we were meant to be together. I was hurt. I was shocked. I was becoming aware that this was a child in a woman's body who had no concern whatsoever for another person's feelings. She let us both down very badly and blamed me for it, as will become apparent in the following letters.

Hi David,

After speaking with you last night, I couldn't sleep. Something just wasn't sitting right with me and I thought about it all night long. Nothing about what you want scares me, however your intense reaction to certain things does. It's a trait I don't admire in myself and I certainly don't want that in the person I'm with. It's drama and something I'm trying to avoid. I've had way too much of that in my life. The fact that you can get that way when we haven't even met is troubling to me. Before last night, I absolutely did want to meet you and it was no lie that I couldn't get anyone to watch my son today. I am sure that you are every bit the attractive and wonderful person you say you are, but I'm going to have to go with my instincts for once and listen to them closely. Something I've never done before. I can imagine what you must be thinking of me right now, and I'm truly sorry, but I have to do what's best for me.

Take care David and I wish you the very best.

Anna

◆   ◆   ◆

I was going to wait for you to call, but your e-mail has forced my hand. You really need to look at yourself in the mirror and take a long hard stare. You need to ask yourself what you're so desperately afraid of and why you chased me away even before this message to me.

Lets just look at the facts, shall we?

You contacted me first.

You sent me sexy photos, six of them, portraying a certain image that was undeniably sexy and forward. I never asked for them. You volunteered.

You, after only speaking for one day to me, went out and got a definitive analysis of a possible relationship together. It was so totally positive that it reinforced the tiny positive feelings I was already having towards you.

You showed my photos to your mother. YOUR MOTHER! *sheesh*

Why in Gods name would I NOT develop some feelings for a woman who shows me that much attention? Damn right I liked you! Drama you say? Not even!

And here's the big one. You were completely and totally selfish, with absolutely no regards to my feelings, or my time. Upon realizing that our date was off you did not call me and in fact did NOT intend to! Your words! I asked you after I woke you up and you said that perhaps you would have called me in the morning. In the morning? Perhaps if you had a sense of anyone else's feelings you would see this the way I do? This was all your doing. I am innocent of everything but hurt feelings and a sense of emptiness that I'll perhaps never meet you. You have proved everything about women that I said was true. Had I acted aloof, and not upset, that our date was canceled, you would have had no problem. So it really IS true. The assholes DO get all the girls. You have taught me a valuable lesson. One that I will learn from despite the letdown.

What a shame…………D…………..

So we spoke on the phone yet again. This time was like the other times, laughing, joking, silly, and fun. It ended badly however, for at this point she was just waiting for the other shoe to drop, and drop it did as I jokingly said that, "I would hate her if she screwed this up for us both." I was laughing when I said it. It was meant in jest. She did not take it that way.

I did take a good hard look at myself and for once I'm doing what I feel is right for me. Something I've never done and have always had many troubles for it. I had very good feelings about you at first and never intended to hurt or disappoint you in any way. But then you started showing a side of yourself that struck me as obsessive. I didn't know exactly what it was at first, but now I'm sure. Yes, women are looking for a man who's passionate, considerate, loving and all that we spoke of, but he's also got to be a strong man and I'm not talking physical. You seem to have been wounded by life, just as I have and you need to be mentally strong before you can have a healthy relationship. Something I feel that we both need to work on before finding "the one" If you asked the women that you say ran from you that you almost fell for, I'm sure they would agree that you have a tendancy to be obsessive. That is the clear signal I'm getting from you. I have been guilty of being this way myself in the past and that is why I recognize it in you. I completely see parts of myself in you. It's something I'm not proud of and have worked very hard on changing and I'm still working on it. Now could you imagine two people getting together that have a tendancy to be this way. For your own good and mine, I feel this is best at least it is for me.

I have taken that long hard look at myself and maybe I have you to thank for that. I will be removing myself from that dating site as soon as possible. I don't think I will be dating anyone at least not seriously other than friends for a long while until I feel that I am completely strong enough myself. I thought I was, but I'm not. I think you should take a look at yourself as well.

I am very sorry it turned out this way. All I ask is that you understand what I'm trying to say. I do think you're very special David, I sincerely do.

Take care,

Anna

◆   ◆   ◆

I should have listened to you. You're not ready. I was joking. I had a smile on my face, but you couldn't know that, how could you? I hate nothing for there is too much love in my heart, but how could you know that as well?

I will listen now. I will leave you alone. I remain open to meet but I don't know why. You scare me now. You have been damaged badly by your past and seem to look for negative where there is so little of it. If you look hard enough you'll see cracks in even the brightest of diamonds. I am not perfect, but I could have made you happy. I'm sorry that you can't open your heart enough to even attempt to see that.

I wish you happiness and joy. Don't cry please as there are happier days ahead......

bye...D...

Yes, she cried on the phone after basically saying that she'll never meet the man she seeks. At least, not while she keeps chasing away the nice ones. Then, as if by divine intervention, my friend Sharon sent me the following note. She is another one of those Internet buddies that I adore as she is a pistol and smart as a whip. It seemed fitting so I decided to send it to Anna. I do not know who authored it, but he/she is a genius!

> This is a good one for you. Perhaps you cut the ties a bit TOO soon. Time will tell here it goes: Pay attention to what you read. After you've finished reading it, you'll know the reason it was sent to you!
>
> People come into your life for a Reason, a Season or a Lifetime.
>
> When you know which one it is for you, then you'll know what to do for that person.
>
> When someone is in your life for a REASON, it's usually to meet a need you've expressed. They have come to assist you through a difficulty, to provide you with guidance and support, to aid you physically, emotionally, or spiritually. They may seem like a Godsend, and in fact they are! They're there for the reasons that you need them to be there for. Then without any wrongdoing on your part, or at an inconvenient time, this person will say something to bring the relationship to an end.
>
> Perhaps they've died. Perhaps they've walked away. Sometimes they act up and force you to take a stand for your own rights. What we must realize is that our need has been met, our desire fulfilled, their work is now done. The prayers you've sent up have been answered, and now it's time to move on.
>
> Some people come into your life for a SEASON, because your turn has come to share, grow, or learn. They bring you an experience of peace, or make you laugh. Indeed they may teach you something you have never done but they usually give you an unbelievable amount of joy. Believe it! It is real, but only for a season.
>
> LIFETIME relationships teach you lifetime lessons: things you must build upon in order to have a solid emotional foundation. Your job is to accept the lesson, love the person, and put what you have learned to use in all other relationships and areas of your life.
>
> It is said that love is blind but friendship is clairvoyant. Thank you for being a part of my life.
>
> David...

◆   ◆   ◆

Perhaps I did, but there were things about you that were just not sitting right with me. I may be completely wrong, but it's what I felt. Yes, time will tell….you're right about that.

Hope you're well.

Anna

◆   ◆   ◆

As I had said previously, if you actively look under enough rocks, you'll eventually find yucky stuff. My final words to you that night were said in jest, and also said over an hour past the time I had already told you I was exhausted.

I have moved on and already have other dates set up including one of the "playday" variety today. You send so many mixed signals to a man in such an aggressive way that it's no wonder I screwed up a bit. I stood no chance. Funny thing is we formed a bond, or so I thought, of fun and laughter over the very few days we spoke. I hate to lose that and would still welcome your friendship, but would not meet you at this point in your life. I will confide with you, I will laugh with you, I will tell you stories and listen to yours. I will be your friend as that's what I think you need right now. I think you need to start trusting the fact that there are sensitive, passionate, wonderful men out here, like myself, who would NOT hurt you.

Someday when you begin to trust again, we can meet, but I fear I'll be in a relationship by then as I never stay alone for too long. You have an adorable way about you but you need to stop judging a word here and a word there. I made you laugh regularly, and feel good for the most part, so stop looking at tiny pieces that are totally inconsequential at this point in time.

Any time you need to talk I'll be here for you. I already consider you a friend, albeit a confused one. Join the club.

hugs

David….

Did you see anything nasty in the previous letter, anything at all that you would need to attack? Did I not leave the door open for friendship as well as a future meeting? Did I not admit that I myself was confused? The following is her response, along with the "crash and burn" variety of letters that she needed to get off her ample chest.

Funny how you don't seem to take the blame for anything. I am not at all confused about what I see in you. I'm not at all a stupid woman and I've seen a lot and I saw someone who was a bit obsessive and somewhat insecure and desperate not to mention pushy. I was married to a man who started out like you did and I saw all the signs there in you. I'm usually never wrong with what I feel and my only problem was that I never listened to what I felt in the past and got into relationships that weren't good for me. I have the right to change my mind about someone and I have.

Take care David and good luck.

Anna

♦   ♦   ♦

I don't recall being rude to you. You obviously have much deeper issues than I was aware of. I never said that I was perfect but that horoscope you received was not arbitrary, they know what they're talking about. I'm sorry that you feel the way you do but there was no reason to attack me the way you just did. You have opened up my eyes to the person that you truly are, one that I would not have in my life in any way. Please get the help that you desperately need.

You truly need to re-read the last full paragraph of the horoscope you sent to me. It was right on the mark, but you chose to ignore it completely.

David

♦   ♦   ♦

I don't recall saying rude and I don't think I'm the one who needs help! Take a look at yourself. Don't write me again.

Please go away. You're starting to resemble an obsessive nut.

Anna

♦   ♦   ♦

Yet you keep responding! Get over yourself already!!! SILLY GIRL!

David

◆   ◆   ◆

You're truly a sick man…and for your information. I'm not wrong about you.
 Anna

◆   ◆   ◆

So angry, so judgmental, what a shame as you are so off base………. oh well!
=) Still smiling on my end! Gotta scoot!
 toodles!!!!!…D…

And that my friends, was that! Just where did all her anger come from? Did she truly not understand that after two passionate days on the phone, with all the accompanying accoutrements, that I would not be upset with her ignoring our first face-to-face meeting? Perhaps it's just me, but if I have to break a date with a woman, I am going to call her at the earliest possible opportunity after finding out I cannot make the date. Am I crazy here? Did I not have ample reason to be upset? Even if we did not have such passionate conversations, even if she did not garner the horoscope evaluation and even if she did not send me all the sexy photos, is it not simple courtesy to pickup the phone and call a person to tell them that you will not be seeing them the following morning? Izitonlyme here?

Does the possibility exist that when she finally got her first positive response from her astrologer that she became scared that I might indeed be the one she was seeking and started to create excuses to not meet me? In one paragraph she managed to call me obsessive, insecure, desperate and pushy! Yet she was the one who contacted me first. She was the one sending all the naughty, suggestive photos. She was the one showing my pics to her mom. She was the one seeking out professional guidance even before we met to see if we were compatible. Everything was fun and positive until she decided that it not be so.

The entire scenario confused the hell out of me and left me mentally and emotionally exhausted, as well as less trusting of women. That indeed is the sad part. Why do we do this to each other? Do we not all realize that when you let someone down, or even hurt them deeply by changing directions suddenly and for no apparent reason that you screw them up just a wee bit more for the next lucky person who comes into their life? Thanks a lot Anna! Ya big poopy head!
 'Nuff said.

For all the women out there shaking their heads right now, prepare yourselves. For all the men thinking I should have just swallowed my pride, relaxed, and met this woman who may have been a bombshell in bed, learn a lesson from me. I sensed once the problems between us began that perhaps she wasn't really mad at me but just venting in my direction. I sensed some very deep issues but ignored them as the sexy photos progressed one after another to my inbox. Stupid. Really, really, stupid. You're right girls, we do have two heads, yet often think with the smaller one!

So I began to date a girl who lived quite far away. We were not very compatible, yet we seemed to make each other laugh. She sent me a very cute joke online that I forwarded to my entire contact list…which Anna was on. This was the sort of e-mail that usually garners no response from your friends and contacts due to its very nature.

Imagine my surprise when I received the following response:

> Hi David,
> How are you?….thanks for sending this…I enjoyed it!
> Anna

What??? Five weeks had passed in the interim. This girl was not even on my radar screen, and yet for some reason she chose to contact me. Considering the strong negative comments she had shot towards me I did not expect to ever hear from her again. Being a writer though, my curiosity got the better of me and I figured that the worst that could happen would be more cannon fodder for my book. Boy, was I ever right. My initial feeling was that this truly was a very confused, disturbed young lady and I'd better tread lightly in my responses to her.

> I Know! Wasn't that just TOO funny! My friend Linda sends me stuff like that all the time as do lots of my friends. I know people from all over the world and I get some stuff from Europe that just about kills me because I laugh so hard!!!
> Nice to hear from you. I miss our talks.
> Toodles….
> David…=)

Yes, that was very funny. Did you ever finish your book?
  Anna

I write nearly every day and yes it is closer to completion. My editor seems to have disappeared too, so I actually edited over 6 chapters myself over the weekend. UGH. I do NOT want to be an editor! It's really hard critiquing yourself and removing anything that is not awesome, as well as making sure that grammar and punctuation are perfect, but it needs to be done.
  You didn't tell me how YOU have been doing?
  toodles......D...

Yes, I imagine that editing your own book would be a real pain. I'm doing okay. I had one more run in with my ex Simon that I told you about. We saw each other again, but I decided that it's not the right thing to do. In fact it's a big mistake. Maybe I needed that closure. Anyway, I'm just working and seeing friends. Not dating anyone seriously, just go out with some male friends of mine from time to time. Nothing major...how about you? Have you met anyone on Match.com. I'm now off of there.
  Anna

Not dating at all really, too busy with my book, my new digital photography equipment, my softball team, kids, Coalition, 2 jobs, yada yada. It's a funny thing though as I joined one of those "alternate" dating sights for a kick!? I looked at the profiles first that the guys were putting up and laughed my ass off! All they talked about was how big their, um, equipment was and how wonderful they were in bed. "I can go all night long"..... *sheesh*.... So I took the opposite tack, put up some cute pics and just talked about what I was seeking and OY VAY did I get inundated with e-mail from 23 year old girls seeking my wallet, 35 year old girls seeking?????? I dunno??? and massive women in their 40's and 50's who are all "very oral and swallow hard" and will do "just about anything to please my man"……. *yikes*

The funny thing is that some of these girls may actually be legitimate (ver-rrrry few!) and e-mail me nearly every day. I seriously doubt that I'll meet any-one but I do enjoy reading some VERY naughty messages when I get home at night, and I give as good as I receive! HEY! At least it keeps me writing!!! *grin*

So, sorry about your "big mistake", we all make them, it's part of being a human being.

Hollah back y'all…..

David =)

◆   ◆   ◆

Well that's interesting. I don't think I'd join another dating site. I think I'll find someone in person. That's pretty funny about all those responses you're getting. Although, I've found that if people brag about how great they are and all that they can do in bed, that it's usually not true…it's just talk. I think if you're truly that great at something, you need not say a word. At least you're having fun reading that stuff. As long as you don't take it seriously and I don't think you do.

Anyway, I hope there's no hard feelings between us. Sorry for the way things happened.

Anna

So this went on for a while as we e-mailed back and forth several more times. You need to know at this juncture that her "run in" with her ex included him stopping by for a romp in her bedroom with her. She changed the direction of the chat with her statement, "I hope there's no hard feelings," et cetera. She began to hint cutely about a meeting and of course I took the bait. She men-tioned that she was at work and left a number. I called with a cute accent and pre-tended to be a guy working at a deli. She laughed her ass off, as usual. We talked. It was cute and light. I then asked the question that was on my mind since the moment the first e-mail arrived, WHY?

She stated that a girl has a right to change her mind, that she had been think-ing about me and that even if I didn't send that joke e-mail to her and dozens of others, she had intended on calling me very soon. The reason she stated for not calling up until then was my possible negative reaction upon hearing from her. She was relieved that I reacted with humor and grace.

I explained that I was busy with my kids much of the week, but if she wanted a safe date then we could meet with our kids on the weekend, like a play day! She liked the idea but since her son was busy asked if she could meet me with my kids only. I agreed.

We spoke briefly (for us brief was 90 minutes) on the phone that evening and just before bed I shot her the following message.

> OK, I have something to share with you and PLEASE try not to laugh your guts out over this one! We may indeed be meeting this weekend, but how will I know who you are as I've never seen a photo of you clothed! I mean perhaps if you walked up to me backwards and butt naked I'd say "HEY, that must be Anna! I recognize the tooshie!!!" hehehe......"Sammy, meet Anna, Sherry this is my friend Anna"........ and they're thinking to themselves "daddy where are her clothes????"
>
> So unless this is a scenario you're comfortable with *sheesh*, then perhaps you'd like to shoot me over a pic with your sweet face prominently displayed, orrrrrrrr......you could attempt to describe to me what that same face looks like.....um, from the front! (too funny!)
>
> Okee dokey Smokey?
>
> The guy from the Deli.......... oy vay................

◆   ◆   ◆

> You're a complete nut job...LOL
>
> I don't have a pic on here. I have no digital camera. However, I promise that I'm attractive...at least to most people. I'm kind of hard to miss...I have long brown wavy hair...I have big brown eyes and I'm curvy...all over. Most of my friends compare me to Sophia Loren. I look Italian too! If I wear capris, well I have a tattoo above my left ankle of a purple rose with a curved stem wrapped in barbed wire. I have a feeling you'll recognize me.
>
> Anna

So Anna said that she'd call me early Sunday morning to firm up our plans and where we were going to meet that day.

I had my kids with me from the following morning and would not be bringing them back to their moms until the following Tuesday since they were off from school and we always have a blast together. So I didn't call her for several reasons. First, there was no reason to, as she had stated that she'd call me. Second, I was focusing on my kids, since I don't see them as much as I'd like (which would be all the time) and third, because I really didn't desire a repeat performance of our communication five weeks earlier. I though it wise to just meet and let nature take its course.

Of course, with my silence she was building all sorts of scenarios that I was unaware of at the time, but which would become blatantly apparent shortly.

The following discussion took place three days after our last contact, and on the afternoon of our planned rendezvous.

> Hi David,
>   I'm e-mailing you from my brother's house. I didn't have your phone number on me and I tried getting your number through information, but they couldn't find you. Anyway, today is not going to be good for me as I have a personal family matter to tend. I just found out a little while ago, so no, I didn't know about it last night or early this morning. I apologize for having to cancel.
>   If you want to try again for next week, let me know. Hope you and your kids are having a good time together.
>   Anna

◆   ◆   ◆

> No problem Tooshie, just call me later tonight at home after 11:00 or so and we'll chat. I hope everything works out with your family. They can be such pains!
>   Laters!....D...

She seemed to like this response, casual, no big deal, see ya later, whatever. I figured that's what she was looking for and it was also the truth! The following message came about 8:30 that evening. I should have listened!

> Hi David,
>   I just got home and I'm on my way out again in just a little while to a friend's house. Today was a `very trying day for me, first with my family, then with Simon. While I was at my brother's he saw my car there and I had a run in with him again. He lives right near my brother. After today, I think I'm about to lose it. He doesn't seem to want to go away and my state of mind is very fragile when it comes to him. I've come to the realization that I don't want anything to do with anyone right now. I simply can't handle it and I have to listen to my intuition for once and it's really strong right now. I'm still far from being over him, yet I'm not going to be with him either....even if he

doesn't seem to want to go away completely. It's unfair of him to keep popping back into my life. Needless to say all the other crap I've put up with from numerous men in my recent past. I'm just going to take myself away from it for a good long time until I know I can move through it completely.

This has nothing to do with you David. I'm sure you're a nice person and you have all good intentions. It would be completely unfair to you for me to get you involved in all this, even as a friend right now. If you're ready for a relationship with someone right now, then you should find someone who's completey open to it. I'm just not that person and won't be able to be there for someone like that for quite some time, I'm sure. I need to heal myself from all that has happened to me over the past few years.

I'm truly sorry. But better I do this now, than later, after you've met me. I don't want to lead you on or anything like that.

Take care of yourself and I truly wish you luck in finding the right woman for yourself.

Anna

Oy! I'm thinking, here we go again! But you know what, she was being honest. She was telling me the truth. It came out in her messages and over the phone that indeed she was mad at him while she vented out her frustrations on me. It should have been blatantly obvious to me at this point that indeed, she was two people in the same body: one person that was gentle, silly and kind, who I liked a great deal, and another who was bitter, confused, venomous and nasty, and scared the crap outta me. Now understand that the last time she had a "run in" with her ex it included a romp in the hay. I'll have to assume that this time was no different.

I arrived home quite late that night with my kids and did not check my messages until the following morning. I should have let this lay where it was. I should not have responded, but we had a spark that was undeniable when we spoke, so I wrote the following, for good or for bad.

My, my, my my......such drama!!!! Grab a cup of tea, sit down, take a breath, SMILE at how silly life can be, and then read my little note that follows. Oh, before you answer it, give it some time to sink in, read it AGAIN, and then respond like a friend would, as this is not an attack, just my feelings, right or wrong.

This comes as absolutely no surprise, in fact I expected this. Perhaps you wondered why I have not picked up the phone to call you since we spoke 3 evenings ago? I simply did not desire to invest any more time in something that I was convinced was a complete waste of effort. We could have been friends. Really, really good friends, but you even closed the door to that. Sometimes I truly don't think you remember what you said yesterday, or what you were thinking last week (it's an analogy, don't hurt yourself thinking too hard! *grin*)

For example: you let your pain and hurt from past relationships give you false viewpoints about who I am, as you say that you always follow your intuition and it's never wrong? Well, it was wrong about me. You've never followed the advice given to you by your astrologer, and get burned every time you don't, yet when she tells you how right I would be for you, you can't run away fast enough? *sheesh* WTF?

I've already told you that I have great trepidation when it comes to you, and seek only friendship at this point, exactly what you SAY you seek, but you're still bookin' on down the road?

I'll tell ya what I think, and you're not gonna like it, but I care enough to tell you anyway even if you rip me apart in the process (no doubt you have the skills). I think you are doomed to forever be with aloof men. I think it is in your makeup, your destiny, your unspoken desire that only YOU and a great guy can change. I think that as soon as you indeed DO find a nice guy that seems to possess all your dream qualities in a man, that you find excuses to NOT like him and rip him down, or just outright run away.... like you're doing right now.

I cannot believe that you would be afraid to have a cup of coffee with me? Fer Kripes sake Tooshie we don't even know if we'll BE attracted to one another? I mean what is the worst that could happen? We meet, I'm exactly how you'd hoped I'd look, act, feel, speak, everything.......and I don't feel the same? Is that what scares you? I know that you said this has nothing to do with me but running away from me just the same because your ex is making you nuts, will not make it any better.

I'm just a human being. I have feelings, strong feelings. I am everything I say I am, and so much more. I make mistakes. I screw up royally and sometimes hurt people in the process. I apologize and sometimes they understand and a friendship gets stronger. Sometimes they don't and a relationship ends. But I survive, I learn, I grow, and I move on better for the experience. I try very hard not to judge and always give people enough rope to hang themselves with. They often do.

I don't know why we seem to keep making these little cameo appearances into each other's lives. Things happen for a reason. People enter our lives for a reason. Your horoscope said that "this wasn't over yet" for a reason. It also said we had a "double sun/moon connection" for a reason. Your intuition has been wrong before. Perhaps you need to listen to your heart and who makes you laugh and feel good every time you speak to him. Who is much better in person. Perhaps you should look at ALL the positive facts screaming at you instead of only focusing on the negative ones.

I understand that you're going through a trying emotional time. Guess what? I don't know anyone that isn't! Join the club but do not stop living your life just because you're hurting and confused. If I could give you one final suggestion it is to call your astrologer who you trust, one final time and ask yet again about us and see what she says. And LISTEN and act on the advice.

I'm here if you need me and I will listen. Believe it or not!

Feel the fear and do it anyway.

Semper Fi.

David…=)

To say that her response was brutal is an understatement. She indeed had already corresponded with her astrologer about "us" (what a surprise), and based on her negativity of men and her hurt heart, got a very negative response. Our e-mails went back and forth for several hours until I simply could not accept the attacks anymore. She stated that the reason I hadn't called her in three days was to show how aloof I was, to prove something to her, to continue the "game" that I was playing, and also my way of controlling her. Sheesh! She even had an official background check done on me and my business and found a negative note on an obscure website from eight years ago. She checked on my ex-wife. She mentioned things that scared the hell out of me so I just stopped responding to her e-mails.

I just wanted to have coffee with her or hangout shopping at the mall, or whatever. This was one very sick individual who sucked me in with sexy photos and a made up personality. She had me snowed. I guess in the final analysis I really didn't need to look much further than her simple e-mail name, "WickedOne." What was I thinking???

So ladies, the next time you complain about what bastards men are and the games that they play, remember this story. I am barely scratching the surface of what transpired on that final day, but the e-mails are very lengthy and I just do not want to dedicate that many more pages to a very disturbed individual.

So, on the heels of this fiasco and while I was *very* busy in my two careers, came the following. Every now and then, I just let my personality loose and just see how a woman will handle it. I use all the little "emoticons" and the like to portray my feelings at the time I'm writing to them.

An "emoticon" is a sort of makeshift graphic created by using the common letters, numbers and symbols you would find on your basic keyboard. For example, if I were to write "=)" to you, I'm not writing "equals end parentheses." If you tilt your head to the left, you'll see that it's actually a little smiley face. This little icon is useful in showing others that, whatever else it maybe that you are typing, you're saying it with a smile. Emoticons come in a vast variety. There's "8)" for a smiley face with glasses. There's ":-O" for a yelling face, or ">:-O" for an angry yelling face. The possibilities are limitless.

Usually these can be used to convey what sort of tone your e-mail is meant to be read in, but every so often, they read only the words, and not the sentiment behind them...thusly:

> Too good to be true?
> I won't lie...I'm outside your "profile" by three years, but my close friends tell me I put other 49-year-olds to shame, so if you want to chat or find out more, write me. My computer crashed last week and I lost most of my picture files, so I don't have a picture up on the site yet...you can read my profile, though, and if you'd like to chat...well, I think we'd have plenty to talk about!
> Amanda

◆   ◆   ◆

> Well. So your computer crashed and you lost ALL your pics, eh? Uh huh.....8-I
> AND, You put other 49 year olds' to shame?????......I see......8-O
> Also, your profile somehow mysteriously disappeared off the Internet when I attempted to check it? How EEEEEnteresteeeng!!!!! 8-S
> Not to mention that we'd have a lot to talk about!!!!?????
> Well, aren't we cocky!!!!! *grin* I do SO adore a woman who has a positive image of herself.... even if she won't tell me what that image is!!!!
> Perhaps you'd like to share a wee bit about yourself so that I'm not sitting here clueless and wondering if I'm being contacted by a hairy, bald, smelly, 55 year old man!!!!
> If you have a sense of humor then I'm sure I'll hear back from you.
> If not?.... then we wouldn't get along anyway!!!!
> Later gator!
> David...=)

◆   ◆   ◆

> "WE" aren't cocky at all...you don't know me. I have NO idea why my profile isn't online...I only signed up last night. As for the picture, it will be uploaded tomorrow or friday, when I have the time in between working and helping my daughters with their homework. I'm not hairy, I'm not a 55-year-old man, and if you're THAT cynical, you must have been burned a few

times…I feel sorry for you. I've been married twice…once for six years, the most recent for 16; so, I've been out of the "dating" scene for many moons, and since I don't drink, what's the point of going to bars to meet drunkards I wouldn't date anyway?

So, if you still want to "chat," have a little faith and patience.

Amanda

◆   ◆   ◆

I was joking. Anyone with a sense of humor would know that! It's not to be my dear!!!!

Good luck to you!!!!8-S

Why, oh why, oh *why* do we do that to each other? Could it have been more obvious that I was joking, between the "emoticons" and the "grins"? Why do we assume the very worst of the person writing to us, and attack so easily? "I've been burnt," she says. "I'm cynical," she states. What did that have to do with my e-mail? I was attempting to be cute!

The funny thing here is that even though I am aware of this type of attitude online, and even though I understand completely that sarcasm is almost always misunderstood on the Internet, I keep doing it anyway! Believe it or not, I occasionally get back an even more sarcastic, but adorable response from a woman. That's the one I will run to because she "gets me," a rare but beautiful thing.

On the other hand, when a woman tells me that she feels "sorry for me," and then in the very next sentence asks me if I still want to chat? Sheesh! What *was* she thinking? The problem is we usually don't think. We react, we type, we hit the "send" button, and then it's too late.

Abraham Lincoln was our President during perhaps the most difficult period in our young country's history. Many years earlier, and during one particularly grueling run for a lesser office, he wrote a scathing letter about his opponent and dropped it on a road in town. The letter was published in a local newspaper, anonymously, but the gentleman figured out who it was and challenged Lincoln to a duel to the death! As they were pacing off the moments to an ending that may have decimated the future of our nation, their "seconds" raced in and stopped the insanity. Lincoln learned a hard lesson that day in that we are all responsible for the words we utter and once sent, they cannot be withdrawn or retracted. He authored many letters of this belligerent variety during the long years of our Civil War. He sealed the letters, put them in his desk, and never sent one. He got the anger off his chest by expressing it in his eloquent writing, but they were for his eyes only. Smart man. He learned from his mistakes. I wish I could say the same for the rest of us, myself included!

4

"Um, like, how old WAS that photo?"

The Samoan Wrestler

I had been chatting online with a girl for a couple of weeks. We took it to the phone for a few conversations and it went well. Her picture was kind of fuzzy and non-descript. She seemed pretty exotic looking! I really couldn't get a good idea of exactly what she looked like but she had a pretty decent personality. She was very outgoing, you know, very out there, and I figured, "Okay I'll give it a shot." She lived in Brooklyn, which is always a warning sign for me. (Relax folks, I'm a NYC kid) Sort of a death knell, because I've never had a good date with a girl from Brooklyn (Well, until last week, but she came *here*).

Anyway, I drive all the way out there. It took a real, real long time as I was living in Jersey and I finally get there and I park. She didn't want me to meet her at her house for some reason. She wanted me to meet her on the Boulevard or something. So I pull over and I'm just waiting, and I'm kind of leaning up against my car, trying to look cool, trying to look cute. I'm looking around, and I really don't see any girl walking by herself.

So I'm waiting and waiting. It's like fifteen minutes and I'm getting ready to call her from my cell phone, and finally, um, some girl comes walking down the street. She was sort of short and comes walking over to me, and I really didn't think this was her. This girl had a *shocking* mop of chocolate brown hair in these ringlets. She looked like a Samoan wrestler. I mean birds were fighting to nest in this woman's hair. It was huge! You could have taken 500 bald men and supplied a never-ending amount of hair transplant material. It was absolutely unbelievable!

Now, that in and of itself wouldn't have been a problem, okay? But one of the things she said to me on the phone was that she liked men who were very clean cut and closely shaved, you know things like that. So she shows up, get this, with a *beard*. Oh yes. Oh no, I'm not kidding! With a beard. That wouldn't have even been that bad, but it seemed that pieces of it have been shaved and some areas were missed, like she ran out of the door in a mad hurry! So, it was an ill-kept beard.

Now ladies, if you're going to have a beard at least trim it well. Not for nothing, but it'll cut down on the razor burn…Yikes! Now the beard didn't phase me, but the *sideburns* were just too much to take.

So I'm kind of looking at her and I'm freaking out. Now at this point you're probably saying to yourselves, "Why did you stay?" Well, because, I just did. This was pretty early in my cyber-dating career and I really didn't know how to handle it, and I didn't want to be rude. I'd driven over an hour and a half to get there anyway, I was hungry and I didn't want to drive all the way home just yet. I had packed a picnic lunch, as the plan was to meet and go to the park to have a picnic. So what, you may ask, saved this date? Her two-year-old daughter who she just happened to bring along in the baby carriage. Yes, this gets better! Her daughter was absolutely adorable and friendly, and being a daddy I just couldn't resist hanging out with her.…. and mom went along for the ride.

I played with her most of the time we were together. We put the carriage in the car, put the baby in the car seat, and drove off to the park. So mom is grabbing me and telling me that I have very nice hands. I have the hands of a contractor, as that's what I was then. So she looks at my right hand as I'm driving and proclaims "Oh my God! You have dirt under your fingernails! I really like a man who's well-kept, hmph!" Well, she knew I was a contractor and that I was coming directly from a job site. Sure I wash my hands when I'm done, but if you've ever been an outside contractor you know that your hands never quite get squeaky clean. She's sitting next to me, I'm thinking, WITH A BEARD! Sorry my fingernails are dirty!

That just goes to show you, that there really are people out there that have absolutely no concept of who and what they are, but all the while will judge other people!

Fortunately, the date went very well as the toddler was a pisser, and the girl *did* have a great personality, as well as being, um, affectionate. We got along fine. I drove her home and never saw hide nor *hair* of her again!

Yeah, I know, your sides are probably splitting and you don't believe a word of it! Believe me that was light stuff! You would *not* believe what some of the ladies go through. One of my friends from Philly actually had a guy arrested for attempted rape on a first date while in a restaurant parking lot. It's not even like it was something she had intended. This lunatic who was very nice through dinner just got carried away as they were kissing, and would *not* take no for an answer. Fortunately, as he was tearing her clothes off, with her trying to escape, a waitress who was going home saw what was happening and called the police. They carted the loony away as he screamed curses at her and threatened her life. Nice evening, eh? I'll take the bearded lady instead!

The So Ready Girl

I had gotten an e-mail from an attractive brown-haired, brown-eyed beauty. Her letter was upbeat, friendly, intelligent, and seemingly everything I was seeking in a woman. She pretty much told me that she was perfect for me and that we needed to meet ASAP! So, not being one to argue, and after speaking very briefly on the phone, (always a mistake) we decided to meet midway between our homes for coffee. One of the things she did say in our brief telephone encounter was how "so ready" she was to date since her breakup nine months prior and that I was going to be her first online date. She was *so* excited. Hoo boy…I pull into the parking lot and as I get out of my pickup truck she pulls in next to me. She was just as attractive as her photo online except for the deep black circles under her eyes, circles created from years of intense stress and unhappiness. We hugged, as we were pleased to meet and entered the coffee house.

Once inside, now seated with our drinks, she proceeded very joyfully to tell me several times all the reasons why she was so ready to be dating now. After briefly relating the story of her past relationships and once again how wonderfully good she feels after the nine months of therapy, ("Can't *wait* to tell my therapist about our date!") and how healthy she feels about dating now, she started to ask me questions about my past relationships. Now I don't know about you but I tend to keep the conversation a bit light on a first date and she was getting very personal with her questions. When I began to gracefully change the subject she began to tell me that perhaps I should see her therapist and then I could feel as healthy as her, and thus be able to spill *my* guts to everyone I met (on a first date…ahem).

For at least the next thirty minutes, she gave me all of the wonderful advice that she thought I needed to hear. Understand this situation, folks. We had just met. She knew nothing about me. She had been totally destroyed in her past relationship but was somehow "better" now and needed to share her wisdom with the world, a world which of course desperately needed to hear what she desperately wanted to share with it.

By this time the hackles were rising on the back of my neck. I was really beginning to dislike her and was even a little afraid since her eyes were starting to bug out of her head. In all the excitement she didn't perhaps realize just how loudly she was speaking. There were two girls sitting at the table just behind her who, by now, were holding back tears and motioning to me with their heads, "GET THE HELL AWAY WHILE YOU STILL CAN!"

Then I did something that I've never done before, only because I couldn't stand it for another second. I put up my right hand and said, "STOP!" I proceeded to tell her that I've *never* been more uncomfortable on a date in my entire life. It was like a physical wall slammed down between us and I felt that I really needed to either stop her from talking or just leave right then. I said, "You know nothing about me, my life, my kids, my friends, yet you're judging me and everything about me. How dare you give unsolicited advice to a total stranger who hasn't even said two words yet."

Well, let me tell you that a look came over her face I can only describe as sheer *terror*. She realized in that instant that she was *not* ready to date, not ready for a relationship, and *really* not ready to stop seeing her therapist. She started to cry, got up, and as I attempted to hold her hand she screamed, "DON'T TOUCH ME!" and ran briskly out of the door. Now that I think of it, she didn't even take the time to throw away her coffee cup. Personal judgments I can handle, but messy dates? How rude!

I just sat there with a shell-shocked look on my face realizing that I had blown another evening. One of the young ladies at the next table who had witnessed the entire scenario sat down with me, touched my hand, and said, "Be very grateful it came out of her tonight. It hurts a lot worse to find out later that they're nuts!" So true, so true.

The saddest part of this whole thing was that she probably was a very nice, loving woman. I enjoyed her writing and the phone talk, but when we met she turned into the therapist from the netherworld! I felt really bad going home but did learn a valuable lesson. Never meet someone on a date until after you've had several long phone conversations, because things that you need to know will tend to come out of people as their comfort level with you increases. Live and learn folks!

The next story comes from my friend Phyllis. She's petite and adorable, and what I'd consider a "gym rat" since she just about lives there. She's going to kill me when she sees this, but count how many times she says "like" in the story!

Mobility

So like, I'm at the mall, and I'm like, waiting for this guy to show up, right? Well, I'm looking at my watch, and tapping my foot, and looking at all the people looking at me! Oh my God! So I'm waiting for this really nice guy, Jim. We'd talked on the phone, like, a zillion times over a few months, sometimes for like three hours or so.

There was always something bothering me about our phone talks though. Like, he would change the subject when I asked certain questions. I just figured he was a little shy. So like, his pics were really gorgeous, and I'm like, *really* looking forward to meeting this guy!

Then, like, this weird thing happens. Some lady comes over to me, and says that some gentleman is waiting for me at some access station or something. She was a security guard or something, so I followed her. So like, we get to this customer service thingy, and there's a guy waiting there in a wheelchair. The guy was Jim!

I can't even express my feelings at that moment, like, all the life just left my body. Here I am, running marathons and he shows up in a wheelchair. Well, I gave him a kiss on the cheek and we went and got some coffee at the food court down the hall. I didn't know what to say to him, I just felt really, really uncomfortable. So finally I asked him if he had an accident or something and he tells me that he was in a car accident years ago and he'll never walk again, but that he functions quite well in all other areas, and he smiles.

I just couldn't like, stand it any more. I had to leave. I felt so angry that he didn't tell me he was permanently disabled because I know that would have ended it right there. I mean I'm a really nice person, you know? But this was just too much too soon. He should have told me. Am I wrong here? He didn't seem to have a problem with his disability and like, that's good, but it wasn't fair to assume that I would just be okay with it.

So I walked him to his car and kissed him goodbye and he called me for months after that. I wouldn't see him again because even though he was nice, I didn't want to, like, lead him on or anything, so I just let it go.

I still feel kind of bad about it, but I don't know if I'm mad at myself for not giving him a chance, or if I'm mad at him for putting me in that situation. I ask a lot more questions now before I meet anyone, and if they won't answer me I just assume they're hiding something, and I move on.

Whoa! Disclosure! I can't say that I agree or disagree with what Phyllis did on her date. What I do disagree with is Jim not telling her about his disability first thing on the phone. It was very unfair to put her in that position, no matter how comfortable he seemed to be with his situation. A nice person will think in advance about how someone will react to a surprise of that magnitude. Also, to tell her that he "functions quite well in all other areas" with a little smile is major sexual innuendo, and that was certainly uncalled for. Imagine this girl's feelings!

I know Phyllis for quite some time now and she is a living doll and would never hurt anyone's feelings, but this was just too much for her to handle. Not cool.

Honesty is the *only* way to start a relationship folks. We're not talking about vomiting out total disclosure of your entire life on a first date, but if there's something major like a permanent physical disability, you need to tell that to your prospective partner up front on the first phone call. Anything less is a lie of omission and blatantly rude to the other person.

Now if you have a hang nail, that can wait for the actual first date! Second dates are good for disclosing that your sister *just* got home from the institution and she's doing *just fine*. Third dates are for crying on your partner's shoulder as you open up to them about the closet that your parents made you sleep in as a child. Fourth dates, if you ever get to one, are the high water mark. When two people get to that point, they usually stop counting what date number they're on. Fourth dates are for all the relationship stories you didn't want to *ever* hear. This is truly the point where you're deciding if you want to stick it out with this person or run screaming from the restaurant and move to New Zealand!

WAITAMINIT! What happens to me if I get *past* a fourth date? Well, then you're not cyber-dating anymore. Then you're in one of those things, what do they call them? Hmmm...Oh yeah! A relationship! One of the most amazingly awesome places in the world to be. Your stomach is doing flip-flops, you don't know whether you're coming or going, and you feel kind of like you have the flu, but...you wouldn't trade it for the world. Because when she comes slowly up behind you, places her hands gently on your neck, and rubs all the stress of the day away into oblivion, you know, you just know, that no amount of money could buy the feeling you have right at that moment. 'Nuff said!

This story is from Bridgette. She lives overseas, and although we've never actually spoken on the phone, we have chatted constantly online for 6 months or so. That's the coolest thing about certain dating sites, the international participation.

You see, on some sites you can set your parameters for local people only to view your profile, or you can have a little fun and set them to unlimited!

Chatting with people from many other cultures can be fun as well as informative. Once you get past the cyber language barrier you'll discover that everyone has a similar sense of humor. I have ongoing "cyber-relationships" with women from Russia, Great Britain, Singapore, Hungary, Australia, Canada, Taiwan, China, Ireland…and have also chatted with women from some countries I've never even heard of!

Now back to my friend Bridgette. She describes herself as being a *very* forward woman, large and muscular, (she's a personal trainer) voluptuous, short curly blonde hair and emerald green eyes. When she sees something she wants, she goes after it and isn't shy about letting a guy *know* that she wants him. Geez! I *sooo* love a confident woman! She sent the following to me with several other stories as an e-mail attachment. I needed to change some of the words because she is a wee bit graphic in her writing style!!!

Third Time This Week

By Bridgette

I wasn't having a good week. I'd already had two dates with studs who turned out to be duds. Why do men put up ten-year-old pictures anyway? Do they really believe we're so stupid that we won't notice? It's a Saturday evening and I was to meet Nigel at a shop at the east end of a local town. We were going to meet for tea and just take it from there. He shows up looking very dapper, in a pair of blue britches and a white collar shirt, open at the neck and with a red ascot thrown across his shoulder. OH MY! He was a handsome devil and looked even better than advertised. "About time!" I thought. At least this one told me the truth! I had NO idea. I was wearing a very low cut blouse which Nigel seemed very pleased with and mentioned several times.

We drank our tea fairly briskly and since it was a nice evening, decided to walk along a riverbank and talk. Well, I can tell you the conversation didn't last very long. Nigel was a few years younger than I but not shy at all where it counts! We began to get very close to each other and before long were doing a very nice tongue dance! He was an amazing kisser and when he attacked my neck….. well I can tell you that it just set me over the edge. Not being a shy woman I looked around and decided it was fair time to see what stuff Nigel was really made of!

I slowly slipped off my blouse to the utter delight of my, hopefully, excited friend. His hands seemed amazed at the utter joy of touching my very large, firm breasts. Didn't feel too bad to me either! By now I just couldn't stand it anymore and started to slip and slide my way down his body to his mid-section. My hands hungrily began to feel for the expected erection. Imagine my surprise when I didn't feel one! I just figured that he needed a wee bit more motivation, so I slid down the zipper of his trousers with my teeth, opened them up, and felt the teensiest wee willy I have ever had my hands on.

I looked up at Nigel, wiping my face to hide the tears, and asked him if there was a problem. He said, "It's not the size of the boat that counts, it's the flow of the river," and I damn near fell down on my bum! I was laughing so hard to myself that I needed to walk away for fear of insulting a nice guy. Nigel zipped back up his trousers, realizing by now that he wasn't going to get his willy wacked tonight! We walked back to our autos and said our goodbyes as I felt silently to myself, "Third time this week, I MUST be cursed." Suffice to say, that in the future I'll know that the more men brag about their prowess the smaller their willy probably is! Oh, how cruel is fate?

Poor Bridgette! What's a girl to do? I mean after all not every guy is hung like a bull! I didn't fully understand the entire scope of this story until I spoke to her this week. I was under the impression that his "wee willy" was small, as well as not erect. She corrected me and said that the reason she was holding back tears of laughter was that his pee pee was *so* small that even though it *was* erect she could barely tell.

Now just think about this for a minute ladies. What would *you* do in a similar situation? I know most of us wouldn't *do* that on a first date. So let's just say it's the fourth date and everything had been moving along smoothly so far. You're at your apartment and he's over for the first time and things get frisky. So there you are and there it *isn't*. Yikes! If you were thinking about having a relationship with this guy, is this something that would end any romantic notions? Do you have the "I just wanna be friends" talk after the occurrence?

This is a very *hard* (pun *absolutely* intended) situation to even think about. Hopefully you wouldn't be bothered with such *little* things! Hopefully you would *rise* to the occasion mightily! Assuredly, you would be *big* about it!

Oh, I've gotta stop! I'm killing myself here!

The next story is e-mails only and shows a bit of just how nasty people can be online with absolutely no possibility of any repercussions. Prepare yourself!

Hello, how should I address you?

Trying to think of a way to make a connection of some sort,,,,,,,,you are complex as I am…simple also in the same sort……well,,,,if you think you might like me,,you've got my name,,,,Eilene

◆   ◆   ◆

Hey Eilene…did you realize that you sent me the same message 3 times?? Weird. I guess you REALLY wanna meet me…well, that's not out of the question, however your timing sucks. I'm very busy with a new business venture online, and since it's global, I can as easily be working at 11 pm, as 9 am…I've got my kids this weekend, and have plans down the Jersey shore the one after that….. soooooo…. if ya wanna keep chattin me up….. and you've got the patience of a saint……Y'know what I mean….. talk to ya soon! David…

Simple enough. Right? No problems here? Check out her response!!!

Sorry you mistaken the wrong person,,,,this is the first message I have sent you,,,or for that matter (any one of interest) in a long time,,,,,,You after your writing to me,,,don't appear of my class. I found your approach rude,,,,,No way do I want to meet a person like you,,,,,and god forbid the other woman!!!!!! You sound like trash,,,,,,,,Eilene!

Ouch! Where did *that* come from? Her profile did mention how sensitive she was and the only thing I can assume is that there was a slight language barrier here and she misunderstood my silly sense of humor. It gets better. At the time I was checking this e-mail, two of my friends were standing in my office and they were not pleased with her response to me, so they had a few things to share with her.

Sensitive you say? I have 2 of my best friends standing here with me. Both are women, they would like to say something to you……

Girlie…you really blew it!!!! You have no idea what a nice decent guy you just blew off, and SO RUDELY……. Anna……. (Yes, my ex!)

I'm not as nice as Anna, you cow!!!! This is a man who works 80 hours a week, and still finds the time to raise his 3 kids, since his separation. You are a total freaking idiot!!!!! Have a nice day PORKIE!!!!……. Ariana…….

◆   ◆   ◆

I feel sorry for you......I hope you find help,,,, Eilene.

◆   ◆   ◆

You need to understand the difference online, between humor, and reality. My 2 friends are REALLY here, and they BOTH would like to rip your head off, because I said NOTHING to you, to elicit such a rude response. I am not the one who needs help my dear.... but good luck anyway.... David...

◆   ◆   ◆

Really, you know...I'm not out to get anyone in a bad way. I'm sorry we didn't click and you took me for another person. I wish you harmony...,for real...hope you find what you are looking for...Eileen...

Well, at least we ended on a good note. The funny thing here is that she never did admit to actually e-mailing me in the first place. So instead, she decided to start e-*mauling* me. Hey, I like that! I've gotta remember that one, e-mauling! Could start a trend!

Online misunderstandings are so rampant that you really do have to be careful what you say to someone new. Even someone who's known you for years can take something totally out of context. Sense of humor does not translate very well in cyber-space, thus you really must tend to over use things like "LOL," and "*grin*," and "*smile*," just to avoid getting your head ripped off! Oh yeah, and sarcasm? Just forget about it. It will get you in trouble *every* time no matter how well someone knows you! Doesn't even come across too well in real life sometimes either!

I can see how Eileen could have been offended by my response to her e-mail. Instead of saying that her triple received message was "weird" perhaps in retrospect I might have simply told her that perhaps she just hit "send" a few times too much by mistake or something. Saying that her timing sucked, well, I can see now that those were not the right words to use, with her anyway. The good thing here is that the type of woman I seek would probably have laughed at my silly response and taken no offense at all, quite the opposite. There is of course an alternative explanation, one that more easily explains her vulgar response. She could just be a loon! *smile*

Now it's high time we brought our friends back into the fold. Here is one story each, garnered from taped interviews, from Swayne, Linda, Charley, Anna, Freeda and of course Brando.

Fly Like an Eagle:

By Swayne

I had been chatting with a very pretty blonde both online as well as on the phone for about two weeks. My initial feeling towards her was to run because she clearly stated that she had only been separated for three months, but this was not a problem as both her and her husband knew it was kaput for years.

Since she was both intelligent and funny, as well as verrrry easy on the eyes I agreed to meet for a bite. I felt this was a mistake all the way to the restaurant but ignored my gut instincts. It WAS a mistake! When I arrived she was already seated at a table, looking around like a wounded animal and tap, tap, tapping her fingers on the table…to stay calm I guess? Her first uttered words were, "You're late, sit down and we'll order."

Now I'm pretty easy going and all but it became very apparent to me that I felt sorry for her husband of twenty years! She was bold, loud, manipulative, but also very confusing because as much as she seemed a bitch verbally, she was also sending all the "I'm cute, come get me" signals with her eyes and her movements.

Dinner arrived about thirty minutes later to her chorus of, "Shit, it's about damn time!" Now at this point I'm realizing that it was a mistake to meet her in a restaurant that I liked because I knew several of the other patrons, as well as all the waitresses and help. I was beginning to feel a bit uncomfortable when she turned up the heat. She related to me every detail of her ex-husband's sexual problems, his infidelity, no doubt to retain his sanity, his business failures, his gambling debts, and despite this all she remained a good and loving wife and mother. She then said that she was "free of his shackles and could now fly like an eagle without him holding her back." At this point she was speaking at a very elevated level and seemed extremely pleased with all the heads turning her way.

I wanted to crawl away. I wanted to go to the john, open the window, and head for other parts. I stayed. I ate. Then it happened. A moment I will never forget as long as I live. She got up from her chair, flung her wineglass into the corner, spun her napkin over her head in large circles and began to sing Steve Miller's "Fly like an Eagle" at very high operatic volume…I wanted to die. My anxiety level was such that I could *hear* my heart beating so loudly that it nearly drowned out the sound of the bile dripping into my stomach. It did not unfortunately drown out her voice.

Upon completion of her performance, she gave herself a standing ovation. I asked for the check. She asked me if I liked her voice. I excused myself to the bathroom to relieve some pressure that was surely going to kill me if I didn't release it SOON! Several people I knew followed me to the men's room and attempted to console me, but they were all laughing too hard for that! I guess I realized the humor of the situation at that point and returned to the table to find her gone. I thought that perhaps she had also gone to the bathroom but the waitress said that when I didn't return for five minutes, my date left in a "huff" muttering something about my gastric problems!

She did not call to thank me for dinner, nor did I call to thank her for her performance. To this day I cannot listen to that song without a terrible urge for an antacid and a trip to the little boy's room! My my….

Deer and Elk

By Linda

I talked to this guy online for a while and he seemed okay, I guess. This was very early in my Internet experiences, perhaps the second or third time, I dunno. I hadn't seen a clear photo of him, but I really wanted to get out so I accepted his invitation for coffee at a bar nearby.

My initial reaction upon seeing him was that he was an overweight caricature of Don Johnson from the eighties! You know, the tee shirt and sports jacket with the sleeves rolled up! Oy! Looked great on Don. Looked stupid on him! The penny loafers with absolutely no socks were a nice touch too!

One of his first subjects of conversation was how men are like "deer and elk" and should be able to do what they want with the female, "spread their seed" as it were, and then go off and do their own thing without having to think about that anymore! Well David, you *know* me and I'm just sitting there thinking, "Oh shit, you did NOT just say *that* to me!"

Another comment was that he had problems with his wife for years and his wife thought that he was cheating on her for years, but that she "never had the video to prove it!" To me when a guy talks like that right off, I mean that, that's a goodbye, but that's who I am. I mean maybe somebody else would've been okay with that because that's what they're looking for, but I felt it was *really* irritating and I never had any contact with that person ever again! Deer and Elk my ass! What a turd!

Tumbleweeds

By Charley

It was um, like…I think you were my second…My first…I think you were my second Match.com date? My first Match.com date, I met him at Ruby Tuesday's. I sat at the bar and waited for him to show up. Five, ten, fifteen, twenty minutes late in he walks. He made sure to tell me that we weren't going to go to dinner. We were just going to do drinks. So he proceeded to have a few martinis, then he proceeded to get a little buzzed, so at that point, I guess after an hour he said, "Would you like to go to dinner?" So I joked around and said "Gee, I guess I passed your test?"

So we walked outside to his parked Pathfinder. He opened the door and I immediately noticed that it reeked of dog, and it had tumbleweeds of hair everywhere. He had two gigantic dogs that he owned that he used to let ride around in his car all the time and the car stunk to high heaven! It's winter, I'm in a dress, I have dog hair in unmentionable places, and it's too cold to open the window…so I thought. So we get out on the road and he's accelerating rapidly. At that point as we entered the highway he decides to open *my* window just as I take a breath and get a mouthful of dog hair which is now whipping around his car like one of those whirlwind vacuum cleaners…*gag*

So I just kinda sucked it up and we arrived at an Italian restaurant. As if he wasn't already buzzed enough, he now proceeds to have a glass of wine…and another…and another…and another, five in all. He's now completely bombed and I know I'll be getting a cab or just walking back to my car. All he was talking about at this point was his ex-girlfriend, about how they used to go on ski trips and they used to take the bus up and fall over the luggage when they got to their destination, "Oh, it was *so funny!*" and back and forth. He went on and on about this ex-girlfriend.

At this point he got a quizzical look on his face, excused himself to the bathroom and never did return. I threw a twenty on the table, got up laughing hysterically, returned to my car and was just very glad the date was over. It could not have ended soon enough!

One Minute in Windy Town

By Anna

I am not a stupid woman. David can confirm that at least! So why is it that our mind shuts off when our hormones take over? After David and I had broken up, it took me a while to get over him, and believe me that's no easy thing. I refused to allow him removal from my life because he was sweeter as my ex-boyfriend than he was as the incumbent. He helped me put up a profile on Udate.com and, in fact, shot the photos as well.

It was rather silly. We would sit back to back in our shared office chatting incessantly with members of the opposite sex and sharing notes and laughing at the plethora of incompatible species online. So I chatted and chatted, and after a handful of weeks was contacted by a simply gorgeous man from Chicago. We seemed to click from the word "Go," and took it to the telephone after a few days. He was extremely passionate and very eager to meet me as soon as possible. We had telephone conversations that would melt the polar ice caps if they were in proximity. I am talking *graphic* sexual content.

I was not seeing anyone except on casual dates, and with the constant reminder of David around me on a regular basis (and he wouldn't even give me a quickie! Something about protecting my feelings! *The bastard!*) I was getting very agitated in the randy department! I have a rather busy schedule, but there are advantages to being the boss, so I went with my instincts and booked a flight to Chicago to meet this hunk of a man!

Occasionally we should listen to our friends. David had great trepidation about this man. At first, I thought he was just being over protective, but in retrospect realize that he saw clearly what I did not in my over-zealousness to meet a compatible man. So I flew to Chicago.

The first thing I noticed about Gary was that he appeared older than his photos, not ancient by any means but not as gorgeous as I had hoped. He also seemed to have put on a few pounds around the middle. Perhaps if this were a coffee date in New York I would have politely declined, but after flying half way across the country I was going to have fun if it killed me, so I made the best of it.

We arrived at his "bachelor pad" and changed for dinner. The conversation at dinner was light and not the expected passionate intercourse one would have expected, but pleasant just the same. He was very confident in his male walk and thus grew on me as the evening progressed. Never underestimate a confident guy as they usually get what they want. This situation was no different.

We went to a local club at that point and danced and drank for a few hours. I was getting a bit tired though, after the flight and gave him the look that said I was ready for bed. We arrived at his apartment and our clothes were quickly strewn from the front door to the foot of his enormous bed. The mirrors over the bed did not go unnoticed. A shame I did not get to utilize those erotic tools. We embraced, he entered me, and it was over. He yawned, rolled over and went to sleep.

Understand two things here. First, I had recently ended a relationship with a man who was unbelievably passionate in bed and got *very* used to "all-nighters." Second, he so bragged about his sexual prowess over the phone that I thought I'd need a walker to get home the next day. So I got up and walked around the apartment to find all the things a woman does *not* want to find in a man's domicile. I felt like a complete idiot. I was in Chicago, frustrated, and in the apartment of a lifelong bachelor who was the very nightmare that women attempt to avoid like the plague, a "one minute man" in every sense of the word.

I left early the next day and this idiot called me for months, to no avail. He was just a jerk looking for a piece of ass. I had to look at his stupid-ass grin the following morning and he had the nerve to ask me if I slept well! Can you spell clueless? Ugh! What a dope!

I returned home to find David waiting there for me with a big hug, always my savior. Only the women reading this will understand this next statement. In his arms and choking back tears, I had never hated him more.

The Geezer and the Cheater

By Freeda

Do not get me started on horror stories! How much room is left on that tape? Okay, so I chatted for a week or so with this guy from Sullivan County. Well, I think that's where he was from but you never know. His photo online was not very clear, but he seemed always happy to hear from me when we chatted and seemed to seek me out every time I was online, so I guess I just relented and booked a dinner date with the guy.

We met at a diner where a bunch of my friends work because I didn't know him and just wanted to feel safe, and since I don't drive, I cabbed it to the diner and waited. He walks in with this gray scraggly beard, and blue jean overalls looking like he walked right off the set of a hillbilly movie! He was unkempt and smelly, and his hair seemed like it hadn't seen a comb in a very long time! I was floored. I wanted to crawl under the table as all my friends looked on in disbelief and just walked away hiding the tears of laughter in their eyes. What do you say at a time like that as you're sitting there in the freakin' twilight zone of dating hell misadventures!

I just ordered a salad and coffee. I ate *very* fast and he wanted to pay, but I said, "Oh no, that's quite alright" and paid the bill myself. He offered to drive me home but, I decided to stay for a while as I didn't want grandpa Clam Pit to know where I lived!

That's light stuff dude, I have more!

I was chatting on Yahoo and this older guy contacts me. He had a really sarcastic personality and was very forward and silly. His photo was attractive, so we decided to meet for coffee at Starbucks. My first clue about this guy should have been obvious. He turned *every* conversation around to sex. Now usually that wouldn't be a problem, (you know me David!) but he wasn't joking when he said it. You know how it's okay if you know a guy and it's in a light and silly way? Well, I just figured that he was a little nuts, but it seemed okay since he had a fun personality and we had that chemistry.

So, at the last minute he cancels the date saying he needed to take care of something, but could we have a picnic in the park tomorrow? I said okay, as it was in a public place and that seemed all right. So he picked me up and we drove to the most abandoned freaking place I have ever been to in my entire life! The guy was really big and very loud and scared the hell outta me at first but kept being silly, so I eventually felt more comfortable. He really liked being in nature and mentioned that crowds made him, well, uncomfortable…to say the least.

So we started to date and within a few weeks got very physical and the sex was amazing! He seemed though, to be getting weirder as the time passed. So it's like about a month into this thing and we're out for a burger in a small local place upstate, the kind of place that you never expect to see more than four or five people at. Well, there must have been a bus tour coming through or something like that, and in walks, like, fifty or so people and a look came over his face that I can only describe as sheer terror. He got real quiet then, and just seemed to go into a shell. I asked if he wanted to leave and his response was *very* loud.

"LEAVE ME THE HELL ALONE!"

Now when I say loud, I mean every head in the place was looking at him. This seemed to make him even worse, and by now he was starting to shake. I mean, the table was shaking and everything so badly that the silverware and plates were starting to fall off.

I just sat there with a glazed look as the waitress came over and asked if there was a problem. It got really bad then. I thought a freakin' alien was gonna jump outta him or something. Then his arms started to flail around over his head and he began to foam at the mouth! I thought that perhaps he was having a fit, so I grabbed a spoon just in case and he suddenly stopped dead, got up from the table calmly and walked out the door.

I followed him out as I had no other way to get home. We got in his car, he drove me home without a word, dropped me off and I never heard from him again!

I found out later online that he was on some sort of medication for a personality disorder and that he had been refusing to take it. I garnered this information from his wife! OH YES! She contacted me wanting to know why I was on her "favorites" on the computer at their house. Holy crap! Do I know how to pick 'em or what??? She was somewhat understanding as this obviously wasn't his first go at it. I now understood why he never wanted to be in a public place with me.

By the way, the group that had come into the burger place was his minister and church group! God works in strange ways, don't he? I now speak to this woman regularly, and I gave her the name of a good divorce attorney. Screw the bastard!

Stiffed Again

By Brando

Do I *really* need to do this? **sigh**....okay...This one will prove beyond the shadow of a doubt how stupid men can be. It has taken me but a few short years of pain to unlearn lessons that took me a lifetime to make sense of.

I had done some consulting on several web-site designs and upon completion received a strange message from a member of that particular firm. She wrote to ask me if I was the same person on a dating site that she was a member of. I confirmed that I was indeed that person and how did she get my contact info? She told me that a woman who had worked with me on the project had mentioned to her that I was single and perhaps looking, and that I was on the same site that she herself was on. As she didn't know what I looked like, she simply did a search for photographers and web designers on the site and up I popped with several other gentlemen. She informed me that she had contacted "all the ones who appealed to her sensibilities,"…an odd statement that for some reason raised the hackles on the back of my neck. I guess it was just the way she phrased it.

Of course, being a male and seeing her very attractive photos, I ignored my first uncomfortable feeling. We chatted intelligently, if not passionately, for several weeks until an evening was agreed upon to meet for dinner. I had previously explained to her that although my life was starting to come together, my finances were extremely limited. She stated that this was not a problem for her and that she would "take care of it," a statement that attracted me to her all the more. We met at the restaurant and I could not help but notice that her appearance was somewhat different from her photos…Hell, let me just say it: she was a dog, "Woof, woof."

Not wanting to be rude, as well as being very hungry after a long day, I decided to be polite and to sit down to eat anyway. I guess the lack of attraction was apparent to her, as I was speaking but not holding her attention via eye contact. We ordered a sumptuous meal, since her words to me were not to worry about the money. She told me in every way that either: A) We would split the check, or B) She would be covering for me this time as it was she who contacted me to begin with.

The conversation was nice, if not very date-like, and we ended on a seemingly good note. Then the check came. It was a little under ninety dollars. We both just sat there looking at it like two idiots. I looked at her. She looked at me. It seemed as if I could *feel* the tension building with every passing second. The sweat started to drip down from my temples as I began to realize that she was *not* going to offer me one red cent.

I had about a hundred dollars in my pocket. This was to be my gas money, food money and the like for the entire week. She then smiled, got up from her chair and said, "Well, thank you *so* much for an interesting evening, but I need to take my leave now. I told you on the phone that I do not do starving artists," or some crap like that.

I paid the check. I couldn't even leave a tip or I wouldn't have money for gas to get home and to work. I felt like such an ass, and that's when I called you sitting on the can Dave. Sorry, bad timing.

I was in utter shock that although she knew my situation, that she decided to stiff me on the damn check. My portion was about 25 bucks. Then there were a few drinks, and the rest was hers. Bitch. When will I ever learn to go with my first instinct about someone?

Since that date, I have followed your advice and simply met for a walk, or coffee, or some other situation that would not put me in the poorhouse for an entire week. *Crap.*

Wow. I could almost hear the whistling theme from a Clint Eastwood movie when he levels off against the bad guy! My poor buddy! Why is it always the girl you don't like who stiffs you with the check? So gentle reader, to avoid these happenings in your own life, here is a checklist of sorts to go over before you get your teeth handed to you.

For the guys: Make sure she shaves before the date, or at least trims well. Clean your hands and fingernails. Ask a whole bunch of questions, get her therapists number, and if she says that she's *"sooo* ready to date," move to Kentucky.

Disclosure! Don't get busy if ya ain't got the equipment! Don't talk about your ex and don't compare yourself to large four-legged animals that drool and smell each others' urine for identification. Meet for coffee. Meet for a walk. Pack a picnic and go to the park, the lake, the beach, wherever, but if you sit down to a sumptuous meal be *very* sure who is paying or you might be eating light for a week or two!

Do not dress like a hillbilly on a first date. (It's okay for the second though.) Do the damn laundry before your date flies in from out of town. (That creep!) Get a clue. Do not scream at your date over lunch. Do not have a shaking fit because it makes the waitress nervous. Be honest because the smart ones can see through the crap. The sweet ones cannot, but since I'll no doubt be their next date, gimme a break and cut out the lying as it screws them up for me!

Clean the damn S.U.V. because that could be my sister you're choking to death. Control your libido until you're sure that *she* is ready or you just might screw up a good thing. I know from experience.

For the ladies: Never reach into a man's pants on a first date…unless you're relatively sure of a Redwood, not a twig. Call your therapist *before* you freak out the coffee house denizens. Confirm the mobility status of your bowling partner. Be nice, everything comes back to you, eventually. Try splitting the check occasionally as most of us *do not* get offended! Do not break into song in the restaurant and always wait until you get home to break the glassware. Ask a hell of a lot of questions before you travel to meet a guy and do not get sucked in by a sweet talker, it's usually *just* talk.

Buying the first drink for the guy is sexier than you'll ever know. Never buy the second though, or he'll think you're easy! If a man buys you dinner, thank him, even if he's a jerk. Jerks work for their money just like you do. You can spit on his car later, though.

Be honest. Some of us see through "sexy" when it's a guise to hide the emptiness within. Always be yourself or you might miss your one chance. Control your libido until you're sure that *he* is ready or you might screw up a good thing. Do not learn *that* one from experience as it hurts way too much.

For both: Lose the aloof attitude. Affection is very sexy, but sex is often not very affectionate. Treat your date like they're the only one there because *everyone* is special. Do not send mixed signals and never wash your whites with a red sock. Never wear red socks.

Make friends no matter what, because we all need as many friends as we can get, especially of the opposite sex. Be interesting and talk about the future. The past is gone and your date does *not* want to hear your horror stories, lest you become one yourself!

And lastly and most importantly, if you let your date suck on your fingers and they tell you that you taste like chicken, laugh, thank them, and be very sure why you let them do it in the first place!

5

"Why is this bar so empty tonight?"

So what's the deal here anyway? Why in heaven's name are there so very many people all over the globe flocking to the Internet to find love? It's almost like they were giving away free money and everyone is getting in line to grab their share! "Gimme some, gimme some!" It's like if you don't hurry it up there won't be enough left for you, and that is *so* far from the truth.

Being the master of the analogy, (and modest about it) I'm going to give you some insights into why this darn thing is so very popular, as dictated to my humble recorder several weeks back.

I guess part of the reason why women go to the Internet to find love and companionship is so that they don't have to deal with hanging out in smoky bars and dealing with assholes, jerks, users, players, dopes and idiots. So why do men go to the Internet to find love? In a word? It's a whole lot safer than being shot down!

Case in point: I am not too hard on the eyes. I have had more than my share of women. I've probably had more, um, relations in my lifetime already at 44, than most men do in a lifetime. I've been real lucky, *heh,* in certain areas.

"So I'm in a local supermarket tonight, walking around and there's this stunning creature walking around with raven hair and charcoal eyes, about 35, sultry, sexy, but sorta sad looking. Beautiful, full mouth, sad eyes, amazing. So I'm just kinda looking at her and she's just kinda ignoring me, walking around and around and around...So she decides to get on a line about the same time as I do.

"I'm unpacking my cart as she's deciding which lane to get on and I'm thinking "GET IN MY LANE, GET IN MY LANE, COME ON COME ON COME ON!!!" So of course she gets on the line next to mine! So I'm like giving her these shy little smiles, but trying to stay 'cool,' ('cause heaven forbid a nice guy should ever approach a girl he finds attractive!) and she's looking back at me for a millisecond at a time, and I'm dying to tell her how beautiful I think she is, but she's busy and any excuse will do.

So she finishes just before I do and I don't see her leave as I'm paying the bill. So I run, ever so coolly, out of the store with my groceries in my cart, and lo and behold, there she is unloading her cart. Do I go over and offer to help? Do I tap her on the shoulder to tell her she's a goddess? Do I even acknowledge her existence? Of course not! I have pride you know! I grab my 8 bags, push my cart aside, and brush past her with total disdain!

We both pack our cars at about the same time as I think to myself, "Say something, say Something, SAY SOMETHING!!!" Yet no sound escapes my manly mouth. So, my car fully packed with hers just being started I think, "Go over and ask if she needs some help," but again do nothing. The excuse this time? Well, any one would do, but this time it even sounds good to me. I'm thinking, "Hey, this is a dark parking lot and she's all alone. What if she thinks I'm dangerous or something?" So I get in my car and drive the ten feet to her car and I stop to look at her.

By now she can probably hear me screaming at myself in my head, "Will you say something to her already?" But once again. no sound escapes, and I drive off. Then, a sudden burst of bravery takes over! I screech my car around the parking lot to make one more bold pass at this beautiful creature. I'm really gonna do this! I'm a supermale!

Then, suddenly, in front of me pulls the Beast! The Beast is an elderly man waiting patiently for this princess' parking space and she pulls away, never to be seen again…and I never said anything, and that is why men go to the Internet to find love. Because we'll see this perfect thing all by themselves in a supermarket, and unless they just happen to be on line with us, giving an excuse to say something cute to them, we don't say a damn thing. You walk away feeling so stupid.

Very few women have ever shot me down. The vast majority of the women I've dated have wanted to see me again. There've been a number of women who have fallen in love with me over the past two years, but when it's one on one and you don't know what their reaction is gonna be, sometimes you just don't say anything. You kick yourself in the ass because you may just have let an opportunity walk right out of your life. Ain't it a shame…

Anna related a story to me, which fits nicely here. This happened at a singles mixer set up by one of the online dating sites. You think this would be an awesome place to meet someone? Think again…

Well, it reminded me of a high school dance where you go to the dance, and I thought this was going to be the be all and end all, because there's going to be men and women in the room that are there for the sake of meeting people and making friends and possibly finding some sort of connection. It was so not like that the two times I went that I was in disbelief and never returned.

The men stay on one side of the room, the women stay on the other side of the room. Of course with my personality, I was just like "Ohhh, screw this!" I went right over to where there were several guys standing and first of all, the initial reaction was, "Oh baby, I'm gonna get lucky tonight." Okay, that's the number one thing. That was the first knee jerk reaction, and the second was like, "Okay, there must be something wrong with her if she's being so aggressive."

Um, we who went were two females and one male, and we all had the same experience. Michael had the same experience with the women, and Sandy and I had the same experience with the men. We walked out of there laughing hysterically and could not believe that we put ourselves in that kind of position, and how our expectation was that everyone was there to kinda mingle and how that was not happening *at all*. I'm not just talking about the three of us. I mean it was a clear delineation of this invisible line, men on one side, and women on the other.

So here we are again, not in a dark parking lot of a supermarket, but at a place where, seemingly, everyone should easily be "hooking up" and getting phone numbers, laughing and having a good time mingling with the opposite sex, but no dice. Instead, everyone needs to show how aloof they are, how non–threatening they are, how cool, how un-needy, and therefore no one meets anyone and all go home unsatisfied and frustrated because, as I've said, when it's one on one, eyeball to eyeball, no one in their right mind wants to get shot down and feel horrible and unwanted. The Internet removes all that from the mix.

Removes it you say? *How?* Simple. Suppose you're cruising the profiles for three hours one night. You find twenty different people that you like for different reasons and send an e-mail to every one of them. The next day as you arrive home from work and log on to your computer, you have seven new e-mails waiting for you. Two of them are junk mail, but *five* of them are from women! Three of the five are return letters from women that you wrote to, and the other two are from brand new women who sought *you* out!

At this very moment do you think you're upset about the 17 girls who didn't e-mail you back? *Hell no!* You're flying high about the three who did, and the two new ones who want to talk to you all at their own initiative. Is there any doubt in your mind why this mode of meeting is so very popular?

Brando gave me his eloquent prose as to why he believes the Internet is such a popular medium for meeting. By the way he likes to fish (You'll soon see why).

We're all seeking. We're all searchers. We're seeking a connection, we're seeking meaning, we're seeking to learn more from others, safely, and we're seeking to grow personally. This is a tool. The Internet is a way of connecting with other people. It's a tool that can allow us to choose potential new people to learn from, to share with, to experience with and to hopefully grow our lives.... possibly forever with that person, most likely not...but it has just become another tool in the arsenal of personal growth.

So do you feel it's a means to an end?

Tools are tools. It's a mechanism for expanding one's network should one choose, potentially finding a compatible partner, if one has a clearly defined need for one thing. Perhaps, y'know, throwing...casting a wide enough net to be able to find that one specific "something"...like the women who post on five different dating sites? It's also a tool because you throw it out there and you never truly know what you'll pull back in your nets.

Cyberspace has become a decided force, and the difference, as far as I can tell, is that it's become acceptable in a way that it just was not for the longest time. There used to be the terms "computer dating," and this and that, like, "Well geez, who would I meet computer dating? The only people I'd meet are other people who wanna do computer dating and I don't think I wanna meet people that do computer dating because I'm not a computer dating type of person so I wont even bother." But nowww...all those barriers have come down. Almost everybody's got e-mail, surfs the web, very comfortable, got a computer sitting there and have all their friends and stories and it just becomes such a mass kind of acceptance that, um, it's all out there.

Whether this is good, bad, it's gonna continue. It's the way it's gonna be from here on out. I've had many people say, "No, we still think that the best way we like meeting somebody, y'know, an unexpected situation, or you're introduced. Y'know, it's good, you hit it off, there's good chemistry or you're attracted to somebody." But to some other people it's the same litany. "I'm not out there, I'm working, blah, blah, blah. I want to just broaden my horizons." So it's less like "Why?" and more like "Why not?" I could cover that much more ground, those many more bases, meet people I wouldn't have otherwise.... There it is!

There it is indeed. Here's one of the many conversations between Linda and Charley, this one specifically pertaining to why they started to date via the Internet as opposed to other options available to them.

Linda: The good thing about Internet dating is even if you don't wind up meeting the person online that you wind up with, it's easier to get back out there and start dating again and not have to be so afraid. 'Cause for me to go out to a bar when I was first single again was like "I'm not doing that, that's TERRIFYING!" Where online you have that buffer where you don't have to give out so much information. They can see your picture, they can get basics on you but they don't get anything else unless you want them to…where in a bar they see you, they can see what car you're getting into, that's a little scary. So it gives you the initial way to "get back out there" and maybe have a few dates and maybe start feeling comfortable with dating again.

Charley: Maybe just e-mail back and forth and begin a conversation. You just e-mail back and forth and that's kinda like the "ice-breaker" and then if it's going well, then that's when you go onto the phone. For me, that first phone call is everything. I really need to hear his voice and the Internet is a way to get to that point.

Linda: But y'know, what I'm saying is it teaches you that a little bit, so even if you don't wind up using the Internet, if the Internet doesn't work for you as far as meeting somebody, it's giving you some knowledge, and it's giving you some background and some confidence to go out there in the real world and becoming a little more open and outgoing, or a little wiser when you're meeting people.

I think it's a very useful tool in that way, so even if you don't meet the man of your dreams that way, you still can go out there and practice a little bit and get some confidence…When you're first single you don't have that confidence. I dunno about you, but I was terrified to go back out there and date again! "How do you start, where do I go, what do I do?" So that was safe, that was a safe venue to go out there and start talking to men again and start feeling like, "Okay, so if I mess up online, so big deal! Who's gonna know?" Y'know?

We know Linda, we know. So, you wake up in the morning, go take your laundry out of the dryer and curse at yourself for forgetting to do it last night because everything is creased now (you dolt!). Then you sit down and log onto your e-mail server, and there's another message from someone new, someone you've never heard from before. Well, you've been doing this Internet thing a while, and you've already got a herd of women chasing lovingly after you from eleven states, so you roll your eyes and open the e-mail to find something wonderful like this:

> OMG! Marry me!
>   ok ok i'm back now, i was gone for a minute there, but i'm back. just reading your ad made me realize what i'm missing in my life. not that i dont know it of course, but you put it so well and with crescendo! <sigh> i long for all those feelings you describe (as do we all!) and could be the woman you are looking for, who knows?? take a moment if you would, and look at my ad. hopefully you may see something there, a spark, that could burst into a wonderful flame! and if some kissing happens along the way...all the better <wink> ~debi

Whew! Whether or not you ever meet this person does not compare to the knot you feel in your stomach when you read something so amazing and then prepare to click the link to her profile, which has the photos that you are *dying* to see!!!

Now I don't know about you guys, but when a woman shows me that degree of interest, sight unseen, it stirs my soul and gives me a strong desire to meet the person who could write such inspiring words. Okay, so my photos aren't too shabby looking, but it's the written word from my heart that elicits a first response like hers.

The amazing thing about the Internet is that you can totally express your feelings to someone you've never met, openly and without fear of repercussions. The worst thing that can possibly happen is that you simply don't get a response, and that happens to everybody. On the other hand, the best thing that can happen is that your letter reaches someone who truly appreciates the sentiments that you wrote and responds in kind, leaving you all squishy inside!

Upon looking at someone's profile, you never truly know what the person is like in real life. You can make no assumptions about a person based on their looks, because you really have no way of knowing where they are emotionally in their life. You may come across a photo of someone who seems totally out of your league in the looks department, but so what? Send them your heart and you may be surprised at the response. You may very well have just sent a letter off to someone, who so desperately needs affection in their life, because they feel unapproachable to the opposite sex *because* they're so good looking. I have heard this a thousand times from women, and have dated some incredibly attractive ladies with awesome personalities and charm to whom I would never have walked up to in a bar and introduced myself to.

Am I making my point here? The Internet levels the field for those of us, (the *vast* majority) who don't have a perfect face, perfect teeth or huge muscles, but are sort of okay looking with a nice personality. (Could I make myself sound anymore like a dweeb here?) It is the great equalizer, and although it is not perfect by any means, the Internet is perhaps the best way to meet that special someone in a day and age where almost no one stops to smell the roses anymore.

"WAITAMINIT!" you say. "What about us folks who are not particularly attractive and have bad breath and a foul temper and no job and a total lack of personality and who just want to get some nookie? Huh!?"

Well, you'd be surprised at just how many sites are out there that cater to folks just like you and can satisfy your every desire. I have a female acquaintance who is only interested in other female companionship. She is short, not very good looking, kind of rude, and has body hair in places that a woman *really* shouldn't have any. She manages to get more nookie with amazingly attractive women than you could possibly believe. She meets these women online in alternative lifestyle meeting sites and chat rooms, (I've got to be politically correct here or she'll smack me!) and does so well that it makes my head spin. She's a good friend and we don't judge each other at all, so I'm going to share her first e-mail to me with you, gentle reader. Prepare thyself!

> Hey you nut!
> While I was perusing the fine ladies of AFF, I somehow had a momentary lapse of reason, and read your dopey profile. Whew! You must get major action from the way you write. I mean I actually had to stop and read it again to make sure I wasn't dreaming! You're not too hard on the eyes either! Too bad for you I don't like guys! Gotta go bury my head in something sweet now, stay kewl, and get back to me if you dare....
> Laters,
> Vixen...

Well, how could you, as a guy, possibly respond to that? My response follows:

> Dear Vixen type lady!
> Man you have got some balls girl! Sorry to interrupt your muff diving activities but I'm kinda at a loss to understand what you expect from any relationship between us!!!?? *smile* You obviously have a killer personality and are no doubt someone who I'd probably like to throw a few beers down with!

Now THAT would be a pisser! Get back if ya wanna chat some more and maybe we can exchange muff.... Oops...I mean war stories!!!! *tee hee* See ya on the flipside kiddo!!!...David...

Her answer to that e-mail could not be printed in this chapter as it would probably offend every person reading it, though it would probably also make you laugh until you stopped breathing! A later message is printed however in chapter ten (which is aptly described as the X-rated chapter).

Vixen is a very tough, hard-drinking, foul-mouthed, naughty girl with an interesting way of describing certain things. We have become close friends and speak every few weeks. This is a person that I would never have met anywhere else and I count her as one of my trusted friends and confidantes.

You see, for every love interest you find on the Internet, you will find five people who have the capacity to be close friends, providing you keep an open mind and an open heart. The capacity for growth as a human being is boundless as you bond with people by listening to their stories and you, in turn, share your own. However, if you come online with an agenda and keep a closed heart and mind to everyone who doesn't fit your mold of a love interest, you are doing yourself a great disservice. You're likely to be in for a very painful ride because your expectations will be far too high, and may even border on unrealistic.

You see, you've got to have fun with these things. Make pals, share stories, chat overseas, cry with someone you'll never meet, get naughty online with three people at the same time, and laugh until soda shoots out of your nose! *Enjoy this stuff!* You never know what's right around the corner, so live every day like it's your last. And for cripes sake, don't sweat the small stuff! You'll live longer and probably have less online misunderstandings.

Did I say misunderstandings? Well, not only is the cyber life is rampant with them, but it can assuredly be said that they are the soft white underbelly of online communication. One of the best examples of a lack of communication and understanding is my early relationship with two young ladies who are some of my best friends, Peggy and Toni. The following e-mails sent and received over a two to three week period, should be self-explanatory. Enjoy the insanity that is my life!

You must have beautiful eyes!

I read your profile and all I can say is WOW. You have described everything that I want, everything that I am. I keep asking myself if this could be real, it seems like a dream. You write beautifully, it seems straight from the heart. What more could anyone want? If the eyes are the window to the soul and you seem to have such a beautiful soul, then you must also have beautiful eyes. Is it true?

Peggy.

◆   ◆   ◆

Hey Peg!!!

I cannot say that I have beautiful eyes, however, I have been told that one could get lost in them…. whatever that means!!! *grin*. Since you didn't see fit to leave a link to your profile, I have no idea who you are, or, indeed, what you look like…I will endeavor to look you up later. I do hope, in the meantime, that you'll see fit to write me again, and tell me something about yourself.. my woman of mystery…*giggle*…gotta go shower, just got in from a power walk through the woods with my kids…see ya soon!!…*hugs*….

David…

◆   ◆   ◆

ahhhhhhh David. It's the getting lost in the eyes that I'm talking about. hmmmm nothing better. To be honest, I have no idea how this stuff works. I have no profile, I joined because it was the only way they would let me e-mail you. LOL. I am just a hopeless romantic and the things you wrote were so beautiful I just had to write and say hello. I am going to try to attach a pic to this e-mail but I have no idea if it will be there when you open it. You can write me at Angelyadayada@whatever if you like. That is also my Instant Messager name. Feel free to pop in if you see me online. Oh yeah I almost forgot, a bit about myself. I am 44, tall and thin with blonde hair and green eyes. I have 2 daughters. My 15 year old lives with her dad in Ct and my 13 year old lives with me (most of the time anyway) Tell me about yourself and your children. Would love to hear about all of you. I live in POdunkie, which is probably about 40 min north of you. I know absolutely nothing of the Bronx, only that I pass thru on my way to the GW when visit my family in New Jersey. I look forward to hearing from you. Take care David.

~~Peggy~~

[Unable to display image]This was taken over the summer. I won this kayak and was testing it out. LOVED IT!!

◆   ◆   ◆

Hey kiddo, loved your response, but I'm really gonna need some photos B4 we go any further with this, as I'm sure you understand. You may send them to starfighter@whatever.com as, obviously, your attempt to attach them here was, er, unsuccessful!!! Oh well!!!! See ya in the funnies!!!!...David...

◆   ◆   ◆

Unable to display image]
    This is the best pic I have of myself. I would rather be taking them of other people. so I don't have many. Take care David. ~Peggy~~

◆   ◆   ◆

Dear Peggy...sorry kiddo...no photo attached here either.........oh well!!!...D....

◆   ◆   ◆

I'll give this one more try, and I hope this one works...Peggy...[Unable to display image]

◆   ◆   ◆

Peg, I have every software package for photo's on the planet. If I can't open 'em, NO ONE can.... sorry...I'm just too busy for this, good luck in your search!!!.... David...

One must understand, at this point I really thought she was playing games with me, because in over a year on the Internet I had received hundreds of photos and never had a problem opening one until Peggy came along. She on the other hand, was incredibly frustrated, because not only did she join the site and spend money just so she could contact me, but she thought I was playing with her as well. So, she sent my last e-mail to her best friend Toni, who already had heard about me, and the following e-mails were sent. Just watch as the fur really started to fly!

> Read this Mister!!!
> You dont know me but I have something I want to say to you......
> You are what gives men a bad name! You are so narrow minded that without a pic you cant get to know someone? that is so pathetic! I just want you to know that you missed out on a chance to know a very wonderful person who is as beautiful on the outside as on the inside all because you are one of those small minded men who think looks are the most important thing in a relationship (which is probably the reason you are up "for sale" for a relationship.)
> I dont want you to be confused about who I am so Im putting a pic with this e-mail excuse my bluntness but my friend is too good for you you wrote off knowing a terrific person just because you couldnt open a freakin' picture! how pathetic!

Toni did indeed send two photos of herself and her daughter, both of whom are absolutely adorable and then sent another message immediately after the one above.

> OHHHHHHHHHHH and PS.....
> I just wanted you to see what you missed out on! Its too bad that you based everything on not getting a pic, being that looks are so important to you as you can see she looks like a barbie doll and she's just as beautiful on the inside. Your Loss Big Boy
> Peggy's friend Toni...
> I wanted you to see who is talking to you so you will feel more comfy let me give you a clue....NEVER mess with a southern woman or a southern woman's friend here in the south we know how to handle a man like you sweetheart ;)

Ouch! Now *that* hurt! Who is this Southern firecracker anyway? And why is she sticking her nose in my business? With the second e-mail came another adorable photo of this feisty woman and, finally, a photo of Peggy, but from a distance. The following was my response, which began a three-way friendship that is very strong and lasts to this day.

Toni,

I spent the better part of the last 2 weeks in the hospital with my 85 year old aunt Jeanette, loving on her with my kids, because my cousin's were "too busy" to visit. I have in the same 2 weeks moved a business, moved my residence and uprooted my entire life so that I could spend more time with my children who adore me as much as I do them. I am putting my eldest daughter through college, and crying with her on the phone every day because the love of her life left her for his ex girlfriend, and she is so devastated that she cannot function. I wish I could just hold her and make it better….. I am a passionate, caring, gentle man, who you have misjudged, brutalized, and hurt deeply with your words. I hope you feel like a better person because of it. Your photos, while cute, hide the terrible ugliness beneath, as I never gave you cause for the words you said to me. I am a published writer, who's latest book is on internet dating and the misunderstandings inherent in this medium. Your e-mails will DEFINITELY make it into one of the chapters. Thank you so much for giving me more fruitful research material and the tears inherent in your content, sincerely, David

◆   ◆   ◆

David, Please forgive my rudeness.

I'm sorry but I was a bit upset that my friend Peggy (Angelyadayada) only joined that site/program whatever it's called because she read your profile and your words melted her heart. Peggy has been going through some really rough times herself, which is why I was so defensive. She recently lost her mother, found out her sister has cancer and was treated badly by someone she was in love with.

I truly am a very nice person for real ;) I am however very sorry to hear about your aunt and I am sorry about your daughter my heart goes out to her, I know what its like to be "dumped" for someone else when you have given heart and soul thank God that one day she will be able to move on.

Again I am very sorry I exploded on you but I was very upset that you blew my friend off just because you couldn't open her picture.

Oh and thank you so much for putting me in your book I feel "special" lol. hey let me know when its done I want to buy a copy for myself.

Toni (from Arkansas)

The following is an excerpt of the response from Peggy as the entire letter is *way* too long. I felt that this was really getting interesting since I've never had a cyber three-way before!

Dear David, I am so sorry about this whole drama that transpired as a result of my reading your profile and being so touched by your words that I took a chance and joined Match.com so that I could possibly meet you. I talk to Toni almost every day and she urged me to go ahead and do it once I had told her about you and how I felt about what you wrote. I knew you wrote me off once you said OH WELL after several attempts at sending you my picture. I told Toni that and she was trying to convince me that you didn't. The last letter you wrote I forwarded to her, which is how she got your e-mail address. I had no idea she would react the way she did. She was just protecting me because she is my friend and she cares. I felt as if you thought maybe I was pulling your leg or that I didn't really want the picture sent. Not true.

I am having problems sending pics to people who have a different ISP than myself. I was very hurt that you would base any further contact with me according to my looks. To me it's superficial, what matters most to me is what is in a person's heart. I do truly have a beautiful heart but I guess that is not your main concern. That could be a man/woman difference, I really don't know. I am not saying that because I am not considered attractive. I get plenty of offers and cat-calls, etc. That is not what I am looking for David. I have never had a one night stand in my life, nor do I intend to, I am looking for something meaningful, such as you describe in your profile, which is one of the reasons I was so touched by what you wrote. The one thing that kept coming back to my mind is how you said you were looking for someone who would not run when there was a problem, but would stay and talk it over and work it out. I felt that was the first thing that you did, you ran when you could not get a visual on who you were talking to. I think that with everything going on in your life perhaps it was just the wrong time to contact you. My heart goes out to you and our aunt and especially your daughter since I just experienced heartbreak myself and although I am fine and probably all the better for it I know how she feels. Please tell her that although it doesn't seem possible, it does get easier with time and she will meet the person who is right for her and who will take her heart and soul and cherish it always. My feeling is that if someone could have the heart to hurt you, that capability will always be there so he really did her a favor by showing his true self now before it went any farther. David, I wish the best for you and your family. I hope you find the person you are looking for and that she makes you very happy. Please accept my sincere apologies for any stress or upset that I have caused you. I would never intentionally hurt another person. Sincerely, Peggy

Let me interrupt here just a bit to clarify a few points. When you send a cyber apology to someone, before you click "send," you need to make sure that it's *just* an apology. If there is *any* finger pointing or accusations whatsoever, all of the good stuff gets lost, because there is no face attached to the words, nor any emotion. When Peggy said that she had a beautiful heart, she added that it was not my main concern: not true and not fair. Strike one.

She also stated that basing contact with her according to her looks was superficial. Well, she's not a man who's dated as many women as I have, women who show up for the date looking about my mother's age. Not fun. Strike two.

Then she really went for the throat, though I know now (since I know the *true* person) that it was innocent. She said that she liked the fact that I don't run from problems, but was running from her due to a lack of a photo. Strike three, yer-rrrrrrrr out! So for cripes sake folks, *post that photo online*, and you too can avoid headaches like these!

Well, I accepted Toni's apology and we started to chat very nicely over the weeks that followed. Unfortunately, both Peggy and I seemed to be focusing on the negative in our e-mails and not the positive, so things went downhill fast. Many detailed letters followed until she became bored and started to date other guys. She had a good date with one, but he disappeared after a bit, so she wrote back to me and we started over.

Well, after a ton of very nice letters sent back and forth between us, and after she checked herself into the hospital to kick pneumonia, we decided to finally meet. The following letter was sent from Peggy to Toni, after our first date together.

> Hey T,
> I am off to my sisters' in Jersey. Just wanted to give you a quick thought about last night. OMG, T, David is THE MOST sexy, passionate, beautiful man I have ever met. He has beautiful eyes, an incredibly gorgeous body, heart, mind, and soul. All I can say is OMG! Needless to say, I just got home, so it went very well. ☺ Talk to you later. Have a great day. P.

Well, suffice to say, we've had several more, um, *really* good dates, including New Year's Eve together, and have become extremely close friends. All three of us! (And *no*, there's nothing funny going on here!) So why did I put you through all of those *boring* e-mails? To make a simple point. People screw up, all the time. In our case, we were adult enough, or lucky enough, or perhaps patient enough, to get through all of the misunderstandings, to actually meet, to like each other a whole bunch *in person*, and that's as it should be.

We both seemed to want to meet, yet despite writing nicely for the most part, we *both* concentrated solely on one small perceived negative in an otherwise pleasant correspondence. It is very easy to misread content in an e-mail, and because I was thin-skinned during a very difficult period in my life, with things going on that had nothing to do with Peggy, I took it out on her. How childish, how silly, and yet how very human.

6

Can I get another hit of that?

When you decide to dedicate as much time to writing as I do, you tend to ignore some of the things that you enjoy most. One of those things is chatting online on one of the interactive sites.

These are locations where as soon as you log in, everyone on the site can see that you're there...everyone of your sexual preference or geographic preference that is. So, last night I decided to log on to one of these sites, the one I have the most "friends" and they just about killed me! If I could print out everything I typed last night in the two or so hours I was there, it would no doubt fill two chapters of this book. I chatted with nineteen different women, not all at the same time, but usually eight or nine at a clip. Some of them were new friends, but most were ladies I had spoken to on many occasions, and several were women I had dated or were still dating.

To fully understand the scope of what occurs on these interactive sites, I'll need to paint a picture for you. You log onto your site and immediately the site first tells you which of your designated "friends" are online. Before you can catch your first breath, several of them have already said hello and you have responded. Within five or ten minutes you are involved in conversations with eight or nine women. The speed at which you need to think when conversing with so many different personalities, many from different countries, is mind-boggling. It's no wonder that interesting mistakes happen on a regular basis, mistakes like sending the right mail to the wrong person!

Now before you rip your hair out, understand this, each of those women in turn are chatting with eight or nine (or more) guys as well, and the guys are chatting with more women, and on and on and on. In reality, you're only chatting with one person at a time, with everyone else awaiting your response. This can create a scenario of animosity for the many who are indeed only chatting with *you* and are waiting quite some time for your response as the pendulum eventually swings back their way. It is a wild and crazy-fun environment that can become as addictive as any drug and indeed becomes a world all its own. Two of the more popular sites that I've experienced are at www.kiss.com, and www.udate.com. They are truly unique sites that I decided to leave because I was getting addicted. (Yes, they're that good!)

When you have warm feelings for several people you are chatting with, and some may even be love interests, you can find yourself online until hours of the morning you never would have thought you would be up until. Log on at 11:00 P.M. and the next time you look at the clock it's 2:30 in the morning…and you need to get up for work at 6:00 A.M. There are people who actually stay on these sites chatting for the better part of the day, six, seven, eight hours at a time or more, all in the name of finding love.

Love is the most wonderful thing in the universe, but when love does not seem to be forthcoming online, there are so many opportunities to replace it with lust instead. I am no longer amazed at the sheer number of women who initiate online naughtiness very early in a cyber conversation. Sometimes, even when you're not attracted to the person, you play along. Why? Simple. We're all adults and it's a release of stress, as in fun! I won't do this with a young lady who lives locally, because my intention is to meet and perhaps develop a love connection. If however, I get a naughty lady from California while I'm in New York, (not a rarity) and I know that there is little to no chance of a meeting with her, I will take it as far as she willing to go, or beyond! It really is a blast as a writer to be able to drive a woman nuts with my words and knowing that if she calls my bluff I can back it up with action.

The very best of the Internet happens though, when a person of the opposite sex whom you have befriended is having a rough time, needs to talk to someone, and you are there to help them through. The conversations here can get so deep and personal that the inevitability of a bond seems almost pre-ordained.

You can usually tell you're going to have one of these types of deep conversations when the only message to you is something like, "Hi, can you talk now?" and you just know. There is only one major rule that I live by online, and there is no deviation from this rule. This rule is as follows: Those friends that have come first and have been there for me when I needed them take priority over anyone new, no matter how attractive the new person is. You never forget your history here, as there are some folks that you'll get *so* close to emotionally, yet will probably never meet due to the distance between you and the lack of time that we all have in our lives to pursue anything at a distance.

Well, being a sort of a nutty guy, I just started to copy some instant messages on one of these sites a couple of months ago. Most of them are not the complete conversations, but you'll still get a pretty good idea of what goes on in that little section of the universe called cyberspace.

The first woman was a friend and customer of mine many years ago. She had been widowed two years earlier and decided that she had waited long enough. While she was cruising the profiles, she found me and we both nearly died! It is a total blast finding an old friend in a dating site online! The following two short chats online ensued after several weeks online:

Eve:	I had one guy blow me off, I blew off one guy and a long take with my date for next week, and a weak offer from a guy that I sound like fun, hot fun! That's a quote!
David:	oooooooooooo......be careful hon.... Lotsa dogs out there, and some of them bite!!!
Eve:	I bite back! One guy told me to meet him in Manhattan NOW! I told him "do I give you the impression that I can be told what to do?" and that one is STILL talking to me!
David:	Did I tell you that I was writing a book on Internet dating????
Eve:	You only mentioned it. What angle are you taking on it?
David:	Can't really talk about it in detail (I signed a paper!) only that nothing like it has ever been written, from the same angle.... Not even close!!!
Eve:	Excellent!! Do stories from other people help? I am endlessly having weird experiences already and I've only been doing this for two weeks!
David:	SAVE EVERYTHING!!!!! You just got one of those angles!!!!! But not the rest!!! *teee heee*
Eve:	Great! This is a really strange experience. I like it, but there's no way to really get it until you try it.
David:	keep on pluggin', no one ever figures it out...it's just being lucky enough to click on the Right profile on the RIGHT day and say the RIGHT thing to the RIGHT person.... Not an ez task!!!

The following conversation occurred a week later, and no, I'm *not* making this up!

Eve:	Dude! Had my first date…went amazingly well!
David:	Da Bronx is in da house!!!!! Kewl, 'fess up!!! Details, I want DETAILS!!!!!!!!!!!!!!!!!!!!
Eve:	Had a 5 ½ hour lunch, got me some, a tall, skinny, charming, funny, delightful man.
David:	got you some….WHAT? *tee hee*
Eve:	I got SOME!!! Ring the bells the dry spell is over!!! He needs practice, but he has some wonderful skills already.
David:	Eve! You DEVIL you…. On a first date???
Eve:	OH YEAH!!! Isn't that what first dates r 4, to see if you want a second date? How ELSE would you know if you want a second date?
David:	Perhaps we're not on the same page here. I know you long enuf to be to the point…YOU SCREWED????? Or just short of it??? Or????
Eve:	Got laid baby!! It was delightful!!
David:	GO EVEY GO EVEY GO EVEY!!!!

All I can say is I *really* wish I had saved the rest of that conversation!!!! I must get her to sit down with me and re-tell the rest of that story!

The following conversations took place over a three-day period with a young lady in Florida who I can only describe as drop dead gorgeous. We love to tease each other and have been doing so for about six months now. Even though these are some of our more sedate conversations online, I still needed to slightly change a few words, because we did get a bit graphic. I pray that I do meet this girl someday to call her bluff, though if she's *not* bluffing I'm not too sure if either one of us would survive the meeting!

David:	You changed your photos!!! Whassuuuup?
Breezy:	LOL! You hate me!
David:	Why? You hurt me to the quick, my princess of pleasure, my pee pee in the potty, my….. can't top that last one…………LOL!
Breezy:	OMG!!! Have you been drinking again (smiling)
David:	Only to excess, but I'm with the girls, and they watch out 4 me!!!

Breezy:	How are you David?? Is it getting cold???
David:	Well it WAS, but now that YOU are here my love, my heart is warm indeed!
Breezy:	LOL, you are soooooooo full of crap!!!! That's why I like you:)
David:	I am not full of crap, but there are a few things that I'd like to fill YOU up with!!!! *grin*
Breezy:	laughing <—stop teasing me!
David:	I only tease in person, with my eyes, and my tongue, and my mouth, kissing and probing and caressing every passionate inch of your supple body, as I drive you to the very precipice of an orgasm, only to let you slip back down, so that I can take you there again, and again, and again......
Breezy:	GULP!
David:	and just as I have you begging, pleading for a release "PLEASE DAVID, NOW, NOW, NOWWWWWW-WWWW!!!!!! I'll thrust the full length of me DEEPLY inside of you, only to withdraw, slowly, and gently thrusting only the head inside of you..... it's agony you're thinking, but it's not over yet, because every tenth thrust will be the DEEPEST you've ever felt.... and then....
Breezy:	hey!!!!! You are making me wiggle in my office chair! LOL!
David:	Not as much as you'd be wiggling if you were here in my arms!!!
Breezy:	awwww, there is nothing I would like better:)
David:	I think you would BETTER like to feel what my tongue can do to arouse you, as it circles it's way around your neck, nibbling at your ears, then down to your luscious breasts, circling all around the outer edges while you pray that I touch your nipples, sometime before you die of desire....
Breezy:	wow!!! You are in some mood tonight, huh babe:)
David:	if you were here looking into my big brown eyes, you'd be put into the same mood, if not more so.... Come on silly!!!! Play with me here!!!

Breezy:	play with you?????? C'mere and pull down your pants...then I will play with you:)
David:	Gee I don't know...I'm such a GOOD boy, d'ya think I really should? I mean after all, what if we have S-E-X? someone could get hurt! *smile*
Breezy:	Let me assure you that the "soreness" you would feel after being with me would be WELL worth it, :)

Do you believe that I stopped printing at that point? I guess the chat started to heat up a whole lot more. This was the next day, somewhere in the middle:

Breezy:	I heard about the storm you are going to get...it is pouring here...I love it:)
David:	you are a sick puppy!
Breezy:	nooooo, I meant the rain we are getting! Grrrrrrrrr........
David:	exactly! The only thing I love about the rain, is being in upstate N.Y. and dancing naked in a downpour, preferably not alone, and then making love in it...without drowning, hopefully!
Breezy:	wow, do you have an erection right now babe?
David:	no, why?
Breezy:	hmmmmmm...just wondering:)
David:	so.... If it's pouring down there.... *smile*, does that mean you're all WET???
Breezy:	well lets just say I am moist:) hehehe
David:	I luv ya kiddo!!!! You is da BOMB!!!!
Breezy:	and you are AWESOME!!!
David:	oooooo...a mutual admiration society!!!! Guess what? I got my first, totally nude, unsolicited photos from a girl in Asia this week!!!
Breezy:	okay I take that back...you are such a dog!
David:	I said UN solicited, you dork!!! That means I did not ask 4 them! She e mailed me on my other site, and asked if she could send me some pics.... Sounded pretty normal, then I opened the file..... and BAM!!!!!! Pussy parade!!!!! I TOTALLY laughed my butt off, 'cause she was pretty laughable looking, but I guess some guys are into that stuff!!!!

Breezy:	Damn, I hate when I miss the annual (or is that anal) pussy parade:)
David:	not this one…She had tread marks on her stretch marks, and I won't even guess what her cup size must be, as she was HUGE!!!! EEEEEEEYUCK!!!
Breezy:	LOL, I love the way you explain things on the computer babe (kinda makes me wanna throw up) thank you soooooo much for the visual!
David:	HEY! I work out every day, not my fault she's a piggy!!!!!
Breezy:	>>>>>> laughing my little butt off!!!! You are sooooo funny!
David:	yeah…like I BELIEVE you have a little butt!!!
Breezy:	HEY!!!!!!!!!! You leave my LITTLE butt out of this Buddie!
David:	You left yourself SOOOO open to me in that last one, but the response on my lips would make you laugh so hard, that your breasts would start to vibrate, and cause an earthquake that would give Georgia ocean front property, as Florida slipped into the sea!!!
Breezy:	baby I have perfect breasts and they do not vibrate <grrrrrrrr>…now why the heck am I trying to defend my body??????
David:	if you were with me right now my love…you would be doing a lot more than vibrating……and I am most sure that they ARE perfect!!!! BTW, I may be visiting Fla. In about 3 months…*grin*
Breezy:	David, I have to run upstairs and take a shower (alone, boo hoo!) and then snuggle with my comforter and pillows…sweet dreams xoxoxoxoxxx's…ohhhhhh and if you visit Florida, I will run to New Jersey…we can't be in the same state at the same time <kisses>
David:	wanna bet??????????????? *grin* nitey nite luv!

Actually got to the end of that one! The next day, after receiving one of the most erotic e-mails ever from her, (which is printed in it's entirety in chapter ten, which my equally erotic response) the following short conversation ensued.

Breezy:	Hi punkin! Did you get my letter? I wrote it for a special horny guy in New Jersey!
David:	OMG….. I haven't quite recovered yet!
Breezy:	LOL! You deserve it and it's long overdue!
David:	flatterer!!! My loins ache for you my darling….. it's sooooo very difficult not to feel you in my arms….
Breezy:	geez, where do you get this stuff from??????? (laughing!)
David:	just kinda OOOOOZES out of me…. But only with certain girls…
Breezy:	ahhhhhhhhh, I get such a kick out of your personality!
David:	if I were with you right now my love, you would be getting a kick out of SEVERAL things about me….
Breezy:	somehow I believe that!
David:	You'd better! Believe something else too, if someone doesn't snatch me up (and many are trying!) in the next few months, you WILL be getting a visitor!!
Breezy:	I would not mind you visiting me at all!!! Just remember this David…don't blame me if you fall head over heels in LUST with me (giggle)
David:	is that an invitation??? 'cause airfare to Fla. is not very expensive…. But can I ask you a question? My love? Why hasn't some Floridian stud swept you off your feet yet?
Breezy:	Perhaps if I could find one with your personality and charm, they would?
David:	*blushing*

Well, that's that for now. We really haven't spoken for a few weeks, and I'm no longer on the site that she's a member of, but I get the feeling I haven't heard the last of my Southern friend, not by a long shot.

The next victim…er, girl…is from Singapore, clear on the other side of the world. After receiving her initial e-mail, I clicked on her profile to see what she looked like and almost passed out. There, looking back at me, was the most perfect face I had ever seen in my entire life: perfect shiny black hair in sexy little curls, perfect blue eyes that are as big as the ocean, perfectly round, red lips, that beckoned, "Kiss me once, and you'll be in my power forever." Her head was tilted sexily to the left with her beautiful locks just slightly obscuring a wee bit of her left eye.

Now, being a professional photographer for seventeen years, it was apparent to me that she had an excellent makeup artist, great contact lenses, an amazing photographer and a talented airbrush person. Funny thing though, knowing all this did not detract from the sheer artistry of her photos and the latent beauty that needed to be there to begin with.

I am going to print her words to me exactly as I received them. I don't want anyone to be offended by this, so you should understand that her English is *much* better than my, um, well whatever they speak in Singapore. Give her credit for trying as hard as she did because she is a very sweet girl and I do hope to meet her someday. As usual, it begins somewhere in the middle...

Bunny:	oh sound great to me...so hows ur date going?
David:	I have my third date with Maria tomorrow night. She's very sweet, and EXTREMELY sexy, and we like each other a lot! There's also a MAJOR sexual attraction going on...I don't think we'll be able to STAND it much longer, without...you know!!!!
Bunny:	Maria sound great...well go for it then if the mutual understanding is there.
David:	I think that mutual horniness is there!!! But we do talk a lot on the phone, and make each other laugh.... A little.
Bunny:	oh mutual horniness...so r u on the phone right now with her?
David:	NO, I'm chatting with YOU, my goddess of the orient!!
Bunny:	Oh tot normally u do 2 thing at one time.
David:	I do 2 girls at one time! *giggle* but never 2 things at one time!!!!!!! I would REALLY love you to be one of those girls, but alas, you live on the other side of this big blue marble!!!
Bunny:	Well as for me I don't like to share my men...I rather have u alone with me all by myself...(LOL) maybe we can meet in a dream...
David:	I will dream of you, my goddess of Singapore, through the long dark night, as I lie next to you, and

slowly caress your lovely face, run my fingers through your beautiful hair, and as you awake...I am gone...like the wind, as I was never truly there...

Bunny: Please don't go! It nice to have u with me...hmmm I'm enjoying what u have do to me...arrghhh...

David: What time is it there? It's really late here, 3:25 A.M., so I DO have to go in a little while! You're so sweet!!!

Bunny: ok hunny, gud nite...mwahhh...

David: Silly!!! I'm not going yet!!! I really wanted to KNOW what time it is there, as I'm curious!

Bunny: It's 3:30 P.M.

David: So you are EXACTLY on the opposite side of the earth!!! WOW, can't get any further than that! I will dream of you anyway, as the lion dreams of the lamb.... Or as the prince dreams of his princess, as I await your gentle caresses in my dreams....

Bunny: yes WE ARE...IT MY PLEASURE...and WILL ALWAYS WAIT FOR U...

David: if only...if only that were true, I would fly to you, on gossamer wings of love, and sweep you up and away.... To a baseball game in Tokyo!!!! HAH! Didn't expect THAT one didja???

Bunny: HAHAHHAH! That is like a slap on the face...well u sure are good with fairy tales aren't u?...like u a lot!

David: I like u 2. It really is a shame you're so far away, as it would be so lovely to sit with you, by a lake, and just look at the stars...

Bunny: yeah I know wat to do...we can only create all this on this site I guess, well at least we are having fun.

David: Fun is the main ingredient, in a happy life, but I SWEAR to you, that if I do make as much money in the next year as I hope to, I'll be on the next flight to Singapore!!! Or.... Bring you here to me!!! New York is AWESOME!

Bunny: ok, we meet for sure...

David: Have you ever been to New York, or you haven't ever left your country? Been anywhere else in the world? London? Brussels? BROOKLYN?????

Bunny:	Sorry Honey, the nearest is only Phuket in Thailand, and Kuala Lumpur in Malaysia…the rest only god know when…
David:	I've never been to those places, perhaps,…you can take me there…someday…I'm exhausted baby…really gotta go now! Please talk to me again soon, you're a LUV!
Bunny:	ok, talk again, gud nite…a kiss for u. mwahhhhh
David:	back atcha!!!! MMMMMWWAAAAAAAHHHH!!!!!
Bunny:	OH! Your lips are so moist! Mmmmmmmmmm mmmmmmmmmm…….

Now how cute is that? Why does this adorable creature with a matching personality have to live on the other side of the world? The point here is that we brightened each other's day…um, night *and* day, and would never have spoken at all, if not for the Internet…nuff said!

Now just for a wee bit, I'm going to get off the beaten track here, and talk about two things that happened last night. Call it filler, or call it a study of human nature, but a story is a story and for some reason I need to tell these.

I was visiting my 86-year-old aunt at the nursing home where she resides. I was there because she called me at home and said she was lonely. So, I finished what I was writing, grabbed a bite, jumped in my car, and went to visit one of the people I love most in the world.

My aunt is a talented artist who draws all the people at the home and can get very upset when they move too much and mess up her drawing. One of her proudest days occurred when I brought two of her paintings there and hung them on the walls of her room. She had me parade them around for everyone to see and just beamed with pride! So, she saw me last night, and it was like sunlight hitting the petals of a flower.

"David!" she said loudly, "You came!"

"Yup," I said, "of course."

She asked me about the book I was writing and we walked the hallways back and forth until she decided to go back to her room. I helped her off with her shoes as she complained that her feet might smell…they didn't. Then she climbed into bed and I read one of my children's books to her while she laughed at the content.

Her roommate was not feeling very well and complained of the light, and the talking, and the company, and everything. They started to argue with each other and something suddenly occurred to me. They were behaving so rudely, like two six-year-olds who had absolutely no compassion for the other one's feelings.

How amazing that our lives come full circle. How incredible it is that children can be so horrible to each other. They never once think about the damage that they can inflict on each other in their ignorance through harsh words and insensitive actions. Watching my aunt, who I have known to be the very sweetest person I have ever known, yell at her roommate for disturbing our visit was an eye-opener for me. I hope that someday they find a cure for dementia, and Alzheimer's, because it makes children of parents, and parents of children.

Earlier during our visit, we were sitting in the hallway near the nursing station, when out of her room comes a tiny little lady, perhaps about 4 feet 6 inches. She may have been a bit taller, but due to the osteoporosis she was completely bent over. She began to shuffle down the hallway, but kept veering to the left, correcting her trajectory, and continuing her voyage.

Upon arrival at the nursing station, she looked up from her walker, caught my eye, and said, "Can you please help me with a drawer in my room?" I said okay, and she began the long return journey to her room.

She walked about three feet, turned around to look at me, and I said, "It's okay, I'll be right there," and she continued on. Every three or four feet she would stop and turn to see if I was coming. I continued to encourage her on in her quest as I sat with my aunt watching her draw a picture of the nurse on duty.

The woman finally arrived at her room, so I got up and walked over to her. She gave me the sweetest smile and pointed me to her bureau with the bottom drawer open half way. The drawer would not open fully because something was blocking its progress. I cleared the obstruction and prepared to leave, but she wasn't done with me yet. The contents of the drawer were adult undergarments!

I smiled. She asked me if I could take them out, as it was difficult for her! So, I reached down, took one out, and stood there holding a diaper in my hand. Well, I can tell you I felt a little weird! I started to hand it to her and she proclaimed, "No! I need the whole package!" So I put the diaper back, grabbed the full package, and now stood there with a month's supply of these things.

"Put them on the bed" she said, so I did. Now here I was putting diapers on the bed of a 90-year-old woman and wondering, "Why do I *do* these things?" I prepared to leave as she thanked me, and then she gave me the cutest wink. A wink you say? Yup! She may have been 90, but she didn't forget how to flirt! Women!

I returned to the nursing station and told them what had happened. They were rolling on the floor in hysterics!

"She does that to every man who lets her," they said. I felt *so* used!

"She's just a geriatric slut," they all laughed, and we went back to our drawing with my aunt who seemed to miss the entire event.

People are just people folks. We need affection and attention, and when we get it, even just for a moment, whether it be online or in "real life," it gets us through just one more day.

This next girl contacted me from a personal ad on www.craigslist.org, the most amazing site on the planet! If you've never been there, just log on and click on the city nearest you and find something you're seeking. Just don't expect anything from Craig because his favorite response is, "David, I don't get it." He is a great man indeed. I am *not* jesting here! Craig has created something totally unique there in San Francisco that has literally spread around the world like a plague…er, a good one that is! This was the only IM conversation (for those less than internet savvy, "IM" stands for "instant messaging") I ever had with this young lady, which is truly a shame as you'll figure out, (especially the guys) after reading the very naughty content. We exchanged several photos via e-mail, with hers being a bit, um, provocative, though not in a seedy way.

> Michelle says:
> I like your hair on the pics where you are on and over the chair…..it's very….well classy and sexy looking…..nice….thank you
>
> David says:
> But you saw that one already?
>
> Michelle says:
> I am a woman who just loves the 50's……everything about it……the way they dressed and the way they wore their hair and to see your hair and you in that t-shirt reminds me a bit of that look
>
> David says:
> Funny how every woman seems to like me with my hair slicked back…….
> Like a BIG city guy….. and me just an ol' country boy!!!
>
> Michelle says:
> LOL…….it looks rugged yet sexy and classy all in one!!!!
>
> David says:
> *sheesh*………..

David says:
I am all of that, of course!

David says:
thank you madame!

Michelle says:
Well see then it just fits your personality perfectly!

David says:
Perhaps WE can do a little fitting ourselves.... ahem..... OOOOOOOOo
was I getting naughty??????

Michelle says:
LLLLOOLLLLL nawwww not really.......perhaps we can....(did I say
that?).....xxxxxxoooooo

David says:
I'm sure that we could drive each other nuts online or on the phone. Fun, but
in person is sooooo much better

Michelle says:
I know it......and I think you and I would get into a lot of trouble in person.....I am talking about closing the bedroom door and not coming out all
weekend trouble......lol

David says:
no doubt. Just looking at your photos, the first thought I had was turning you
around, hitting my knees, pulling you strongly to the edge of the bed, and
burying my head where the sun don't shine.........if ya know what I mean
jelly bean?

Michelle says:
(blushing again).......I have to tell you I have a very HIGH sex drive.....some
guys I have dated in the past loved it....others were annoyed with it.....NOT
that I have slept with a ton of people.....8 to be exact, but I think you know
what I mean.......I LOVE getting it from behind and my hair being tugged a
bit and my ass being slapped not hard, but just right.......oh yeah......lol

David says:
oh my.........

David says:
I think that perhaps I'll need to mail you a plane ticket!

Michelle says:
LOL……..One thing I am as well is EXTREMELY responsive……moaning, touching and letting you know it feels good, not just by telling you….I like to show it

David says:
I'm the same way. I don't think you'll find a guy that gets such a major kick out of pleasing the girl I'm with. I loooove to tease! I will get you VERRRRY close to orgasm, only to smile, wink at you, hear you moan, and move on to a different area until you settle back down…….. just so I can take you there again. There is NO orgasm that feels better than releasing after a period of frustration,

David says:
brought on by a talented lover

David says:
purposely!

Michelle says:
Of course………and I love to hear the response back as well…….that turns me on soooooo much……I love to give head as well……that really turns me on and for a guy to totally get into me while I am doing it as well…..

David says:
I have been with VERY few women who truly have the skills to give an amazing blowjob.

David says:
Some get so into it themselves that they fail to realize I just MIGHT like something different!

David says:
There is a certain technique that ALL my friends agree sends us right through the roof,,,, but few know it, and fewer still have mastered it…. boo hoo….

David says:
I have been told by some women that I am SO good with my techniques, that they get so VERY into it, they just sorta forget to reciprocate!

Michelle says:
I don't brag and I won't brag about it……i will say that I love to do it and well……the exhusband….(sick pig) has on several occasions (even though he is remarried) has asked me to give him a blowjob because he says no one will ever or has ever been able to top me…….I hang up on

him......LOL>>>.never in a million years would I degrade myself to doing that.!! but like I said I don't brag

David says:
You either type VERY slow, or you are multi tasking!

David says:
I understand. I have yet to be with a woman who satisfies me orally as well as my ex wife did. OMG!!!!! She was SOOOOOO amazing!!!!!

David says:
I miss her mouth SO much!

Michelle says:
LOOOOLLLLLLL

Michelle says:
I think it's an art as well as kissing......you need to slowly take the shaft and put it in your mouth......(not to mention all of the other kissing down the body and licking the nipples and things first).....and then.....

David says:
uh huh?

Michelle says:
Good you are paying attention

Michelle says:
lol

David says:
come again? hehehe

David says:
GO ONNNNNNNNNN!!!!!!

Michelle says:
I LOVE sucking and playing with a guys nipples.....It turns me on....some don't like it others do......????

David says:
do

Michelle says:
lol

David says:
I love when a woman plays with my balls, caressing them gently as she takes the full length of me deeply inside her mouth, gently twisting in circles with her tongue........

Michelle says:
I love to take my tongue and run it along the inner thighs then......on to the ball area where I gently lick in between the two balls and then take one ball and gently glide it in my mouth with my lips and suck gently....that's just a warmup

David says:
a warmup to?

Michelle says:
then after the balls have danced in my mouth for a bit I then take my tongue up and down the shaft and then insert that lovely cock in my mouth.....

David says:
and what do you do once it's there????

Michelle says:
I then take it and run it gently to the back of my throat up and down and start sucking and feeling his reaction on where he likes it....some like it more towards the head....but my bigger success has been to take it with one hand and stroke as I have it in my mouth going up and down as well at the same time

David says:
uh huh....

David says:
you're in the ballpark girl!

Michelle says:
It depends on the guy and how he likes it.....after all that is what it is about....and I feel for the response from him.....

David says:
wanna hear what I like to do to YOU?

Michelle says:
Sure!!!!!!!!!!!!!!!!!!!! ;)

David says:
Everything begins with the kiss. I love to make a meal of a woman's mouth. I spend a great deal of time caressing, licking, suckling, nibbling, and exploring every inch of her beautiful lips and mouth.

David says:
Just when she is frenzied, I attack her neck. The response I always get is moans of happiness, arched spines, and a ton of goose bumps along the arms.

David says:
As I kiss and nibble my way around the back of her neck, eliciting groans of "MORE", I gently smile at her, and remove her blouse. I kiss my way to her full breasts, gently removing her bra, and kissing all around the outer areas, but NEVER touching her nipples, until I feel her hands on my neck in her frustration PUSHING my mouth gently but firmly over her very erect nipples, as I take one into my mouth, suckling her like a child does with my tongue in ever faster circles.

Michelle says:
I WILL cum from that if it goes on for a while

David says:
She is pleading for more, yet I will not give in....... yet

David says:
I move to her other nipple and give it a gentle bite. She is starting to squirm under my weight as her torso is PLEADING for my mouth

David says:
I lick all around her other breast for what seems like an eternity, but finally start my travels southward

Michelle says:
Ohhhhhhhh-
hhh.........myyyyyyyyyyyyyyyy...............gggggggggggggggggg...........
.....

David says:
I nibble on her thighs, kiss and lick at her belly button, move along and up the back of her knee and swirl my tongue behind it. She NEVER knew about THAT spot and almost cums right there in complete surprise.

David says:
I smile, give her a wink, and move to her inner thigh.....

David says:
I begin to swirl my tongue in HOT, wet circle inside her thighs, brushing against her pussy hairs ever so gently, but never quite giving her what she is by now BEGGING for...

David says:
I bite her just an inch away from her pussy. She moans, I smile, she is SOOOOOO wet anticipating my next move.

David says:
Suddenly my hot wet tongue strokes the full length of her clitoris, as she arches her back and nearly breaks my jaw!

David says:
I smile yet again, and bury my sweet mouth between her wonderful, sexy legs.

David says:
hehehe

Michelle says:
mmmmmm

David says:
more?

Michelle says:
I am going to have to masturbate tonight you know this right?

David says:
I have no idea what you're talking about?

Michelle says:
Sure.......David

Michelle says:
lol

Michelle says:
I do need to get to bed now sweetie.....

David says:
Hmmmmmm....... if you're REALLY gonna do what you just said..... then perhaps you'd like to do it while listening to my voice???

David says:
just an idea….

Michelle says:
Not tonight………but perhaps soon…….It will only take me one
minute…..LOLLLLLLL…..talk tomorrow? Goodnight xxxxxoooooo

David says:
you are very naughty getting me so hot!

Michelle says:
Well you will have to do something about that and when I get there I will
have to do something about that!!

David says:
We shall see my dear, we shall see!

Michelle says:
Ok……night night

David says:
nighty!

Cute, sexy, naughty…everything you'd want to do with a pretty girl on a
Thursday night. We never chatted again and never did speak on the phone. I
guess I'd already given to her all that she needed from me.

So what do we have here? An old friend who believes that sex on a first date is
necessary for further communication, a sexy blonde from Florida who gets much
naughtier than her messages show here, an adorable girl from Singapore who can
only meet me in her dreams and a very expressive, horny woman from Georgia
who I would truly kill to get between the sheets!

Aside from Eve, whom I previously knew, I never met one of these girls, or
indeed the next one in this chapter with whom I had a very heartfelt conversation
with, wholly online, that may indeed have saved her life.

June was a girl that contacted me on Udate.com. We chatted occasionally but
I never sought her out as she lived very far away and my intentions going in were
to find a girlfriend and not just a bunch of "chat buddies." We had chatted for
several months about the men in her life until she seemed to disappear suddenly.
Several weeks later she sent me a note to say that she was head over heels in love
and would be canceling her membership shortly. I was very happy for her, if not

slightly jealous because she had grown on me in the months we had chatted together, laughed, and shared "war stories." Funny how sometimes a person enters your life for just a short time, but the ripples of their presence lasts a lifetime.

June:	David I do not know what to do, I think I will go quite mad.
David:	What's wrong sweetie?
June:	He disappeared. He just won't answer his phone, return my messages,......nothing....... I am going insane with questions. What did I do wrong?
David:	What happened??????
June:	We spent last weekend together and although not perfect.... I think we were both a little nervous, it was still glorious.
David:	Okay, so everything was good? I mean it went well.... Y'know what I mean...your first...."encounter?"
June:	Since we had decided to wait, I had thought that it would be amazing as we were both wound so tight..... I thought we'd just about kill each other..... it didn't go as expected the first night but I really didn't mind considering my past history.... You know......

Just a word to explain a bit. June's "past history" was very colorful in the sex department and included several "adult movies" as well as having been an erotic dancer. Although a wee bit past her prime, she was still very sexy looking and just wanted to be loved for the person inside and not be just a sex object for the rest of her life. She thought she had found this with "Michael." They didn't have sexual relations until they had dated for over a month, thus the content of the correspondence you are reading.

David:	Okay, calm down. Just give me the details so we can discuss it. You know I love ya hon. You're a special person and I'll stay here with you as long as you need me to. Why don't we get off this site and chat on Yahoo so we're not constantly disturbed by everyone else?
June:	Okay let me say goodbye to the other's.....
David:	Me too see ya there in a sec......

◆   ◆   ◆

David:	You there?
June:	Yes….. in body anyway……David I am so confused. I think that my heart is just going to explode……..I don't know how to deal with this. I have never been rejected by a man in my entire life……
David:	Tell me what happened last weekend. I know it'll be tuff but don't leave too much out. At least I can give you a guy's perspective…. Hell I've had girls disappear on me too! You know!
June:	Yes, I do know…. That girl you thought was "the one"…. You always fall for a pretty face!
David:	A joke? Good, you're cheering up already. So talk to me…..
June:	Yaaa sure…We got to the bed and breakfast just before sundown Friday night and checked in. Oh it was so beautiful! It was just outside of Tucson and the desert was blooming like crazy! We decided to stay in and have a late dinner as we were starving after a two-hour ride in the car. It went nicely with a lot of chit-chat and teasing, y'know both of us knowing what the night had in store and all….
David:	Still there? Ya okay sweetie???
June:	Yaaa…. So…whew, David this is hard. Ya sure you're up to this?
David:	Fire away hon…. Nothing I'd rather do.
June:	Liar! That's why I love ya! Such a b.s. artist! Okay. Like I said dinner went well and we had a nice desert and we got a bottle of Chardonet to return to the room with. It was a really tasty wine and we got cozy pretty fast on the couch in the room. We kissed for a while and…well you know where we ended up…
David:	Prey tell, where?
June:	Wiseass, you know! So the clothes came off and we started, um, well we started…. and then he ended….
David:	Prematurely?

June:	Yaaa…kinda. I mean it wasn't instant or anything but it was very fast. I just laughed it off and started to joke because if I were a guy and had to endure a month's wait I'd be pretty excited too….. he started to mope….
David:	Mope?
June:	Yaaa…he just got up and sat on the edge of the bed and was very moody. I waited for a little while and really tried to make light of the whole thing but he wasn't going for it, didn't want to be held and just, well, just didn't seem very happy about the whole situation. I tried to tell him it didn't matter and you know me D…. it really didn't matter to me but I guess it was a major issue to a guy. If this was ten years ago I'd have laughed and bolted, but I'm a different person now…. Looking for more than sex and I got all that from Michael…..
David:	That's sucks. Did he feel better after a while? I mean was that it, or did you cheer him up and have another go?
June:	After some time he came back to bed and we did snuggle for a while. I figured that at this point I needed to be very gentle and not the vixen inside me. We started to kiss slowly and I eventually found my way down stairs (you know!) but he pushed me away and didn't let me touch him there.
David:	Damn! You REALLY need to pay me a visit girl!
June:	Not a chance luv, you're even a bigger slut than me!
David:	I'll take that as a compliment!
June:	Uh, yeah, right!
David:	You should be nice to your east coast friend! After all this is a Friday night and I'm spending it with a beautiful girl who I can't even see, none the less touch!
June:	Hey babe I give what I get!
David:	That's why you've been known to not walk too well the day after!
June:	Now that was uncalled for! Can't a girl be depressed around you, ever?

David:	Not a chance. I really do wish you were here though, and NO not in a sexual way either. I'd like to just hold you and tell you how amazing you are and that everything's gonna be kewl…..
June:	You're already doing that babe. Thank you for being there for me. I really thought Mike was the one. Everything was great until we attempted sex. What the hell is wrong with me?
David:	Nothing is wrong with you. So he got over-excited. It happens to all of us sometimes. There could be physical reasons, or medical reasons or even psychological ones but so what? Did you guys get together again? I mean was that it???
June:	No, not even close. If it were that easy I wouldn't be so upset. You know me better than that and I do NOT give up so damn easy!
David:	Somehow I didn't think so.
June:	Right.
David:	Right!
June:	So he started to warm up a bit and eventually we got around to, well, attempting round two. He seemed pretty fixated at this point on pleasing me and he did a decent job. Not the best but his skills were commendable. It seemed to get him quite aroused and he had a better time of it the second time around with me. Not a marathon mind you, but at least he lasted a few minutes.
David:	Sweetie…. I've never seen you write so "matter of factly" before. U O K?
June:	Just tryin' ta hold it tugetha babe…
David:	Now that's more like my Junie!
June:	So we fell asleep together and had a really nice time Saturday culminating in literally "dancing 'till dawn." We fell asleep in the room and nothing happened that night due to sheer exhaustion. We slept in Sunday, missed breakfast and had to go out for brunch. So we returned to the room and I just attacked him!
David:	You dog!

June:	Yaaa well, it didn't go quite as anticipated as he had a repeat performance of Friday evening but this time he just went into a shell and remained there. I tried and tried to cheer him up but nothing seemed to work. The drive home was a quiet one and he dropped me off earlier than we had planned. We kissed goodbye and he would not meet my eyes. David what am I going to do? He won't answer me?
David:	How long has it been since you last saw him?
June:	Almost six days now. I can't take this. Why? I finally find a man that I love and it has nothing to do with sex and yet sex ruins it????? WTF......
David:	Did you see the movie "Meet Joe Black?"
June:	With Brad Pitt?
David:	Yes. Do you remember the scene where he's kissing the girl goodbye and they're both dying inside because they think that it's over?
June:	Yes but how is that supposed to be helping me now?
David:	I just like the movie!
June:	You are a shit! I am laughing so hard! Here I am thinking that you're leading up to something prophetic and you leave me with that??? If I ever get my hot little hands on you......
David:	Yeah, like I should be so lucky!
June:	Keep it up, New York isn't THAT far away from Arizona!
David:	Yeah but you know I always stay away from gorgeous women on the rebound. They're just soooo weepy! *grin*
June:	I really do not understand why I like you so much. But ya make dis goil smile and dats okee dokey!
David:	Now THERE"S the June I'm used to! THERE"S the June that has my heart in the palm of her hand, THERE"S the June that's too damn cheap to buy a plane ticket to New York!!!! PIKER!
June:	Just you wait. I'll surprise you one day when you least expect it!
David:	From your keyboard to God's ears my love!

June:	Thank you my friend. You have earned your keep for the night. I feel a little better so I'm gonna go now. Any last thoughts for me?
David:	Gimme a sec to come up with a good one......ok......We go through pain for a reason. The smart one's learn from it and the dumb one's take away only grief. I dunno what your lesson will be this time, but remember only the joy and understand that you gave it your best and it's Michael's loss that he walked away from a woman who I would kill just to get a sniff of (got an extra pair of panties laying around?) hehehe......
June:	You never change youuuuuuuuu!!!!!!!! Thanks, you helped me smile. I do love you, even if you are a loser!
David:	Perhaps, but I'll always be your loser......nitey sweetie.....
June:	Nitey....... Loser!!!!! NOT!!! Luv ya peeps......

I saved that for last because I think that perhaps that's the very best of what the Internet has to offer. Sexy chat and silly stuff and glorious fantasies are a blast, but when it comes down to it, softening the heart of a cherished friend in pain is the most I could ever wish for, or hope to accomplish in this life. Michael never did come back into her life; however she did get one final e-mail from him that blamed her for the entire fiasco.... He was *not* "the one" at all.

She has recovered nicely after several phone conversations with yours truly, as well as a chance meeting with a childhood friend that always had a crush on her. They've now been dating for over six months and her sex life is described by her as "simply glorious." I am *sooo* damn jealous! Damn!

7

The games people play.

My friend Freeda could probably write this entire chapter by herself, but she won't. She's going to have help from a host of other folks who have been burned the old fashioned way. They *earned it*!

"How did they do that?" you might ask. Simply by trusting unconditionally, the way we're supposed to when we're attempting to build a healthy relationship with someone new. Except on the Internet, you just never know the degree of fear, trepidation, and borderline insanity typing their way back to you just the other side of your keyboard.

It's a funny thing that I've just come to realize upon awakening this morning. The thing I've come upon is that the acquaintances and friends of mine who have the most to say also seem the have the biggest axe to grind. Yeah, I know they're all going to kill me for this when they read it, (can you say "Run for the hills!") but let me explain.

I have several friends with busy, happy lives who have promised to e-mail me several stories each for the body of the book, yet none have been forthcoming. On the other hand, I have several *other* friends who are pretty bitter right now because they've really been burned badly in their relationships, who have filled up two hour tapes with their words, expressions, rants, misgivings, tears, anger, resentments, and the like.

Why is it that when we are content we don't have too much to say? When we have an axe to grind on the other hand, you just can't shut us up! Show me a happy couple and I'll show you two people who will sit in the park, holding each other wordlessly, staring lovingly into each other's eyes and sighing deeply. Show me another couple who are going through difficulty in their relationship, and they will debate absolute gibberish for hours on end until there is no voice left in them.

Here's part of the interview I did with Leeza a few months ago, and some of her *very* interesting perspectives on both men and women.

Okay, I started dating online about September of 2000. I met a lotta nice people and I've only had one real bad experience because the guy put an old photo of himself online. When he showed up he was 60 pounds heavier, had long scraggly hair with gray in it, and tried to tell me he was the same guy! He insisted on driving me home and I said that I was close enough to walk and I *will* walk! I didn't even want him to buy me my meal because I didn't want any contact with him after that. I bought my own dinner and everything. My girlfriend was freaking out because we went to the diner where she works, and I just walked out...LATER!

Then I met another guy and I actually went to see *him*. I didn't know him and I went to meet him in the Bahamas! He liked me and he was all hot for me and the next thing you know the next day he started acting different. I just kind of ignored it, y'know, I didn't pay too much attention to it.

Within two days we were laughing, we were having fun, we were out, he owned a club, everything was great. I think what happened was he was so used to dating these small, petite little skinny nothings from Canada and his friends said "Oh, she's a great girl, she's got a great personality, she's fun, she talks to everybody, she's all friendly, but she's not the same kind of girl you always date." So I think the pressure got to him. You know what I'm saying? It's not that I wasn't perfect! They liked everything about me. They just said, "She's different from most of the girls you usually date."

I mean the girls he dated, they were like, they had no build, they had no boobs, they had no butt, they wore a size two; they had nothing! And this is what he's looking at and they were 25 years old. I'm 40 years old and he knew it! He knew what I looked like before I got there 'cause I'd sent him recent pictures and everything. So he knew it and he was *fine* with it.

I think what happened was they just made a comment saying, "She's different from anything you've ever dated. Maybe it's a good thing, maybe it's a bad thing. We don't know, we don't have to live with it, you do," and he kinda just didn't know what to do with it so we ended as friends. It's fine, it's no big deal. We're still friends.

Okay, I left it for a while. Meanwhile, I met a guy and I dated him for three months. He lived in New York. Well, he lived in the Bronx, worked in Manhattan,. He worked, um, Monday through Friday. I of course work nights and weekends being in the restaurant business, but I always made the effort to go down there on my day off and stay overnight. Blah, blah, blah. We went out a few times. I tried to be really understanding because he was going through a really hard divorce and he had grown up kids and everything and he didn't have a lot of money, but he would make it up to me in other ways. So it was good, you know, it wasn't, y'know, it was fine.

He left me, and I knew he was cheating on me because in November (pause) he started acting funny, last time I saw him, and I didn't hear from him through Thanksgiving, Christmas, and New Year's.

So I confronted him about it and he said, "I-I-I-I'll call you back." I gave him a half an hour, he didn't call me back. I made him confess! All through the year 2002 he's been asking me to go back to him! THEY ALL ASK ME TO COME BACK!!! They *all* ask me to come back because they realize what has happened is they end up with women who have too much baggage, too many mental problems and women that are needy. I'm very independent. They say they want that and then they run from it. They end up going and rescuing these needy women, they get tired of it, and then they want to come back. Too bad, the door's closed! I don't go there!

Left online dating until July of this year, July of 2002, that's when I met you! Spoke to a lot of guys, went on a few dates, didn't have a lot of time because I was workin' and stuff like that. Y'know, I just got *real* selective. I just wanted to get to know people more. Meanwhile, I met this guy.

He lived in New York but I met him from the computer, but I actually met him in New York. We were friends. I told him I didn't want anything because he told me he might need to go away. He would be back to try to finish up his extensions and stuff for school in February, if he got accepted back to NYU. It's very hard for the kinds of things he's going to school for. He has to go where the work is. Okay. Everything was fine. I'm supposed to go see him in January. "Get your tickets. Get back to me. Blah, blah, blah…" I put the tickets on hold, sent him an e-mail. He said, "I'm sorry I haven't been able to get back to you, I've just been really busy. I'm not ignoring you, I'm very sorry, I'll talk to you soon. Meanwhile, get your tickets."

So I put the tickets on hold for 48 hours. I sent him two e-mails, called his cell phone, and I've *never* heard from him since. He refuses to talk to me! He's now blocked me online on our site! He just won't talk to me. I've sent him e-mails and I know he's read them 'cause he's got the same ISP as I have, so I can check the status of his mail.

Why he blocked me on the site and not online? Why one and not the other, I don't know. Okay, so, the thing of it is, I don't know. Maybe it became too real for him? I know he didn't meet anybody else, so…. I decided I'm tired of men! I just decided I'm tired of people saying to me I'm too nice of a person. I'm too outgoing and I have too much going for me to have to deal with this crap!

So the bottom line was I decided to get even! But not in a bad vindictive way. I decided I was going to set him up! *giggle* Pretend to *be* somebody else, under an alias, change everything about myself, well not my, y'know, and talk to him, and he's falling for it! It's working like a charm! He can't wait to meet me! I have him climbing the walls with sexual innuendo!

He doesn't even know what I look like, he's just going by my word. It's a beautiful thing! He's 6 foot 4, gorgeous. He's a surgeon in a transplant team, he goes to school besides that, he's *not* a dumb man. He made the statement to me that I'm "the sharpest knife in the drawer," and I said to myself, "Hell hath no fury like a scorned woman." Hell hath no fury, you just do *not* know!

He loves everything about this so-called person that he *thinks* he's talking to, Marissa, okay? Meanwhile, she's the same person I was. I'm the same under both profiles. Same sense of humor, same everything about me! He has

NO CLUE! So I'm driving him *nuts* sexually, but I refused to go there until I made a statement of, "What is Santa gonna bring you for Christmas, have you been naughty or nice?' and he took the opening. So I decided to go with it and see how far he'd take it. He took the bait, knowing me only a week, hook, line, and sinker!

Sooooo…I disappeared online on him. I disappear, I don't log off. I just X-out, and I'm gone. He's like "Where'd ya go? You disappeared on me! I hope to talk to you soon!" I was driving him crazy because I kept doing this to him over and over, and he just kept coming back for more! He's *dying* to talk to me, but I told him that, "I like the mystery of this better! I like not knowing what you sound like. I can use my imagination and let it run wild!" He's like, "Oh, okay." He's clueless! He's a *man*! He thinks with his prick!

So he wanted to have sex with me online. So he says, "What time do you get home?" I told him I was going out, I had a date. I thought he was gonna die! I didn't tell him it was with you buddy boy, that I didn't end up going until today! But that's okay. *laughs* So I stood him up again, and he's apologizing to *me* for it!

So he caught me online and we chatted for two hours, and then he wanted to call me. He wanted to have phone sex so he could finish getting off. I told him no, that I was too tired, but I was gonna go do what I had to do and he would just have to finish it himself! HA! Oh yeah…

So meanwhile he wants to meet me. I told him I'm going to Las Vegas. I have no intentions on going. I'm going to sooo set him up! My girlfriend is going to talk to him on the phone, to let him think that I really am a *real* person. Not that he doesn't believe me, it's not a big deal. He says he understands, it's not a problem. So I sent him a picture of my *very* hot 25-year-old girlfriend, but he said that he never got it. I told him I'm a size 0 to 2 and he wants to meet me, but I told him I can't go to California, that he has to meet me in Las Vegas because I'll be there with friends. It would be easier for him to drive there so I'm setting this whole thing up!

I told him that when we meet, I'm gonna lick him from head to head, climb him like a totem pole, and screw his brains out! So he's trying to tell me that it's difficult to get off from work to go meet me, and every time he does I turn up the sexual heat so high that I can almost feel him breathing hard as he types back to me. I think he's gonna have a heart attack! I tell him that I want to suck him hard to soft and hard again, and ride him all night long…there's usually a delay in his response! I don't think he can take too much more of this.

So he's going to show up there, all by himself, and I'll be at home laughing my butt off. Think I'm done there? Not by a longshot pal! When he gets back home and e-mails me to find out why I stood him up, I'm just going to ignore him for a week or so. What he doesn't know is that my friends really *will* be there in the bar having drinks, and when they get home they'll give me one of their receipts that they got at the *same* time he was there.

So I'll fax him a copy of the receipt and tell him that he's a jerk for standing *me* up! That I never want to talk to him again and that he'll never taste the
sweet nectar of my gorgeous firm body! He'll think he's going crazy because
he'll *know* he was there! He's never gonna figure it out, but he deserves this!
Maybe he'll learn a lesson and stop playing with people's heads.

I'm only doing this because there's no rhyme or reason for his behavior.
We were friends, that's it, and he was the one who asked *me*. There was an
interest, but because I knew he was going away I decided to keep away, and *he*
initiated everything! What the hell! I told him maybe when he got back, but
he convinced me otherwise. Then to turn around and do all this to me for
months, and turn around and just flake out on me for no reason...I just don't
get it. But *he's* really gonna get it, and how!

Yikes! I hope this guy never reads a copy of this book! Oh what the heck, he
doesn't even know who Freeda is anyway. I can't defend this guy, or his actions,
(or lack thereof) towards my friend. What I can say, playing devil's advocate here,
is that Freeda has the most honest, in your face, outgoing personality, and that
may be the reason that some men run from her. They cannot take the honesty.
They cannot take her independence. They cannot deal with a very strong woman
who wants a man desperately, but does not *need* a man.

I mean, we're very good friends, meaning *no* funny stuff between us. We like
it that way because we can talk about *anything* together, and we do. We bounce
stuff off of each other and we get a viewpoint that is honest and loving because
there is no ulterior motive there.

Don't get me wrong, this loony tune woke me up at 12:45 the other night just
so she could complain about men! She kept me up until 2:00 in the morning,
and I *hated* her for it. I couldn't get back to sleep until 4:30, and was useless the
whole next day. But you know what? That's what friends are for. Being there and
listening for an hour while your buddy lets off steam over the phone, even
though you're *dying* to go back to sleep.

Every time Freeda used to IM me online, I would just roll my eyes, because I
was not interested in a love connection with her. I never put her on my buddy list
to see when she was on the site, but she *did* put me on hers and initiated conversation every opportunity she had! She was the biggest pain in the butt. However,
she somehow wiggled her way into my heart and I now cherish both her friendship and her amazing perspective on people and why they do what they do.

Freeda is one of the few people I know who has literally no baggage, no
agenda, and a heart as big as Texas, so she looks at things a little bit different that
most of my friends, who are all divorced with kids. She has no kids, no ex-husband, no divorce papers, no animosity, nothing but her adorable puppy. She's

just a good ol' gal looking for a good ol' boy to hang his hat for a bit, stay for a while, and maybe even not leave.

I wish that for her too. I wish it for everyone who is lonely and holds their pillow at night and wakes up in the morning wondering, "Why am I still alone?" Or even worse, "Ugh! I wish I *was* alone! Who *is* that next to me? I'll *never* drink again!"

Did I just say that? You *do* know I was only making an example, right? I mean, that would *never* happen to me! I don't even drink…Well, not *much* anyway.

Now on to my friend, buddy and drummer, Brando. He's a crappy interview, I can tell you! He meanders around, does not answer questions the way I want him to, goes off on tangents that had nothing to do with the original question, but in the end, after listening to the tapes over and over, I did glean some wheat from the chaff.

> So you don't want me to talk about my ex-wife Nazi lesbian bitch and her lover? Why not? It makes such an interesting story. Just think about all the other lesbian, controlling, conniving witches out there that will get a kick out of my story and my pain. You're no fun at all Dave!

So we started talking about sex early in a relationship, or with a woman you'd just recently met.

> I'll opt for standard operating procedures. It's still mostly up to a man to read signals, to gauge…men still have to make the move. Well, probably not always, but I've found that, yeah, women are playing the game like, ya gotta do something, y'know and then I'll either resist or not. There's just a lot of training in that modality that girls fall into and um…They WANT a man to make a move. That's the good part of getting a little older and having a few relationships under your belt. Okay?

Modality? Uh huuuhhh…what the hell did he just say? That's why I love the dude; he overstates everything! Anyhoooo…I just thought I'd chat for a bit about the way I see it, about what sort of games people play online and why. Well, perhaps the "Why" will be a bit more difficult to explain, but here's some stuff to think about.

One of the most obvious situations happens when I'll get an e-mail from a woman that I haven't heard from for a year or so. It goes sort of like this:

"Hey! How are you? I guess we lost touch for a while! I've been pretty busy with my…whatever…. So how have you been?"

Sheesh!…Translation for those who don't get it?

"I just broke up with/was dumped by the guy who I met while I was leading you on last year, but it didn't work and since you were my second choice, I thought I'd just give you a holler and remind you how wonderful I am so that I don't have to be alone thinking about *that* jerk." You got it?

Okay, so that's one pretty sedate way that women, or men for that matter, play their little games in cyber space. Yeah like I'm a *complete* idiot to fall for that! Why the game playing? I mean, can't we just be honest and say that a relationship didn't work out? Why do we need to play all this crap to each other when all anyone truly wants is honesty? I would kill to get a letter from a girl saying, "Hey dude, what's up? I just broke up with my guy and I'm a little sad. Wanna buy me a beer?" That would be so amazing because the honesty would just floor me. So sad that very few have the guts to do that, and yes I do mean from *both* sexes!

I guess to a degree, the posting of a ten-year-old photo is a game, as is a profile that bears no resemblance to the reality of the type of person you are. Game playing online always backfires and usually damages both parties in defeating the very purpose of having an online love profile.

Oh, did I say love? Well, take a gander at dozens upon dozens of sites that cater to married women seeking a booty call, sites supposedly owned and operated *by* married women, (smart girls!) as well as countless sites like www.adultfriendfinder.com, (one of the good ones actually) that will allow you to find any sexual type of situation you desire, without exception! Friend Finder is set up in a very professional manner and has many chat rooms as well as thousands of articles for your entertainment and informational purposes. There are affiliate programs and a zillion attached sites. It is simply huge and is a resource for millions of people, though I don't happen to be one of them.

Now many women will correctly inform you that men indeed *do* think with the small head as opposed to the large one. Take a look at one of these sites and it will be confirmed. You will find enough photos of genitalia, (um, from *both* sexes actually) to boggle the mind. However, you'll find blessed few pics of a face or anything that identifies the person posting there, because many are married or in committed relationships and are just seeking something sexual on the side. Does this constitute a game? I don't know. After all, most usually *state* that they're married and just seeking a booty call and if that's all you seek and you're being honest about it to your potential partner, then more power to you.

Hiding behind your keyboard constitutes a large part of the games played online. After all, when you can type a filthy and degrading letter to someone and then "block" that person, thereby nullifying the possibility of any answer, it not only becomes game-playing at the very rudest level, but also a power play as well. *You* have the power to degrade, and you have taken the power *away* from your "opponent" to do likewise. Freeda was blocked so many times on Udate that they cancelled her membership! Geez, men just cannot deal with a woman who speaks her mind.... and speaks it.... and speaks it...and speaks it...but I digress.

Game playing is rampant on the interactive sites as it becomes a game of "who blocks who first." Every time you get a "block," the site warns you, but does not mention who blocked you. So, if you block them first.... Well, you get the idea. It's so silly!

Freeda sets up alternate profiles, (and actual pays for a second membership) just so that she can mess with the people who blocked her in the first place. You see, on these sites when a person "blocks" you, you can no longer see them there at all afterwards. It's as if they just disappeared off the site. However, if you go back on under another alias, you can now see those people again, thus knowing who blocked you in the first place. I think this is a total waste of time, but I guess Freeda just has more free time than I do.

There are, of course, many games that I refuse to play. Like for instance, Anna talks about being too honest and putting forth information too quickly, as well as learning how to play "the dating game." I won't do it. I've got to be me! There's no one else that I know how to be as well, so trying to be that aloof "New York Guy" has never worked for me. There are women who expect me to be "stand-offish" and to try to impress her with my coolness...Screw that crap! To borrow a word of wisdom from Popeye, "I yam what I yam"...and if I want to attract someone to love me for who I truly am, then I need to show her that from day one, or she might just miss me as I'm attempting to be "Mr. Cool." Now I'm not saying that I'll be an affectionate "wuss" on a first date either, but if I sense affection coming my way, I won't back away from it just to play "the dating game."

One night last year, I was cruising the posts on Craigslist in the "Rant-n-Rave" section. (If you've never seen them, you really need to! They can be hilarious!) Well, it seemed that a certain young lady pulled a fast one on a group of young men in the city. She posted an ad online to meet a guy for a night of...er...well, I guess a night of "no strings attached fun," (also known as "NSA") and seemingly had booked the same date with as many guys as she could. Seven or eight, (or more) of these poor schmucks showed up outside some warehouse downtown, and of course the young lady was nowhere to be found while this bunch of poor jerks just stood around staring at each other while the man-hating girl and her friends were no doubt watching them in utter hysterics from a hidden location nearby.

Okay, perhaps that was a harsh judgment on the girl, but these guys were *pissed!* A bunch of these characters posted later in "Rant-n-Rave" about the incident, (I wish I had saved those posts as they were delicious in their venomous blasts!) and were none too happy about wasting a Saturday night in the city alone…Well, alone, except for the company of other hapless and hopeful men they were sharing the conspicuously female-less sidewalk they were milling around on. Dangerous fun to be sure, but that's not and unusual escapade for cyber life. It can be sick how some people need to hurt others just to make themselves feel alive.

Swayne shared an interesting story with me a few weeks ago. This didn't happen to him, so it's second-hand; however I've heard similar stories from others and nearly had one similar to share myself.

It seems that one of his buddies was new to the Internet and did not as yet understand some of the vernacular inherent in that medium. He met a "T-girl" online and just assumed that the "T" stood for something erotic. I suppose it *could* stand for something erotic, particularly if you find "T"ranssexuals a turn-on, which Swayne's friend does not.

Well, the "she-male" that was chatting back to him must have known of his naiveté, yet still played along enough to book the date that evening. They met at a local bar and he was blown away by the beauty of this creature as they drank, danced, kissed, and ended up back at his apartment, stewed to the gills. One wonders at exactly what point this guy realized that his "girl" for the evening had an even larger erection than he did!

I guess the lesson to be learned is to assume nothing, to ask a lot of questions before meeting and, particularly in Swayne's buddy's example, to ask about anything you don't understand. Perhaps if he had, he would have realized that his date wasn't the sex that he was assuming her…uh, him…to be.

Of course, if the person you're chatting with is intent on concealing something from you, no amount of questions is going to force them to reveal what they don't want to. However, asking the right questions may at least give you the opportunity to get a gauge on whether they're hiding *something* from you. Or it might not. As in life, meeting someone new can be a bit of a gamble. The important thing is to not assume anything, and to not think with anything other than the head on your shoulders. It's funny how we think with our hormones just enough to get us into some sticky situations! *grin*

As difficult as it is for a guy to find the right situation online, I cringe when I think how tough it must be for the women. That tiny fear of meeting a nice guy who turns into a lunatic must be always in the back of their minds, and the more trusting you are, the greater the possibility of your openness getting you into dangerous trouble. This is discussed in greater detail in the next chapter, so I won't go into it here, but girls, be careful for cripes sake and always meet in public places because you never know!

Several women that I know quite well have left dates very early in the evening just because they had a "feeling" that something was just "not right" with the person sipping coffee across the table, leering at them. One of my friends left Starbucks while the guy was in the bathroom and he ended up chasing her to her car like a madman! She locked the doors, screeched the tires and escaped intact.

Sheesh! If a girl walked out on me in the middle of a date I certainly wouldn't be chasing her anywhere. Get the message, dude!

This next young lady needs a good spanking! She's been mentioned earlier in the book and will appear several more times as well. Her name is Vixen and she plays games like we breathe air. It seems that she placed an ad on some obscure "alternative" dating site, (as in *not* hetero) posing as a gay male. This chick just loves to bust chops! She cut and pasted some pics of a really hot guy with a, um, *huge* package located nicely between his legs and received a ton of responses from interested parties. She picked exactly ten men to correspond with and had them all drooling like babies with a bottle with her dripping sexual innuendo over a one-month period. Then she just stopped writing, stopped responding and hung them all out to dry spinning in the wind like pieces of garbage.

That's light stuff for her though, as she's done far worse to hetero males who she describes gleefully as "the bane of humanity" and "the evil scum of society." Nice. She has all but admitted to me that many of the bogus "sex for free" posts on Craigslist are of her evil design. Man alive, not only does she hate guys, but she loves living dangerously too! All she needs to do is to start messing with the wrong hacker who will find her and skin the flesh from her "manly" bones! Pray you never chat with this girl and get on her bad side.

I manage to stay on her good side, (well, if she had one that is) in the hope that I will someday get her to buy me a beer and share more of the misadventures that are her life. Perhaps someday I might even get friendly enough with her for her to allow me to delve a little deeper into the dark recesses of her mind to determine *what* happened to her that makes her hate men with such venomous passion. I can only imagine that it must have been pretty bad. I don't really think she's evil though, she's just drawn that way. (Oh, she's going to just *love* that one description!)

So why *do* so many seemingly normal people turn into game-playing savages upon entry to the Internet? I guess it's due to a certain amount of fear. For men, it's the fear of being too shy, or too bald, or too short, too fat or too thin, or maybe being two cards short of a deck. Perhaps they feel that they're not wealthy enough, young enough, white enough, black enough, or just too disadvantaged in the writing department to express what they feel inside. And so the games begin to hide the deficiencies.

For women, the fears often revolve around being too old or too overweight, (yeah, we know what "height/weight proportionate" and "a few extra pounds" and "curvy" almost always mean). Sometimes they're afraid that they might not be pretty enough, or don't have as full a set of "endowments" as other women have. For all their claims of being happy with themselves, as true as that may be overall, many women have a teeny tiny little voice in the back of their heads that whispers all their (often misperceived) imperfections to them, just as men do. It's out of a fear of being judged that many women feel the need to hide the fact that they're an awesome mom and a smart businesswoman. So, they "dumb it up" just to meet a loser who will never gauge or understand the levels of their brilliance.

On the other hand, there are some really great men and women out there who end up sabotaging themselves out of over-confidence. Because they might have great genes and have always taken care of themselves, there are some who feel that they're so gorgeous that they will only date people who are ten, twenty, or even more years their junior because they deserve a partner who's "hot." What they don't realize is that they're robbing themselves of the opportunity to date men and women who have the goods just as much as they do, with the added bonus of having the life experience and maturity to really create a lasting and healthy relationship.

Many wrongly believe that game-playing is part of the, well, part of the game! But here's something to think about. A game is defined as "entertainment, sport, play and recreation," and there can certainly be plenty of that online. However, "game" is also defined as "meat, fish, fowl, wildlife," with the final two being "quarry and prey." Quarry and prey, yikes! So if you do not want to become one of the final two, then leave your game on the basketball court where it belongs and be honest, as you always get exactly what you give, especially on the Internet.

8

The hook and bait

For the life of me, I can't figure out a sweet way to write this chapter. Let me tell you, it's probably going to piss a *lot* of people off and cost a bunch of young ladies a bit of cash, but the truth is the truth, and it needs to be written.

You see, the porn industry is *massive* on the Internet. All you need to do is click on one site, one time, and you will not *believe* the flood of e-mail you will receive in that inbox every day for the duration of the time you have that e-mail address, and there is *nothing* you can do about it!

Many Internet surfers are well aware of these facts, and keep alternate e-mail addresses for surfing the "unusual" or "forbidden" vistas to avoid this floodtide to their personal address.

Creativity however, is a watchword for making naughty money online and millions of lonely guys looking for love are prime targets, as well as millions of unaware women, who I will discuss a bit later in the chapter.

When you sign up for a new dating site, you will usually get a good amount of responses in the beginning, especially if you have cute photos and intelligent prose. But suppose that you don't. Suppose that you just signed up, don't have a photo posted and don't even have any verbiage typed at all. You might get an unsolicited letter on the site, such as the one I did here.

> Hi, My name is Tiffany. I read your profile and think we have a lot in com-mon. I am 23 with long blonde hair, blue eyes and about 119 lbs.
>
> I work hard all week and really look forward to weekends. I like to hang out with friends and maybe go out dancing or catch a movie.
>
> I am a senior in college and spend a lot of time studying. I am planning on a career in nursing.
>
> If you are interested please e-mail me at tiffany_0000@hotmail.com
> Tiffany

So, what's so unusual about a 23-year-old girl sending me an e-mail telling me how much we have in common? For cripes sake, I'm 45! Yeah, I don't look too bad for my age, but *really* now, there is *no way* this hottie is looking to date me! Let me give you a few more examples of these girls' e-mails.

> Hello there, my name is Bridget and I am relativelly new here. I am sending you this message not knowing whether or not you have found someone! Oh well, I guess that's a chance I have to take! Would you like to exchange pictures with me? If so, send me a note at bridget_0000@hotmail.com. I check my e-mail all the time, I just can't check my messages from matchmaker at work =(Hope to hear from ya soon, B.

Did you catch the subtle similarities between these two messages? First, the sites on which the previous e-mails were posted have a double blind e-mail system, so your personal e-mail address cannot be seen. Why would a normal adult female leave both her name *and* her e-mail address in a first contact with a complete stranger? The answer is simple, they don't. While you may *think* that's what they are doing, what's really happening is that you're wallet is being setup for a reduction in funds via your credit card. You'll see why after I give you a few more examples.

> Hi,
>
> You probably don't remember me, but we talked online a while ago. I don't really know what happened, but I guess we both just got really busy or something. I feel really bad because I don't want you to think I was ignoring you or anything. Maybe I'm being presumptuous by assuming you weren't ignoring me.
>
> Anyway, I know we haven't talked in a while but I thought we had the beginnings of a pretty good thing going so I was just wondering if you'd be interested in getting back in touch. Maybe with a few e-mails first so we can feel each other out again? You probably don't remember what I look like, so here are some pics of me:
>
> http://www.moonlightmatch.com
>
> I hope you're still interested. I'm gonna feel pretty dumb showing you that website if you blow me off.....but I hope that gives you some confidence that I'm for real. I DEFINITELY don't just hand that out to people. I hope this works out for the best, you were the most compatible guy I met on that site and I feel horrible for letting it slide. Anyway, check out the site and e-mail me if you want to get together.

If I'm lucky you don't have definite plans for the weekend and we still have
time to arrange something?
I hope so. Talk to you soon!
Love,XX
Laurie

No, I never spoke to this girl, nor did I "forget her," or "ignore her." She's just
another predator waiting to strike. Next...

Hey, wuzzup?! remember me? I'm Crystal. I'm 23 and I work in the lawn care
area of Lowe's.I really want na to meet you and I thought this would be the
best way to let youno I really wanna get together withyou so I sent you these
pictures (i stole mycheerleading unifrom from when I was in highschool and i
kept it!). I have more pic my profile at OnlyWantSex but I couldn't send them
because they are pretty raunchy and I didn't want yu to get in trouble if you
see them at work :)) Anyways, you can look atthe pictures of me and if you
want we can get together when I'm not at work. My son has daycare all day
and his father takes him on the weekends and some nights so I have the trailer
all to myself whenever we need it. Plus I have my own truck so I can drive to
you or whatever.

XOXOXOXO CandyCrystal***

Not the best speller in the world is she, but at least there's a wee bit of honesty
in her e-mail, when she admits that her profile is listed at "OnlyWantSex." It
kind of gives you an indication of what she's looking for, just not that *you* will be
paying for it.

What ties all these lovely ladies together is the type of site you will go visit to
view their lovely photos. Some will give you an e-mail to make sure of your interest and then get back to you with a site to go to, while others will let you link
directly to the site. What most of these sites have is a brief letter from the young
sexy lady with a cute photo. This will be followed by a naughty photo and prom-
ises of *very* naughty photos if you just visit their "free" photo site.

Funny thing about all of these "free" sites though. To enter them, you need to
verify that you are 18 or older by inputting your credit card number. Hmm...I
was not aware that you needed to *be* 18 to *have* a credit card! When my daughter
left for college at 17, she had an emergency card in her pocket, with *her* name on
it. Age verification indeed!!!!

Guys, I am only scratching the surface here. There are *sooo* many more scams on the web, in the personals…all offering to help alleviate the pain of having a full wallet!

> Did you think I would forget to reply? My name is Sandra, I'm glad that you e-mailed me. I'm looking forward to getting together and having some fun. I am 24and single. I am a secretary at a mid-size law firm. My measurements a 36-24-35. Guys seem attracted to my D cup breasts. But there's more to me than my tatas! I have a personal website with more info about me. It is free, and gives you a chance to get to know me better. I have many of my photos online so you can see what I look like before you decide if you want to meet me. These are my personal pictures, you won't find them anywhere else. My personal e-mail and contact info is also there.

The common ground between the last two letters, was that they didn't attempt to shade the truth too much. Either they came *with* the naughty pics enclosed in the body of the e-mail, or they had a direct link to the site to view the pics. In the latter case, the link did not work. Poor girl, how *will* she pay her bills this month?

Okay, so you say, "Waitaminit! These girls have every right to make a buck!" and you'd be completely right. There shouldn't be any real concern for there being any chance of our young and innocent youth being corrupted by these women, since I doubt that any of these lovely Internet entrepreneurs are e-mailing anyone who hasn't got enough funds for lunch money. We're all consenting adults. Why not answer the ads? If they're offering, then we *owe* it to ourselves to take advantage of the offer, right? So the line of reasoning here is that if you answer a post from a woman half your age who's offering scintillating pictures of herself, then you *deserve* whatever the outcome is. Hmmm…not too sure about *that* one…I'll give you my answer the next time some 21-year-old cutie from Bulgaria offers me "unlimited services" just for sending her a one way plane ticket to New York…Yeah, there's an experience I'm sure we're *all* anxious to have.

This next one was the cutest one I received. It almost seemed real and actually had me thinking for a moment, until I clicked on her website with the "pay to see my webcam" deal. People can get sooo creative when there's money involved!

> Hey!! I got your e-mail a few minutes ago. I just got in a few minutes ago. If my other e-mail confused you sorry, I didn't really know what to say! Anyway, I was just writing to initiate some contact between us. I was extremely interested in what you had to say. Your compliments were quite appreciated…. although I am not sure if I deserved them or not :blush:, but I will take

them....lol. So what would be your ideal night with a woman...and I want both :-) Romantic, and Kinky ;-) If I were to choose a romantic night, it would start with you picking me up, and taking me to a nice restaurant....maybe italian, with some red wine. After that, we could take a nice stroll together, holding hands, stroking each other's backs, kissing playfully. From there, it is onto the carpet in front of the fireplace.....wine and strawberries, and deep passionate kisses.......Hopefully, I am painting you a good picture :-) As far as kinky goes....well, perhaps I could show ya? Hee hee...let me just tell you it involves a bedroom, a padlock, perhaps playful plastic handcuffs, whipped cream.....are you liking what I am saying so far? I sure hope so....I do not want to turn you off....anyway, I am going to chat with my girlfriends on my webcam.....I am SO tired....I just want to relax and hang out....come join me!! It is at: http://www.ComeGiveMeAllYour$$$.net/ I would love to talk tonight....see what you thought of my little scenarios :-) Perhaps you can tell me yours huh? I do not want to be the only one being naughty.......ok, I am going to end this now....it is turning into a novel!!
Hope to talk to you in a bit.
Kisses and Brains,
KatieAnn

PS If I'm not online, check back in a few.

Verrrry cute, especially the pic she had on her site, and she did have me going for a moment, but it passed as soon as I "clicked."

These were some of the more sedate ways that the web is used for monetary gain. Not too honest, but nobody really gets hurt. After all, sex *does* sell, and people the world over are buying it lock, stock and barrel. So let's stop hitting on the ladies for a while, and swing the pendulum back to the guys.

There are some *really* bad dudes on the Internet and they are playing some very dangerous games, as the following stories may attest to. Some of these guys live in chat rooms, some on dating sites, and some take up residence in porn cafes, but wherever they reside you can be *very* sure that you never want to be contacted by one. Their main focus of interest is in the most trusting of the female segment of our population, that being teenagers. If you think us thirty and forty-something folks spend a lot of time online, then just talk to my college-aged daughter and her friends who grew *up* online. They live there, eat there, work there and play there. It is the common ground for all of them and there is a very positive side to most of it, but there is also a more insidious side for the innocent few who visit chat rooms often and trust the "nice guy" they've been writing to for weeks, believing, in their naiveté, that he is another teenager.

This next young lady does not act, speak, or write like an inexperienced teenager. She is the daughter of a friend's friend. Marissa and her mother were so upset about the following experience that they contacted me to interview her for this book because they wanted the story told. This may disturb some of you, so be forewarned.

Tell me something about yourself Marissa, before we get into the details of your experience.

Okay. I'm a third year Sociology student at—University. I'm pretty popular, have a bunch of friends, but haven't really dated much since most of the guys are dorks that I hang out with.

Can you tell me how much time you usually spend online, I mean on a daily basis?

Pretty much a bunch. As soon as I get to my dorm I usually log on to check my e-mail, send a few IM's, finish what's left of my assignments and then spend a few hours chatting to my buds and listening to tunes.

Sounds pretty normal. So what happened to you on that particular evening that we're talking about?

I need to first preface the evening by a few weeks, so you can understand that I'm not an idiot! I spend a little time in chat rooms, but mostly the ones that my friends go to. It's really fun because when you know eight or ten people there, I mean *really* know them in real life, it's a blast dissin' each other and stuff. You can say things online that you'd *never* say to a person's face, *especially* if you don't know them beforehand.

So what happened?

Okay. I was chatting to a few of my friends, but I walked away from the screen for a few minutes to grab a soda down the hall and when I got back, they were gone. There was a message from a guy named Scott who wanted to know what school I went to. He said he was from a neighboring University that I knew, because I had been to some of their crazy dorm parties. We chatted for about an hour, but since other people were jumping in constantly we decided to exchange IM addresses to keep the chat personal. I thought he was sooo funny that before I looked up it was past midnight and my roommate was bitching that she wanted to go to sleep, so we said goodbye and I logged off. We promised each other that we'd chat again soon, and for sure when I got home the next day there were six messages from Scott. This went on for about two weeks. I started to really like this guy because he seemed really smart and silly and wasn't forward in any creepy sexual way. I'm really focused on my studies and I'm not looking for a boyfriend, but I'm not a nun either so we started to chat about meeting. It never crossed my mind to even ask him for a photo or anything, and he didn't ask for one either. We did describe ourselves in detail though, so it seemed normal on the surface.

At this point, Marissa looked down, seeming very sad. I asked her if she was okay, and she nodded yes. She continued.

So, we decided that we'd meet that Friday after my courses were over. It took me like, two hours to get ready, and my roommate almost killed me because I'd never even met this guy but I was so nervous! I decided to just wear jeans and a tee because we were supposed to go for pizza anyway. I wanted him to meet me at my dorm so that my friends could check him out, but he said he was barred from the campus due to a fight his friends got into at a party here last semester. I remembered a brawl I heard about or something, so it didn't seem too weird. I agreed to meet him off campus, by myself. What an idiot!

Shaking her head and noticeably upset, Marissa got up from where we were sitting and walked away, staring into the distance. She shrugged her shoulders, steadied herself, wiped her face because she had begun to cry, and then returned to finish her story.

I decided to meet him on a main road off campus. He arrived five minutes after me in a brand new pickup truck, y'know, one of the big ones? This should have been the first indication of trouble to me, but I wasn't thinking. I go to a pretty working class school, so the kids who even *have* cars have pretty old ones that their parents gave them. No one here has a brand new anything, and this truck cost a bundle with all the chrome and stuff on it. So I climbed up as he rolled down the window, which was tinted very dark. Red flag number two, I ignored now.

He said hello, and I said hello back, and climbed into the cab. I couldn't see him very clearly, but he didn't seem creepy or anything because I really didn't know what to expect anyway. He sorta looked like he described himself, so we drove away then. I asked him where we were going and he told me not to worry, that he had it under control.

As we were driving I kept trying to get a better look at him, as it seemed he had some blonde highlights in his hair, so I asked him about it and he just laughed. It seemed weird to me that he was so talkative online, but had very little to say now that we were together. We drove for what seemed like a long time, so I asked him again where we were going, and again he just laughed. So I began to get a little fidgety and asked if we could pull over because I needed to go to the bathroom, and he told me not to worry because we were almost there. I asked him again where "there" was, and again he just laughed at me and said nothing.

I really should have been afraid by now, but we played a lot of cat and mouse games online so I thought that perhaps this was just one of them. He pulled off the road and went down an embankment, and then onto a really dark beach. He then drove under an old boardwalk that I didn't recognize, as I'd never been to this beach before, and I've been to most in this area. He turned to me then and asked me if this wasn't a really romantic spot.

I was a little bit shocked at his being so forward since this was not his way online. He leaned towards me and put his hand on my thigh and I instinctively threw my arms up, turning on the dome light completely by accident. I then saw that what I thought was blonde was actually gray hair.

Now I was a little scared because I *knew* he was not in college, at least not in my age group like he said he was. I asked if we could take a walk down the beach and to my surprise, he agreed. We left the truck and went away from the boardwalk, but suddenly I felt a sharp pain in my side and realized that something had hit me. Before I could recover, I was hit in the head really hard and I fell to the sand. I must have passed out for a little while because when I got my sense back I could feel my body being dragged across the sand, back to the boardwalk area.

I tried to yell, but it was like I was dreaming or something. The sound would just *not* come out of my mouth. I tried and tried, but there just wasn't any sound. I started to get really mad, and then I just got really lucky. He dragged me across some rocks to get me under the wood in the dark, and I grabbed a jagged piece of rock, or maybe it was a bottle. I couldn't tell. He dumped me just in the water at the edge of the beach and started to take off his pants.

I tried to stay calm, but I was scared half to death. He dropped to his knees, now with no pants on, and began to loosen my jeans. I'm laying there now, really calm, and thinking, "What can I do?" I have this weapon but I know I'm only going to get *one* shot at this guy, so I waited. He got very aroused as he began to slide my pants down. He removed my boots, then my pants and panties, and slowly climbed on top of me. I really thought I was going to die as he tried to enter me, but could not. He started to kiss my face and I just got so nauseous that I couldn't take it anymore, so I swung the bottle, rock, whatever, with all my might and smashed it against the side of his head. He rolled off me and screamed in pain.

I was still woozy, but grabbed my pants and ran up the beach as fast as my legs could carry me. It wasn't too far from the road and I guess I just got lucky a second time, because I'd only been running for a minute or so before a car drove by and stopped when they saw me. I was shaking really bad so the lady put me in her car and I told her what happened and she called 911 immediately.

Well, she drove me back to school and the police got a good description of the truck and the guy from me, as well as his IM address. Turns out he used a computer at the school next door to us, so he wasn't joking about being there, but he was no student. Since this is in the courts now I can't say too much, but they're charging him with attempted rape of me *and* six other girls from colleges and high schools in the area. I'm really glad they caught him, and I'm glad I'm the one who got him caught, but if I could do it all over again....well..... I don't know.... I just don't know...

Marissa walked away at this point, and did not want to talk about the incident anymore. We grabbed a few ice cream sodas and she perked right up, being more the child and less the woman. I'm really glad they found this nut job too, and hope that when he does get to jail, he finds out first hand what it feels like to be sexually violated, and you know what I mean.

Marissa's mom, Jean, who had been with us the entire time, thanked me and asked if she could submit a statement to go into the book. I said sure, and because I have a 20-year-old daughter in college as well, they hit very close to home.

> I want every parent who reads this to listen, and listen good. My daughter got lucky, stupid lucky, because she should probably be dead. For all the parents out there who trust their kids in college, because they're smart and good and honest and nice, and pretty much leave them alone...DON'T! Call them. Call them a lot! Bug them. Ask them *where* they're going and what they're doing and who they're doing it with. If they hate it, TOUGH! At least you might get them thinking *just* enough to avoid what happened to my baby and many others. *Be* a parent, whether they like it or not, so that they have a chance to grow up and fall in love and have kids...and do the same thing to their kids because they'll *be* there to do it!

Truer words were never spoken.

The next story comes from a young lady that I never met. Perhaps I would have, but a predator got in the way and in his haste, ruined her for the rest of the decent guys out here. I will call her Sammie. We met in an Internet chat room that was brand new. There were only ten or so members, with her being only one of maybe two women there. We exchanged online photos after exchanging a few e-mails and then she, as well as the group, just seemed to disappear! I sent her an e-mail asking where the group went, and this was her response to me:

> David,
>
> I don't know what happened to that group. I e-mailed everyone who was on the last round of e-mails asking if anyone knew what happened—last Sat-

urday. Immediately after I sent those e-mails I started getting obscene e-mails and IM's from the BOBBY character who I had never even spoken to or e-mailed directly except to ask what happened to L.E. (who by the way told me that he was the "same guy" who e-mailed me his picture before but was using another name now. You were the only one who had ever sent me a photo). I had posted to the group that I had 4 NETS tickets for Sunday game and asked if 3 of the members wanted to come along and also if anyone wanted to get together to go bowling on Saturday. I was surprised that right away 4 members of the group got back to me—3 said yes to bowling. Then some weird IM came in on my computer but I didn't know the name so I wouldn't open it and rejected it. It was PATHFINDER something. Then, a few minutes later I received an e-mail from this (BobbyFeaster) guy and he said that the IM was his and he was from L.E. So, I said okay and opened it and he said, "Bowling rulez". I told him that he was the 3rd one who had agreed to bowling and that since it was so early in the day I would wait to see if we heard back from any of the others and we would figure out where we would all meet up (same e-mail that I sent everyone back). Then, this BOBBY creep, sends me an IM saying that he needed a picture from me "urgently." Urgently? I told him that I didn't know why he would need a picture from me at all since we were all meeting up later that evening. Then he went on to say that he needed my address and insisted that since he had already sent me a picture I should send him one. Of course I am not going to give out my address and I told him that I had only received a picture from one person and then he said that that was him only he was using a different name now. I told him that I wasn't going to send a picture and if he was the same person then I had already returned a photo. He then said that he had somehow deleted it. I told him that I couldn't see what difference it would make to him since we were all just meeting up as friends later. So, THEN, this guy says—"No, I don't want it to be the group of us. I just want it to be you and me and I want your address and to pick you up in my truck. Those other people are fat and goons and I don't want to hang out with them."

I informed BOBBY that I only offered GROUP outings and wasn't inter-ested in meeting up with him alone or giving him my home address and cer-tainly was not going to hop in the truck of some guy that I had just spoke to over the internet. Well, he started cursing and saying that I was probably a "fat goon" like the rest and sending all of this profanity over the Internet. Each time I blocked his e-mail he came in under some other name and then he kept sending IM's under totally obscene names. This guy was sending e-mails and IM's through for a couple of hours non-stop. AND, he was supposed to have been the new L.E. group moderator? This BOBBY character did not stop until I reported him to the authorities. I don't think that you and this BOBBY are the same being—however, needless to say—I am no longer "enthused" at the idea of meeting others through this arena. Shame too, because the group seemed like such a keen idea and yet there are parasites out there just looking to spoil the fun for everyone else. BTW—the group disappeared after that BOBBY invited others out for Cocktails a couple of Saturday's back. I am pretty certain that he was greatly responsible for the disintegration of the group—because when I asked him if he and the others that had responded affirmatively to meet for cocktails the week before—had ever gotten together, he replied, "I dunno." How can he not know if he got together with others or not?

The experience totally creeped me out.

Samm

Wonderful. This jerk obviously just set up this online group to meet women for himself. He deceived everyone involved into thinking it was a way to meet friends of both sexes and just hangout and have casual fun. It really is too bad because a correspondence was begun between myself and several of the other guys on the site, and before you could spit it was all gone. Just another day on the Internet!

Swinging the pendulum back to the women for just a wee bit, I cannot believe how well some women market themselves online! I received the following message just a few days ago in my *regular* e-mail account, not the alternate one where most of the crap goes. Where *did* she get that address from?

Remember me? Heather from the personals!

Hey there, how've ya been? It's Heather and I'm willing to bet you don't remember me considering it's been over a month since you messaged me. Well, I'm not sure if you remember but I promised I'd send you a link to a site I had some serious success on. I normally don't do this but I tried it a little over a month ago and had a guy waiting for me right outside my office that day! LOL!

If you're looking for someone serious this site is NOT for you. It's meant solely for a no strings kinda deal. Access is free so you have nothing to lose. You can thank me later :)

http://www.meetmeandyourwalletsmine.com

I'll make you a deal, if we end up matching I'll bring the wine! :)

Heather

So why is this different? I ignored it and just two days later came the following...

Hello it's Heather, haven't heard back?

Hey, it's me again...Didn't hear back from you, just wondering if you were still interested...Maybe my e-mail didn't go though or something, but here's the site I was talking about, the no strings one......

http://www.meetmeandyourwalletsmine.com
   Hope we can maybe get together sometime and have some fun......Talk to
you later, Heather

So what's the big deal here? Why is she different from the other Internet predator entrepreneurs? Simple. This girl has an auto responder! That means for as
long as you don't answer her, the messages will keep coming until you do. Brilliant! What a businesswoman!

Knowing this fact, here was my response:

   Dear Heather,
      Perhaps if your desire to meet were genuine, as opposed to a monetary
   nature, then you indeed would have heard back from me. Quite the little
   Internet business-woman aren't you? I suppose since you've been "found out"
   that there will be not response from you, but good luck with your venture!

No response was received. What a surprise! Poor girl will just have to pick
some other poor slob's pocket today!

9

"Did I miss something here?"

Unexplainable events. They happen to everyone, but on the Internet they seem to happen with a regularity that is truly uncanny and…well, *unexplainable*!

The following conversations took place totally online, during the month of September 2002. I'm going to let you make your own decisions on what may have happened here.

> Absolutely knowing…. "that you're loved and you're HOME." That's MY line for when I know it's real….I won't charge you with plagiarism though, especially since I forgot to write it in my profile!
>
> Seriously, liked everything you said especially affectionate (and everything that goes with it), lots of energy, love to laugh and have fun, into sports, you're a writer, musician, cook, loving parent….all of those are me as well (okay, so maybe not the 'cook' thing so much, but I certainly love and appreciate a man who does a good job at it!)
>
> I'm in the HR field as well, consulting as of 2 years ago after a long stint in a Fortune 100 company. The majority of my work is in delivering training and development coaching. I love the flexibility it gives me in being able to choose the jobs I really enjoy and have more time for myself and my children (2 girls). No baggage here either. Have a great relationship with my ex-husband, which we worked to develop. Did all my healing work going through the divorce and have come out the other side (it's been over 3 years now) with all of us in really good shape.
>
> Take a look at my profile (and ONE picture….I'm going to get more up soon…won't be the quality of yours though……know a good photographer I could use?) and write back if you choose.
>
> Mirabella

♦   ♦   ♦

What a beautiful smile you have! Thank you for the lovely message, as I get SO many, that basically just say "HI, here I am! Cum get me"! Effort is VERY much noticed, and appreciated, by the denizens of the female human condition!!! (what-EVA!) Sooooo.... do YOU work from home in YOUR underwear as well? We could e-mail each other naughty pictures on our scanners!! *tee hee* Getting back to reality here, a difficult thing 4 me 2 do (as you're beginning to figure out!) my time is at a premium, as I've got a spankin' new internet venture, that's beginning to really take off, and needs a child's attention. This means, I chat online a lot, and have a WHOLE bunch of late nite telephone conversations, with a VERY few women, I've found that I had chemistry with, and when the conversations get fun and cute and warm and fuzzy...it's time to meet, and only then. I don't date just to kill time. I set appointments, only with those very FEW women who appeal to ALL my senses, not just the visual ones...I seek my one true love, and will never cease until I find her, and become one with her. I am NOT however, like so many here, in a MAD dash, to "hook up"!!! and will continue to casually date (I HATE IT) until the time...that I don't. ("where the hell is he going with this" she thinks?) Nowhere, he says.... just rambling on incessantly!!!!!!! See ya in the funnies!!!! David....

♦   ♦   ♦

Cool! Cool! Cool!..........All of it! My work is based out of my home (and it totally depends on the day and my mood as to what I'm wearing, or NOT!) but being a trainer, I've got to be on site with clients to get paid. Lately it's been 5 days a week which is more than I would like (but you didn't hear me complaining about lots of work!) So, love to chat on line which right now is more towards the beginning and end of the day. Late night phone calls are great with me...I'm a night owl and my 2 children are asleep by then. I'm with you on not dating to kill time......I don't have near as much as I want of that and my life is full and busy already (but would be willing to pare down on some thing if the right guy came into my life!). So, sounds like a plan to me.....Mirabella

◆   ◆   ◆

On the same page with you (page 69 of course....ONLY KIDDING!!!!!) *tee hee*...finding that special "spark" with someone, is a really awesome place to be at. My goal, eventually, is to take that spark, and when it grows into a RAGING INFERNO, dating is done, and that ONE lady, better be ready for the ride of her life..... see ya.... D.... just me...

◆   ◆   ◆

Page 69? Is that where the raging inferno is or is that just the spark? :).......................M

◆   ◆   ◆

Oh you are REALLY askin' 4 it you............NOW it's ON!!!!! D...

◆   ◆   ◆

Oh, no, I'm shakin' in my boots now! Go ahead and bring it...................M

◆   ◆   ◆

Soooo, you're a personal trainer, eh? I'll bet there's a few things I could train YOU to do....*devilish cutesie grin*. So exactly WHAT do you train people TO do? Personally that is.....(*tee hee*). Tag, you're it pookie!!!....D....

◆   ◆   ◆

Okay, so what do I train people to do? Depends on what the clients asks for......:)

For a serious answer (don't know if you really want to know or not, but here goes anyway) generally, the things I get PAID to do are PERSONNEL type stuff. I specialize in flexible work arrangements (telecommuting, part time, job share, etc.) but also train in performance management, sexual harassment (I'm very proficient on that subject.....done lots of research to get it right), team building, communication, that sort of thing. I also play one on one, uh, I mean, do one on one,(no, no, that's not it)........perform (no, definitely not it),........um, let's see,......offer individual coaching sessions for management development. Whoops! This is supposed to be the serious answer..........okay, so let's play pretend......And soooo, you're a photographer? What do you take pictures of.....besides yourself? :) (And no fair copying my first answer).....................M

♦   ♦   ♦

Pillow fights at Ikea, and rolling around on beds like two idiots. Dancing in store windows, just because the music is good. Kissing so passionately hello, or goodbye, or hello again, that a passerby yells "HEY, GET A ROOM!" 'cause you're in a parking lot at the time...Snowball fights, sleigh riding, hitting a baseball at 6 am, on a Saturday morning, the lake, the beach, the pool,...cuddling with someone who REALLY cares about you. Baby kisses on the neck, the ears, and elsewhere...Star Trek, Sci-Fi, Cartoon Network, CNN, my babies in my arms......These are just some of the things, that make me, me.... just thought I'd letcha know..... D....

♦   ♦   ♦

I like it, I like it, especially the GET A ROOM thing! Your babies in your arms? Like we're talking 'children', here? (which is totally okay by me). How many do you have? How old? Or is that info too personal? Mine are 7 and 11. And you didn't tell me yet what you photograph..........or didn't you get that e-mail?.....................M

♦   ♦   ♦

Okay okay, So many questions, so little time!! Sammy is 7, and is almost fearless in social situations. Sherry is 9, and is a little shy, until she warms up to you...then...WATCH OUT! Melanie is 19, and goes to the University of

Pittsburgh. She is the love of my life, and raised me from a pup (her mom left when Mel was very young...), so we sorta grew up together!!! I photograph almost anything, but my favorite subjects are kids, well, people in general, and landscapes, be they 2 miles across, or 1/2 an inch across...Okee dokey? Did I leave anything out? LOL! Gotta run!! See ya.... David...

◆   ◆   ◆

Am I asking too many questions? Sorry, just curious......Thanks for all the info. Your kids sounds great.............M

◆   ◆   ◆

Man, what a strange, and final sorta reply!!??? WHATUP?????.... D...

◆   ◆   ◆

Oh, no, didn't mean it as final or anything! Did I sound like I was being sarcastic or testy or something? I actually meant it sincerely, like really nice and sweet..........I guess I don't know how to do that on e-mail too well, you know, impart tone of voice. Sometimes I hate how e-mail is so limited, especially when you don't know someone! I love to tease and be sarcastic but I have a serious, warm and fuzzy side as well. I wasn't really sure if I was bugging you too much with so many questions, I guess I didn't know from your comments........Plus I really thought it was nice how you told me a little about all 3 of your kids, not only their ages and names but a short comment on each of them, and they do sound great! You sound like they really mean a lot to you and I respect that tremendously in a guy. Anyway, thanks for asking and not just assuming and blowing me off..................M

◆   ◆   ◆

Too late to be witty or charming...I'm sooooo tired, long day...and I, as well as you, really hate this e-mail crap, it's so alien to me. I much prefer the phone, and really don't like to go back and forth more than 3 or 4 times, before a phone # is exchanged (especially, when I can sorta tell I'm gonna like someone, like you, *giggle*) So I'll leave you my #, to call at your leisure. 914-000-0000. If your reply is anything but a phone call, you will not hear back from me, as I'm as REAL as they get, and this is so fake....I think you're very nice (God, that sounded soooo cliche!) and would welcome hearing your lovely voice, and getting to know YOU better.... See ya soon! David...

◆   ◆   ◆

Geez, you gotta lot of 'rules' :) but it's actually pretty good because it's clear what you're thinking.....I like that! And you know what? Parts of this last e-mail were very charming indeed! Isn't that cool when you can be charming and you're not even trying? So, yes, I'll call..........thanks for the number. And don't sweat it, no need to e-mail back
:)...............Mirabella
P.S. All of this said in a very sweet, lilting voice............*giggle*
(I'm learning..........)

She never did call me, and I never heard from her again. She is still online looking for her soul mate, and I won't be the judge here, I'll just leave it up to you why she hasn't found him yet.

The next contact is by a woman named Mary and it's unexplainable due to its innate stupidity, as you'll figure out when you read it and in my reply to it. Another thing that tipped me off to the fact that we wouldn't work out anyway was in her profile. As a hardcore Mets fan, I wouldn't be caught with someone who would *dare* root for the Yankees! (Kidding!)

Hi Yonkers...
Hi how are you? I don't think we would get along, but wanted to let you know I enjoyed reading your profile. I have been having an interesting time on this Match thing, but will give up on it when my membership expires. Not sure online things work that well. Good luck to you,
Mary

◆   ◆   ◆

Mary,
    Perhaps this Match thing, doesn't work 4 U, because you start your e-mails with "I don't think we would get along"!!!!.... and you're a Yankee fan!!!!! See ya!! David...

Welll...isn't that special? She's been having an *interesting* time with it! She doesn't think this thing works? She doesn't think we'd get along? How in God's name can you open up a conversation with someone in that manner, and expect to get *any* sort of positive response? Did she expect me to say something like, "Oh no dear, let's meet and see if an intelligent, cute, forward Mets fan, (yes, I'm cursed, I know, you can stop laughing now!) could perhaps get along with a negative, unmotivated, dopey Yankees fan." Sure, why not? After all, I'm like *totally* fanatical about meeting *anyone* at all! Doesn't this girl have anything better to do, than to waste her time e-mailing me just to say that she liked my profile, but that we wouldn't get along? Doesn't the fact that she liked my profile enough to write to me sort of tell her that we just *might* get along, or at least have enough things in common to start a friendship? Folks, if you're not yet online with your profile but are thinking about doing it, please do not waste your time contacting people for no good reason. It will just make you feel stupid when they respond to you negatively, wastes space in both e-mail boxes, and tends to piss people off because they are looking for love here, not veiled compliments smothered in idiocy...Geez!

Now, misunderstandings are pretty rampant on the Internet, so every once in a while I'll get an e-mail from a woman and sort of "test the waters" to see if she can "get" my personality on the first try. Here's what happens when they do not!

HI!
    Loved your profile; I'm also a creative, athletic, fun-loving and romantic person...AND I own my own baseball glove! Can you imagine I actually read that far? I also enjoy photography, the arts, watersports, skiing, people who make me laugh, pillow fights and many other silly things. Check out my profile and see if you'd like to chat sometime./Katie

◆   ◆   ◆

Soooooooooooo.........ya loved my profile, huh? =) Ya own yer very own baseball glove, eh? =Oo Ya even like all the things I do AS WELL as many other silly things? *grin* Mhmmmmm. You'd like me to check out your pro-file and see if I'd like to chat?

What EXACTLY was it about me that made you think that I was chatty????? So ya wanna chat? Then chat! You do realize of course that since you made first contact, that YOU will be driving to the city to meet me! hehehe....... but the coffee is on me..... perhaps I'll even throw in a danish.... if you're nice! *smile*

toodles!...............David............. =)

◆   ◆   ◆

Wow by reading your profile I actually mistook you for:
#1. Someone who could actually write.
#2. Someone who seemed like a genuinely nice guy (aka, not a Neanderthal).
#3. Someone who is smart and funny, not obnoxscious.

By the way, I did not assume you were chatty, match.com messenger is only a way to communicate which is faster than e-mail..... Katie...

◆   ◆   ◆

Wow, by reading your message I mistook you for :
1) someone who liked to laugh
2) someone who could easily ascertain the difference between silly sarcasm online, as opposed to being an "obnoxious Neanderthal"
3) someone who was sweet, nice, and would NEVER assume the worst about a complete stranger.

Boy did you ever misread me. Have a wonderful life.
=).... David...

I guess the best thing about writing a book while you're still seeking the love of your life is that when a conversation goes that foul, it simply becomes a silly conversation piece, as well as cannon fodder for your book. Oh well!

Back to my buddy Freeda, one of the most colorful people I've ever met. If you want to get a dull party kicking, invite her over. Just let her sit and talk for the entire night. Not only will she keep everyone riveted with her storytelling, but she'll probably leave with two or three guys' phone numbers without ever having to ask for one! She recently sent me the following e-mail to attempt to explain some, er, unexplainable events.

Ok where to begin, I have been doing the online dating thing for about a year and a half. For the most part I have met some very nice people and made a few good friends. But as well I have to add that there are some very odd and strange happenings on these sites as far as people are concerned. People generally start as nice and try to be as honest as possible but then as time goes on you see them for what they really are. For example they use old photo's (pic's) of themselves not sure why they do this for in the end result it all comes out. They will lie about their age as well and I do not mean 1or 2 years more like up to 10 years. lol It sounds crazy but it's true. I have had marriage proposals, recently got 2 in the course of a 24-hour period, boy it's bizarre and scary can people really be that lonely and desperate to find happiness and not really know a person? It's sad that we as people have come to this just to avoid being lonely I suppose. I have men friends on different sites that have told me things like all of a sudden they met someone, things are going great and for no apparent reason they just stop speaking to you and block you from being able to speak to them again or they play games like trying to get you to have sex online and don't want to talk to you again. And some of the people go as far as leading you on and don't show, that has never happened to me but to many people I have spoken with. Now I'm not saying it's all bad, I did meet a person over a year ago it lasted 3 months but hey it was not that bad just not enough things in common. Then met someone who is very wonderful and I care about very much and is going through a very bad time at the moment but we speak often it could work out well at least I'm hoping it does. I guess for the most part it's very easy to hide behind the computer or keyboard as we online put it. Then you have people that cannot appreciate honesty or will read your profile and pre-judge you and block you for no reason. The reason the blocking is a bad thing is not because you can no longer speak to them anymore but because you pay for your membership and after so many blocks your membership is terminated and it's not fair for people to do it for no reason. So I guess what I'm trying to say is why do people act the way they do it's bizarre and beyond after all we are all searching for the same thing and should be more adult about it but I guess it all boils down to people do not like rejection or what they think is rejection and always have to have the last word or get even and being online allows them to do so. I hope this gives you some insight to how I feel about such things online.
Sincerely,
Freeda…

I decided not to edit a word of the previous rant because Freeda's personality comes through so clearly that changing *anything* would be a crime. My editor on the other hand is now in therapy!

Sometimes unexplainable events are *indeed* explainable if you simply read between the lines. We all tend to ignore the occasional glaring red flags if the person is cute enough, charming enough, and a possible love interest. I felt this next woman was wrong for me, but her intelligence level as well as her beauty blinded me to several personality flaws, flaws which were self-admitted by her in her notes to me online. We will call my friend Soraya, because I like the name! She stands about five foot eight, slim yet curvy, with shiny, silky red hair and *very* blue eyes, stunning to say the least.

She contacted me through Match.com and we chatted for several weeks until we met at a local bar. The date went nicely, and we parted after several hours with a very nice kiss. Her final statement being, "I'd better go now before I get into trouble!" Cute. So we spoke on the phone many times, and I was her last call at the airport upon her leaving on a business trip down south. There was every indication that she liked me, although she did her best to display the "aloof New York professional woman" front. She did it well and kept me slightly confused, yet upon her return she answered my e-mail immediately and happily, and we set our second date for that Friday evening.

The following e-mail arrived the night before our date. It was her response to me after having forwarded to me the cutest note about how the best women are the apples at the top of the tree, and that most men just grab the rotten ones at the bottom since they're easier!

> Well, I really just thought that the analogy was kind of sweet. But on giving it a bit of thought, I am a work in progress…so I guess I am working as hard as I can each day to get to the very tippy top of the apple tree. I think I am pretty close but I still have my good days and my bad days. I do struggle with my limitations (and I have always been a little bit afraid of heights)…I can at times be selfish, stubborn, impatient and vain—I am trying to rise above these things
>
> I guess there are several apple tree ascension scenerios:
> 1) We might meet somewhere in the middle of the tree and climb up to the top together
> 2) You might pass me (being a little more self actualized than I) and you hook up with a juicier, sweeter more luscious apple higher up on the tree (from what I have seen so far you certainly deserve this)
> 3) A faster and more clever tree climber might pick (and be delighted by) me first
> 4) I may never get to the top and never ever get picked and/or you may never finish your climb to the top and never get the apple that you desire—but in the long run we will both still be very happy.

5) We might both fall to the ground in our climb to the top (I am unsure what the result of this would be, might be either very good or very bad, it will most certainly leave a bruise).

    I could come up with more..but won't.

    See you tomorrow

    Soraya

I already had plans with a large group of friends to meet for pizza and beer in Manhattan and told her that I'd probably have had my fill at about 8:00 or 8:30 and to call me on my cell at that time. Indeed she did call, unfortunately from two blocks away, just as I sat down to eat a slice with two lovely girls I had introduced myself to.

I informed her that I would finish my slice, pack up my laptop, (I was showing pics to my friends, and their friends, yada, yada) and meet her out front in 5 minutes. Two minutes later my cell rings and it's Soraya again. This time she is calling to inform me that she is now going home since I was rude to be eating upon her majesty's arrival and that she didn't feel she should have to wait even *one* minute.

Well I was stunned that a woman of 45 could be that petty, selfish, impatient..... but wait, didn't she already *tell* me exactly those things in her e-mail? Sheesh!

Now normally, this would upset me, but upon my arrival back at the table, stunned look still on my face, the two women I had had to leave earlier seemed *very* pleased that I was now remaining to talk to them. Judy stayed for another hour and then departed, but her adorable friend Megan remained. We talked, we laughed, we bonded, we left together and had an awesome time at another *very* crowded bar watching English football, (soccer to us silly Americans) and when I noticed for the hundredth time how thick and gorgeous her amazing blonde hair was, I began to run my fingers through it. The results were instantly deadly as she closed her eyes, purred loudly and just sort of laid her sweet head on my chest to listen to me sing.

The evening progressed naughtily until, at my car, we agreed to meet again as we were getting each other very hot and bothered on the streets of New York City ("Public displays of affection" would not suffice to describe our embraces).

We have spoken every night since, and as I write this, she has agreed to join me for dinner at my apartment tomorrow evening. She is intelligent, beautiful, down-to-earth and speaks her mind easily and with a grace that is very becoming. My final point is that even from the ashes of a lost evening may come the beginnings of something far better.

Oh yeah, this was my final note to Soraya the next day as I cut and pasted her description of herself right back at her...and fittingly so!

> Well, I really just thought that the analogy was kind of sweet. But on giving it a bit of thought, I am a work in progress...so I guess I am working as hard as I can each day to get to the very tippy top of the apple tree. I think I am pretty close but I still have my good days and my bad days. I do struggle with my limitations (and I have always been a little bit afraid of heights)...*I can at times be selfish, stubborn, impatient and vain—I am trying to rise above these things* NO, YA THINK?????? Guess what? Ya ain't tryin' hard enuf Tonto!!!!!
> But I need to thank you anyway as after you rudely left me hangin' I met the most amazing girl!!! So I therefore bear you no ill will. Good luck with your ascension and please do NOT feel the need to answer this!
> Later gator!
> A smiling but slightly tired David........ *grin*

No response was received. I do not wonder why, nor do I care!!!

The following is a very erotic story that Charley faxed to me a few days ago. I thought that perhaps it should go in the "X-rated" chapter, but with a simple change of a word here and there, it was rendered a bit more sedate and just seems to be a better fit in this chapter. After reading this story, (*ladies!*) do not feel it necessary to hate the guy, as women do this nearly as often.

> During my weekly Sunday night search I saw Danny's picture and immediately thought he was cute. It was taken with a German Sheppard puppy so I figured if he likes animals he must be a decent guy. I e-mailed him and asked how old the dog was as well as the photo? He replied and said one year. We e-mailed for a few days and found that we had a lot in common as well as only living about 10 minutes away from each other. He then informed me that he needed to leave for Texas on a family emergency and upon not hearing from him for three weeks assumed that I had been dismissed.
> Upon his return however he contacted me saying that he was very eager to meet me...his exact words "I would love to meet you"...so we did!
> We met for breakfast on a Sunday morning due to my schedule as a single mom. It was the soonest we could meet. When I first saw him I thought "wow, he is very good looking and he was much bigger...than his picture...very muscular...great body!"
> We laughed a lot and seemed to have much in common. We parted company but met later that day for a few hours. He took me to a friend's million-dollar home, which was in the process of being built. He also showed me the

"boys hangout" which was a barn that they had converted into a club of sorts, as it contained a bar, pool table, stereo, couch, wood burning stove and an outhouse! No bathroom inside…very rustic. He then took me home and I got a little peck on the cheek! We spoke several more times on the phone and we agreed to meet for dinner the following Wednesday evening.

He picked me up and we went to a local restaurant. I remember being very nervous wondering what were we going to do after dinner…was he going to take me home…were we going to go out somewhere to a club? Dinner went well with lots of laughter and conversation. After dinner we got into his pickup truck and he asked me what I wanted to do? I responded "whatever" so he asked if I'd like to go play some pool? I asked him where he wanted to play and suggested a local place but he countered with the "boys club" at his friends' mansion not far away. I said that it would be okay since it would be private and not as smoky.

It was a rainy night and I was a little nervous going there but once we arrived he made me feel very comfortable. He started a fire and turned on some music as we began to shoot a few games of pool. The games were very close although he won, yet he was very impressed that I shot as well as I did. At this point we were at a flirtatious stage. During all three games he would smack my butt as he passed and I would tap his arm. We were getting very "touchie" with each other but no kiss just yet!

After the third game he was leaning against the pool table looking sooooooo fine and muscular! As I walked by he grabbed me by the waist and we started making out. What a great kisser, things got very heated VERY fast! Before I knew it he had picked me up and put my butt on the pool table. Within minutes my pants were down to my ankles, his head between my thighs and he began to work on me with his amazing mouth. OH MY GOD!!! Then he pulled down his pants, threw my legs over his shoulders and thrust his manhood deeply into me. DOUBLE OH MY GOD!!! He was sure a big boy all over and we had such great sex together! It was so erotic being on the pool table and the spontaneity made it even more exciting.

At this point he picked me up in his huge arms and carried me over to the couch. The lights had gone out as the generator had run out of energy so the only illumination in the room was from the fireplace. We rested for a very short while until I felt hungry and started to taste his huge sausage roll! I call it that since that's what it looked like when soft as he was the first un-circumcised man I had ever been with. He seemed impatient with the results though as once fully erect he pushed my head down, picked me up from behind and entered me from a standing position. He was pumping me so hard that I felt as though he would choke me even though he was nowhere near my mouth. I knew I would have trouble walking the next day but it did not affect my passionate response to his erotic advances. We finished shortly thereafter leaving each other very sweaty, hot, out of breath yet still excited at the possibilities of a future encounter. We both agreed that there was a lot of chemistry between us! No, duh?

It took me a while to find all of my clothing, which had been tossed all over. We got dressed and he drove me home, holding my hand all the way there giving me every indication that things were going to be okay. As I left his car he gave me a very nice, wet kiss and I had a hard time sleeping that night, let me tell you!

What a passionate experience and by far one of my favorites. One of the toughest decisions a woman has to make is "do I or don't I" have sex early on in a new relationship? We had one date for breakfast and another date in the afternoon, so I count this particular rendezvous as the third date. At my age I like to find out if the guy and I are sexually compatible early on because it is a very important part of the relationship. So I worry...worry...worry until the next time I hear from him! WILL I hear from him??? I did as we got together for dinner the following Thursday and ended up back at his place. His room had a wall and ceiling full of mirrors and BOY was it fun watching ourselves in action! WOWEE!

I was going away the following day so I stopped by to see him in the morning for one more rumble. We spoke on the phone a few times thereafter and had plans to get together that Sunday evening. When I returned I called him to no avail. No response. I called again. No response. He never returned future phone calls and I never heard from him or saw him again. There was no explanation or closure, just frustration and unanswered questions on my part as to WHY? What a blow to my ego. I had believed things were progressing sweetly thus far. I guess his being single at 38, no kids, never married should have been a red flag of sorts for me to begin with. I found out later that he was indeed only 34...and me robbing the cradle all that time! I also discovered that he had lived with a woman for 2 years and that she had cheated on him, hurting both his pride as well as his heart. A heart which I can only assume was now well protected and closed to women, except for sex.

OH WELL? I learned 2 valuable lessons from this fiasco.

First: Hold off on sex!

Second: Pool tables are VERY erotic! *smile*

What a pistol! This guy made a mistake too, because I can tell you from personal experience that Charley is a handful in the sex department! I just have to assume that she must have shown him some affection and thus scared him away. What a maroon!

I'm going to close out here with some e-mails that contain a story that will leave you gasping for air! I had been chatting with this woman for several days and it was apparent that our personalities were a good fit. It begins in the middle:

Made it. You're never going to believe this, but I am now the maid-of-honor. I am wearing a dark pink strapless dress (my sister is out of her mind—wait until you see it). I'll send pictures...lol.

Hope all is well.
Sarah

◆   ◆   ◆

Ok, I guess congratulations are in order! Whoopie! So there you are WAY down south (I do so love it there, as you indeed will find out upon your return…ahem…) and you're sending me updates. Lil ol me. I am honored. You REALLY do need to clear your calendar for next Friday night…. or Saturday….. what-EVAH….. I just need about 5 or 6 hours….. sleep well….
    ..David…

◆   ◆   ◆

More descriptive…pink satin, backless, strapless (well a skinny strap around the neck), sleeveless…my sister is crazy! Yes, you get updates…
    Sarah

◆   ◆   ◆

OMGd………. sleeveless pink satin brings back one of the worst memories of my young life. I was at my friend Bobby's wedding in Long Island. To say that his new bride was not the most attractive woman in the world would be a gross understatement. However, compared to her three bridesmaids she was skinny and gorgeous. These young ladies were dually cursed as they were both grossly overweight, yet had no visible breasts. They were dressed, you guessed it, in pink satin tutu's. They basically looked like a herd of pink hippos fresh out of the movie Fantasia as they ran in unison to the dance floor to dance to one of their favorite songs, as all the eligible man ran for their lives for fear of being trampled to death. The thundering sound of their terrible hooves was deafening as they danced to several popular numbers. The few remaining men, and other women on the dance floor were summarily pummeled into a pulp as the elbows and thighs flew around, wreaking a TERRIBLE havoc on the unsuspecting guests around them. When they were finished with their dance of death, and the paramedics departed, it was time for the bride to throw the bouquet. On the receiving end were the herd, and several unsuspecting young ladies who obviously had arrived late, and not witnessed the recent slaughter. There went the bouquet, up in the air directly at a slim vibrant young girl barely out of puberty. She reached, but never quite saw what hit her as the herd enveloped her in a mass of twisting epidermis large enough to shield Manhattan from a typhoon.

The young lady who caught the bouquet was quite exuberant at her good fortune, barely noticing the life she had snuffed out in her terrible haste. Normally all of the eligible bachelors would enter the scene at this point, but none were forthcoming, producing the most horrendous rage from Dumbo (or was her name Darla, ahhhh I forget, the years you know....). So they convinced an elderly blind gentleman to try for the beloved garter catch. Since his only competition was a 3 month old baby boy, gently nestled in his mothers arms, he was the victor!

Then came the moment of truth as it was his time to apply the virgin garter belt up the leg and thigh of the young lady who had slain life and limb for the precious bouquet. He kneeled, and began to push the garter over her foot, then up to her knee where he met some slight resistance, only to press on above and beyond the call of all men before him. He pushed it up, up, and even more up, as in his bewilderment and advanced age and blindness he could not see the young hippo turning blue from the loss of blood flow to her extremities. She would not allow him to stop however as this was the most excitement she had experienced in possibly many years.

As this point the bride, sensing imminent disaster, stopped the proceedings with a grace heretofore not seen since the days of Camelot. Everyone got really drunk after that, attempting to forget everything about the evening, for fear that the memories would return and completely destroy any mood of having sex with their partner EVER AGAIN!!!!

Do NOT let this happen to you!!!!!!..... David...=o)

◆   ◆   ◆

YOU ROCK!!!!!

I laughed until I had tears running down my face! Then I read it to my sister Mandie, and laughed all over again. She has begged me to forward it to her so that she can read it to her classes (she teaches HS English/Lit).

Ok...so now I really do adore you. Lol

Today's the big day, bought pasties yesterday to keep the ol' breasts from exploding into/onto the other guests at the wedding. Because of the design of this damn dress, I am forced to go braless (I did say it is backless, strapless, and sleeveless). I spent the better part of yesterday looking for something to contain these bad boys! So, now I've got these flesh colored strips that you affix to your breasts with glue...GLUE...and the only way they come back off (God I hope this is indeed a fact) is when you take a shower. Guess I'll be putting them to the test later today.

Okay my very, very clever and wonderful friend. Thank you so much for the "pink dress saga" I will save it and savor it for the remainder of my days. It is, by far, the funniest thing I've read.
In adoration,
Sarah

So we took it to the phone. It didn't go extremely well. Personalities may seem to jibe online but in application sometimes, do not mix as well over the phone or in person. I mentioned this in a short e-mail to her and this was her final response:

Sometimes David, things are not about you..... Sarah....

Really ladies, we cannot read minds. We're just guys, and being guys we go with what you give us. We don't think about all the deep issues that exist behind the scenes. We just want to meet, see if you're cute, and determine if you're a good kisser or not. It really ain't that complicated!

10

"Can you put that back on please?"

So, after a long stretch of writer's block, there were two things that knocked me back to my creative senses. The first was a telephone interview with one of the ladies in this book, which went considerably better than was anticipated, and the other was a tiny online ad, that follows:

> **In need of a personal assistant?**
> Ambitious young attracting female in need of some place to live. Will take care of ALL daily activities to lessen the load of your life including cooking, cleaning, plant watering, dog walking, dry clean pickup, and auto mainte-nance. Oral Sex included (M/F).

I have not as yet spoken to this young lady, but I did answer her ad, and have every intention on interviewing her for this little project. Yeah yeah, I *know* what you're all thinking. I just wanna get my pipes cleaned! The thought did cross my mind, as I wouldn't be a normal guy if it didn't, but those bases are well cov-ered…..ahem.

I just need to give some of you a warning about the content in this chapter. **Some of the language and content may be deemed very offensive by some,** and very erotic by others. I decided after a great deal of soul searching, to keep the content exactly as received in my inbox, except for any names of people, or places. The reason for this is quite simple. To attempt to edit the content of someone else's passionate words totally changes everything about the way they said it. The same thing goes for myself. Therefore, I relate these stories in the same manner that I would if I were speaking to close male friends…and then some.

All right, enough of this crap. It's high time I got this chapter going, so I'll just jump right in with some stories I've lived through in the last three years. Some make me cringe and some leave me smiling but *none* will bore you in any way!

There is a link in the Craiglist personals called "Casual Encounters." There are some truly interesting and cute posts there, but that's not the intention of that section. The intention and purpose of C.E. is to find a compatible person that very evening, meet, and be in bed fucking like two goddamn animals very quickly. The daily posts in that one section could fill an entire book with their graphic depiction of desired sexual bliss, as well as the innate stupidity of some men who just want some lonely fat chick to come over and blow them, "just because I'm lonely and erect." Yeah, right dude! Some of the women are just as bad though, and despite a "flagging" option on the list, C.E. has, for the most part, deteriorated into a blatant whorehouse of transvestites, gay men seeking horny drunk straight guys, and Internet whores just looking for their next sugar daddy or a money fuck for the evening.

I usually read the posts on slow evenings to be entertained, but one Friday night, I came across a particular post. It was obviously disturbed, but the way she described herself physically sucked me in and forced me to send her a short note as well as a photo. Amazingly, she responded with a plethora of very explicit photos of her own, and a phone number to call her "immediately." She called herself "Princess Priscilla." Anyone who puts a princess moniker before their name without the slightest trace of royal blood is already halfway to the fucking nuthouse in my estimation, but in total guy fashion I called her anyway. I mean, she had a body that interested me *tremendously* on a lonely Friday evening.

We spoke for a brief period and it became apparent to me that she was indeed a disturbed individual who I only desired *one* thing from. I don't think I need to relate what that thing was. She liked my personality on the phone and asked how soon we could meet. It was around 8:00 p.m. and we had both had dinner already, so I asked if she would like to grab a few drinks together. Her response floored me.

She declined going out for drinks as she had a six pack of beer in the fridge which she would bring over with her. She was very clear that if we were attracted to each other, beer was not the only thing that would be entering her mouth this evening. She arrived shortly after 9:00 p.m. and was driven to my home by her ex-husband, whom she apparently still lived in the same house with. (I found this out after the fact)

She was dressed in a long flowing black coat that hid all the attributes beneath. Her hair was jet black and curly, her eyes a strange combination of blue and yellow, and she was tall. She boasted of her status as a "ring card girl." You know, those girls who walk around in a boxing ring with a card that says "Round Two" or "Round Three," and you all know what those girls look like! They're not in that ring for their brain-power; they're there because they have the sort of body that makes the knees weak. Priscilla was no different.

She entered my apartment and said, "How quaint," in a manner that further fueled my trepidation and growing dislike for her braggadocio and utter lack of personality or brains. She removed her coat in a well practiced manner that elicited the desired response from me.

"Oh my."

She was wearing a skintight white tee, and a pair of jet-black stretchy jeans that hugged her form like they were painted on. She asked for several glasses with ice and I complied. She proceeded to pour the *very* cheap domestic beer into a glass over ice and then asked if I had a straw. A *straw*? Holy crap, did you ask me to get you a *straw* to drink your cheap fucking watered down beer? She did!

So she drank her cheap crap beer as I grabbed a Sam Adams Cherry Wheat, (the best damn beer in the ENTIRE fucking world and I will wrestle any woman in Jell-O who has the nerve to disagree!) and we sat on the couch and talked for a bit. After several drinks my phone rang in my bedroom and I went to see who was calling me. As I was speaking on the phone, Priscilla passed my bedroom door and proceeded into the guest bathroom. I didn't see her do this as it was around the corner, but did hear her in passing.

I returned to the couch several minutes later and sat down without looking at her. Suddenly there was a hand on my inner thigh. I turned to look at Priscilla as she sat next to me with a huge grin, wearing only as towel. I guess I wasn't moving fast enough for her so she needed to turn up the heat a few notches. At this point she got up from the couch, allowing the towel to drop to the floor as she glided across the room to strike a very provocative pose directly in front of my living room window. I live on the first floor.

This was not a shy woman, quite the opposite. Her body was the sort that you see on a regular basis in men's magazines. She had the hourglass figure that we dream of screwing every minute of every day. Her breasts were large and bulbous, yet her nipples thrust toward the sky as if she were still a teenager. Her waist was tiny, yet her hips were of the sort that are often described as "child bearing" in their fullness. Her ass was to die for and it made me dizzy as she caressed it with her hands, moving it sexily to and fro around the living room, striking sexy poses as she went and asking, "So, whaddaya think, hot stuff?"

I knew this wasn't going to be one of those sweet, tender, loving evenings that start a relationship. No this was going to be "balls to the wall, fuck my brains out 'till I puke, throw me against the wall" type sex.

So I threw her against the wall and began to kiss her hard. This elicited the desired response as she was just as rough raking my back with her nails and pulling my hair as we found our way back to the couch. She did not remove my shirt nicely. The buttons were strewn in every corner as it was ripped from my body along with every ounce of our self-respect. I flung her onto the couch and proceeded to engorge my mouth with her left nipple. This did not go unnoticed by her! I bit and licked my way to the center of her body and once there, found a mostly shaven pussy that could have used a bath.

A thought occurred to me at this juncture about cleanliness, but I was just too far gone to care, so I grabbed my beer mug, took a large swig of the ice-cold beer, and spewed it between her legs to remove any lingering scents that were assailing my nostrils. I further took an ice cube into my mouth and began to devour her pussy to the sheer delight of the princess. I don't think she had ever experienced "hot and cold head" before, as the sounds escaping her mouth were loud and descriptive, as well as blatantly foul.

"You fucking scumbag! What are you doing to me? Oh, you bastard! You fucking, fucking bastard! Oh, oh, OHHHHHHHH GOD! I'm gonna cum. Oh God I'm gonna cum. Who, who the fuck do you think you are to make Princess Priscilla cuuuuummmmmmmm...ooohhhhhhhhhhhh!"

So I guess she came. She damn near pinched my head off doing it too. She had very powerful legs that obviously spent many hours every day in a gym and squeezed me like a ripe melon as her juices flowed heartily into my mouth and down my chin. My lack of oxygen did not concern her in the least as she grabbed her mug, picked herself up and walked into my bedroom, waiting for me to follow her.

Follow her I did, but not until she was screaming, "Are you gonna come in here and fuck me or what?"

So I walked into my bedroom to find her spread-eagled on the bed. Strangely, this did not excite me. After having an orgasm as intense as this bitch did, most women would thank you, or hold you, or *reciprocate* in some fashion. Not this girl. She just lay there asking for more. I sat down next to her and started to caress her softly as we spoke to each other until she said, "Oh fuck this," and ripped my pants down to my ankles, putting my flaccid cock into her ample mouth.

She sucked. I don't mean she sucked me well. I mean that she was another one of those clueless gorgeous women who expect that their looks alone will elicit the desired passionate response from any male. So I just stood there, bored to death. She didn't change techniques, didn't use her hands, didn't ask what I liked in her single-minded desire to just get me hard so that I could fuck her. After what seemed like an eternity, I pulled away to her utter amazement.

The conversation at that point did not go well as her mouth became even fouler than before. I stood there thinking what a total ass I was for letting this piece of shit into my house, and how I was going to get her to leave? So I asked her to leave and she got out of the bed, started screaming and throwing things around in her fury, grabbed me and threw me violently onto the bed and attempted to straddle me. I threw her to the floor, and as she picked herself up, she cursed me again and spat on me in total disdain!

She ran into the guest bathroom yet a second time, but not to come out with a towel to arouse me. I was a little afraid at this point that my neighbors would call the police, since most of them are in their 80's and are not too fond of cursing, screaming, incoherent women at 11:30 at night. I got up, laughing, and followed her to the bathroom. I thought she might hurt herself, or my apartment, as I had heard things breaking.

I was surprised at what I saw upon opening the door. I expected to see a violent, brazen, belligerent woman. What I found was a little girl sitting on the bathtub, crying openly. I was shocked! What the fuck do I do now? This is a human being sitting there, and although she was a handful as well as a complete nut job, she was still a woman…and she was hurting.

I gently knelt down and attempted to touch her face and she weakly said, "No," and pushed me away. I stood her up despite slight resistance, pulled her to me, held her in my arms for quite some time as we stood there silently rocking to and fro. This changed *everything* about the evening. She eventually moved slightly away, touched my face for just a fleeting moment and in her best effort at emotion uttered, "You're not too much of a prick."

The combination of her tears on my shoulder, our hugging like true lovers, her touch on my face and her fleeting attempt at emotion elicited a physical response in me that her amazing body could not. We both knew what was now to follow as we became the animals that sought each other out for the evening.

I put her adorable ass up on the sink. Her left leg pointed and resting on the tub with her right leg thrown over my left shoulder, I entered her extremely hungry and wet pussy. I was amazed at how limber this woman was. I was so aroused at this point between the fighting and the making up that it didn't take me more than a few minutes to explode inside of her, almost falling to the floor as my knees nearly buckled. She actually held me yet again after I came and said, "Payback is a bitch, huh?"

We entered the bedroom yet again, but this time with a bit more sexual energy as the angst of the "first orgasm" was passed and now we could truly get down to business. After sharing another drink I filled my mouth yet again, this time with ice water, and spat it on her stomach. She really seemed to like this, and although my apartment was becoming quite messy, it was really not bothering me in the least considering why! We laughed because the worst was now behind us and played gleefully for a short time until her filthy mouth once again elicited the desired result. I had never been with a woman so totally degrading verbally, yet it was an aphrodisiac to me. She didn't want tenderness. She didn't want teasing. She wanted to be ravaged like the primal animal that she was, and was certainly in the mood to bring forth that very animal in me.

Her legs now back on either side of her head, I entered her deeply and violently while she let out the deepest throaty moan I have ever heard a woman utter. Her head was up against my headboard as were her feet. My arms were at her sides, locked flush out holding her legs in place as I pounded her more forcefully that I had ever done in my entire life. Her head was now smacking against the headboard with every vicious thrust of my cock, but she didn't seem to mind, no, not at all. In fact I think the pain added to her excitement as she screamed, "That's all you got? You fuckin' pussy that's all you got? Yer fuckin' me good huh? Real good huh? You fuckin' piece a shit! Bring it. Bring it! BRING IT DAMN YOU! AAAAGGGGGHHH!"

Holy shit, I was totally out of control. I had never in my life been with a woman who I really didn't like, respect, or have any intention of ever seeing again, yet here we were having the kind of sex that people only dream about!

I began to respond in kind. "Yeah you fuckin' whore, ya like that huh? Ya like my cock filling up your wet pussy? Your pussy likes my fat ass cock pounding away? Huh? You bitch?"

I never spoke to a woman this way before, but this was like a fucking boxing match.

Believe it or not, we actually climaxed together after what seemed an eternity and lay there completely spent and exhausted, yet knowing instinctively that the evening had just begun.

We fell asleep for a few hours in a puddle of juices that could feed a small army of starving ants. I awoke several hours later to find her staring at me on one elbow. At that point, she looked in my eyes and uttered the only words that could be considered even close to a compliment.

"I'll give you one thing. You sure ain't no limp dick!"

I just shook my head and lay back down as her hands slid down south and began to rub me back towards another erection. There was no stopping this fucking slut, but who am I to judge since I was matching her every step of the way. I do not know why.

After my missile reached the desired trajectory, she climbed on top of me and began to buck like a bronco, having an orgasm almost instantly. I rolled her off and turned her around so that I could enter her dripping, hot, sweaty ass from behind. I was so engorged at this point that she complained slightly as I eased my way inside her slowly. I truly do not think that women understand the feeling a man gets when in that position of power. You are ramming your rock hard cock inside a woman and slapping her ass, pulling her hair, and she is so totally loving every inch of you that you cannot believe you're doing this! She had such an amazing ass that although I was suffering from sleep deprivation and tired from earlier activities, I did not want to stop and indeed went well beyond the point of physical exhaustion. After all, with all the slurs being hurled at me, I couldn't let this bitch down, could I? When I started it was 2:35 A.M. When I finished with her it was nearly 3:30 A.M. I was shocked. I thought I was going to surely die or never have sex again. I collapsed after coming inside her for the third time and did not hear another word she said until I felt a strange sensation a few hours later. The sensation was ice melting and being dripped on my balls and stomach. I looked at her with one eye open as that's all I could manage at that point.

"Have mercy," I said. She had none to give. She wasn't done with me yet.

At this point I was truly wondering if you indeed can die from engaging in too much sex. She sat on my face and would not move until I either suffocated, or turned her over and ate her bald box once again. I ate. She came. Again and again she came until, finally awake and thirsty, I got up for a glass of water. No ice this time!

I sat next to her and just stared at this machine who had taken the very best and the very worst of me, and spat it right back at me. Then we were doing it again. We did it on the floor. We did it standing. We did it kneeling. We did it in the bathroom, and just before the paramedics came to take me away, we came together yet one more time while she rode me backwards, on top facing away from me.

"How dare you fuck the princess like this? No one fucks the princess like this and gets away with it! You better buy me coffee you shit bastard!"

We got dressed. She didn't want to shower with me. In fact, she wouldn't allow me to shower at all. We dragged our asses out to my car. I held onto her as neither one of us was walking quite normally. She didn't seem to want me to drive her all the way home, but instead had me stop at a local deli near her house where I gave her a dollar for coffee. She didn't want me to come inside with her. She never called me back and I never called her.

Her last message to me was as filthy and degrading as one would expect from this fucking lunatic. Since I never wanted to see her again, I did not respond. This was something that was alien to me as I have been told I'm a very gentle lover. I enjoy slow. I enjoy teasing. I enjoy living for the pleasure of my partner. None of that existed between us. It was merely an athletic competition. More so though, it was like an audition. I do believe I passed!

At completely the opposite end of the sexual spectrum stands Melissa. I met her online and we chatted sweetly for several weeks until I suggested a meeting. Because we lived several hundred miles apart and I was moving that weekend, she volunteered to help me move if I would drive the ten hours roundtrip to pick her up. She had a look to her that I found very appealing, so I agreed. It was indeed a crazy thing to do, but I have few regrets, as she was the sexual opposite of Priscilla in many ways.

I arrived at her humble home to find laundry strewn in every conceivable direction. I'm thinking this girl must be a complete pig since she was expecting me and didn't manage to tidy up. Messy yes, pig no. When she told me to come in, I sat on a chair and she just ran into the room, became airborne and landed squarely in my lap! She's about five foot three and 105 pounds dripping wet, with long, straight brown hair and *huge* brown eyes to match, petite to the nth degree. She kissed me passionately on the mouth, giggled playfully, grabbed me by the hand and dragged me down to the beach two blocks away to watch the tide coming in. We walked around town while she finished her chores and she barely left my side for a moment as her affection and desire to please me were very apparent.

We gassed up the car and she even paid for it! We stopped for a late lunch on the way down and arrived at my new, yet filthy apartment just before sundown. She was very playful in the car and I was starting to like her a bit more as time went by. There was something a little strange about her though. She seemed to have an energy level that was almost inhuman.

We watched the sunset through my living room windows and then got down to some cleaning. Afterwards, we had a quick bite for dinner. I was tired from driving most of the day, so I decided to lay down in my spare bedroom, (the only one with a bed at that point) and she came in to join me. She caressed the hair away from my face as I sighed in appreciation, and then started to nibble on my neck.

Oh man, when a woman does that the right way and at the right time, it just gives you goose bumps all over! I turned onto my back and she straddled her way on top of me and smiled in the most naughty way, sending further delightful goose bumps everywhere! She lay on top of me, kissing me gently at first, until we could not take it any longer and began attacking each others' mouths with reckless abandon. I began to attack her neck, which seemed to be something that she *really* liked. I let my mouth devour her in ever-widening circles of tongue movements, nibbles, and hard kisses that elicited the cutest sounds from her petite frame.

We suddenly stopped and regained our composure for a moment. I asked her where she wanted to go with this, and her answer was immediate. She smiled, opened my jeans, and slowly, with almost painful leisure, slid the zipper down with her adorable mouth. This was passion. This was teasing. This was *so* me!

We spent the next half hour fighting off each other's advances, as we each wanted to be the first to please the other. I finally fought my way between her legs, but she said to me that she could not ever have an orgasm until her man had one first. Where the hell have *you* been all my life? So she pushed me onto the bed and oozed her way between my legs. I knew I was in deep trouble when she gently but firmly took my cock in both hands, caressing in opposite circular motions, and finally thrusting her sweet mouth over the head and slowly all the way down the shaft, leaving my eyes firmly planted at the back of my head. She circled her way back up the shaft, never leaving an inch unattended and smiled.

"I can tell you're enjoying this," she said.

"You are simply amazing. Your mouth is the dream of every man," I returned.

She had that magical talent of feeling every pulse of my penis and, amazingly, responding to it in ways that few ever do. She loved what she was doing and wanted it to last a very long time.

"You are so dead when I get to you," I said.

She giggled and decided that it was indeed time to "bring me home." With one hand caressing my balls and the other working in concert with her perfect mouth, she gave me one of the most intense orgasms I ever experienced. It was just a preview of things to come however. She swallowed everything I had gleefully provided, and immediately allowed me to taste myself as she kissed me passionately. My head was spinning. This girl was a dream!

I removed her shirt to find the teensiest little breasts I had ever seen. I slowly began to kiss every inch of her body as she responded with moans of appreciation. She took as well as she gave, and it seemed that I gave as well as I took too!

I teased her with my mouth for quite some time, circling her inner thighs with my tongue, caressing her pussy lips and blowing gently on her clitoris but not giving her what she desired. Not just yet. I had become erect once again, and decided to tease her with only the head of my cock. I rubbed it playfully across her pussy with particular care to gently caress her clitoris several times. She was getting a little agitated as I smiled and joked about payback! I returned to my knees and gave her that one, wet, deep, long lick that her body desired on that one spot we all know so well. I smiled.

As she said, "I am going to kill you soon!" I buried my head where the sun don't shine and my swirling, wet tongue brought her to the place she desperately wanted to go.

We held each other gently for several minutes and then watched some television. Unlike Priscilla, Melissa was in no hurry and seemed very content to just be held in my arms...for a while anyway!

We had some amazing sex that night, but it was sweet, passionate and caring, not at all like the marathon I had with Priscilla. Yet it lasted almost as long, in a more gentle and kind way. Melissa was the type of woman who would look directly into your eyes while fucking your brains out. Do you have any idea how erotic that is? She'd stare right at me and say things like, "You like that don't you? Uh huh! Uh huh! You really like when I fuck you like this don't you? Isn't my pussy soft and wet and doesn't it feel sooo fucking good?" She made me feel like a God. It was so special being with her that it's difficult to put it into the correct words here. Priscilla was erotic in a very different, very angry sort of way. There is a place for the type of sex I had with Priscilla, but nine times out of ten, if not more, I would prefer the primal yet gentler fucking I received from Melissa...hands down.

We cleaned and moved the entire next day, as she seemed almost furious in her passion to help me. I was amazed at her inhuman energy level. She never seemed to stay still for a moment, unless that is, she was still in my arms. Nice; very, very nice. Yet something bothered me in the back of my mind. Something I ignored partly because this girl was a dream in bed, and partly because she wasn't too shabby out of it either.

I discovered on that second day the level of this woman's naughtiness as two cable guys came over to install my cable TV. They were both working in my bedroom running wires when Melissa grabbed me by the hand and walked me into the bathroom, which was also located inside my bedroom. The two Spanish guys just looked on. She closed the door, but managed to leave it open just a crack. At this point, she pulled my pants down to my ankles and began to give me one of the most erotic blowjobs I've ever had in my life. She was not quiet about it. She did not swallow everything I provided, but instead seemed quite pleased that some cum was dripping off her cheek and down her chin as we exited the bathroom. She gave the cable guys a wink and I thought I was going to die!

This girl was *sooo* bad! She did that on purpose, just to tease the hell out of these poor working guys. Jeez! I will never forget that moment and the look on those two guys as I was obviously blushing pure red. As they prepared to leave, I attempted to tip them and they declined.

"No man, keep it," he said as he smiled. I just looked at the floor and laughed as Melissa shook both their hands before they left, the jizz still on her face. What a girl!

There were many more moments similar to that one in varying degrees. The following night, as we were going at it in my just-arrived futon, she climbed exuberantly on top of me and began to grind me down to hamburger meat with her small, firm and hungry thighs. We loved this position because she's very limber and, being so petite, she was easy to maneuver, so it was fun experimenting with many unusual positions that not every girl can handle. As she was riding me like a prized stallion she suddenly stopped, smiled that naughty Melissa smile, and swung her body around 180 degrees never letting my cock leave the warmth of her amazing pussy. When she looked back at me, I was probably near dead with amazement. What *was* this girl going to do next? Didn't she realize that she was ruining me for lesser women (that being most every woman on the planet!)? Her tooshie was small but very round and adorable, and it looked so wonderful going up and down, up and down on my shocked male member. She instinctively knew when I was close to orgasm and started to rock faster and harder so that we could cum together. We did.

It was possibly the most erotic orgasm of my life and left me shaking with a happiness that I have rarely felt for any woman. Perhaps the happiness I was feeling was not just based on the physical since we had at this point spent over 72 hours together, and a good deal of that time was spent making love, or hugging, or just being together. Once again she did a 180 degree turn without ever rising up and just held me in her arms. Total and complete bliss was what I felt at that moment. It was….. indescribable to say the least.

It was to be our final moment of that sort.

The following day she seemed more agitated and energetic that ever and asked me to drive her to a clinic in Mount Vernon, NY. Since it was nearby, I did, but was surprised that it was in a very bad neighborhood. I suggested that I walk her in, but she asked me to remain in the car and wait. This seemed very odd to me, so after a few minutes of waiting I approached the door and was stopped by an armed guard. An *armed guard*? What the fuck?

I asked him what this place was, and he told me that it was a methadone clinic. I said, "Isn't Methadone just used for heroin addicts?" He responded, "Dunno, but that's prolly true."

I was floored. Everything became very clear all of a sudden. I was really upset because I truly liked this girl in so many ways, but no *way* in hell am I going to stick around an addict of *any* kind.

She returned to the car much calmer and with a big happy smile on her face. I was not smiling in return. She explained that she never used drugs and that it was for other reasons that she was on the methadone, but I didn't believe her. Her lifestyle, which I knew quite a bit about due to our conversations, included biker ex-boyfriends who still wanted her, being a bartender, being in trouble with the authorities on many occasions, and so much more which pointed to the facts that she was now denying.

The growing relationship deteriorated badly over the next few days since I was continuously asking her to leave. She did not want to but eventually went to the city to be with some other guy she had never met, and within a day had taken the bus home north.

We never spoke again, much to my dismay, but I will cherish much of the time that I spent with this little imp. I do miss her, because she was truly unique. My only regret is that we met at a time in our lives where we were both going through very hard times. What a shame. I have never met anyone quite like her since. Damn…

Next comes a letter from Breezy. She's the girl from Florida that chatted with me naughtily online over several months. This was one of several letters that she sent to me of this sort, but this one was the best.

Dear David,
   Y'know when you type all that sexy crap to me I'm always at work! It ain't fair dude! So I figured since you leave me wiggling in my chair as well as moist between the legs nearly every time we chat, that it was payback time. So here's the deal my horny friend as I can write too, and now yer gonna get yers!!!

We're in my apartment and the sea breeze is blowing our hair gently across our naked shoulders as we caress on the soft, large couch outside. You are amazed at the size of my beautiful breasts but even so they seem so firm as your mouth glides gently over their fullness. We explore the softness of each other's mouths, missing not a shape or corner as our tongues dance the dance of never-ending bliss in their passion to taste every nuance of the wetness therein. We embrace in a way that lovers do after many years of exploring each other, yet we have just met so this amazes us both in the most glorious way.

You sweep me up in your firm, muscular arms and lay me gently on the plush rug just adjacent to the dark fireplace, as it is summer and warm both inside and out, not as warm however as our growing passion for each other's loins this evening. I push you onto your back and circle my tongue around your belly button, leaving a silky, wet trail of saliva to mark my path to the final destination of your engorged cock. I put just the tip into my beautiful mouth and you smile that smile that men do when they know they're about to be very satisfied. I lick gently down the shaft keeping always a determined grip on your cock so that the pressure is firm, yet as soft as my beautiful derriere. I then take you full into my mouth swallowing all of you entirely as I gag in appreciation of your size. You arch your back as this seems to please you greatly and I circle my mouth around and around and around again yet never remove it from your hotly pulsing member. I tease you slowly just with my tongue, as I smile that smile that elicits a passion that few know or even understand. Once again I plunge your firmness deep into the velvet abyss of my throat as you release a flood of hot jizz deep into my mouth, sliding down my throat as well as releasing the after flood onto my face and neck. I now share this bounty with your mouth as I smile and ask "well, how do you taste tough guy?"

You don't answer, as you are too busy making a meal of my mouth, then my neck and onto the fullness of my amazing breasts! You tease me for what seems like an eternity as your mouth makes ever wider, ever hotter, circles on the fullness of the globes that you have been blessed to be caressing this very evening. You then smile naughtily and lift both my legs behind my head and enter me with a fullness I have never felt before. One thrust and you remove your entirety to tease me with only your velvety soft head. I sigh in frustration as I realize now that your skills may indeed equal my own. You slide gently, slowly, carefully down my body, caressing with your hands, your mouth, your tongue and yes even your teeth in a seething frenzy that is making me very compliant. You arrive at your destination and draw wide circles on my inner thigh with your dripping wet tongue. "OH it feels soooo good David!" I sigh, and you smile in gratification. You glide slowly, ever more closely to that one spot on my pussy that you seem to know, as if you had been there for years and not just arrived for the first time this night. You lick my clitoris with a firmness that sends my thighs careening toward the ceiling as you laugh at my lack of resistance. Circles. Wet, hot, spinning, caressing, fulfilling, blinding, amazing circles of your tongue make the very meal of my pussy that women only dream of as they squirm in their erotic sleep….. but you are not allowing me to release as yet and back off to tease me yet again with your rock hard cock. You slide inside me violently and ride my sweet box with an abandon and lack of caring for it's sweet gentleness. You truly care not as you are now feeling the glow of a beckoning explosion, but yet again I am bewildered as you exit me and smile yet again. "I HATE YOU" I elicit as you feel your way back to the promised-land of my now very frustrated, very abused, extremely wet and drippy pussy! You engorge me with your mouth. I have never had my pussy sucked in just the right way in just the right spot before. I cum in a frenzy of screams and agitation yet you refuse to stop. "NO MORE< PLEASE NO MORE" I say, yet you hold me down with you arms and continue the barrage. It tickles in a way that is nearly unbearable, yet I soon settle down to the warm glow building steadily inside my rocking torso and soon explode inside your mouth, yet again, with a flood that leaves you gasping for air, yet desperately proud of your accomplishment.

We hug. We lay exhausted in each other's arms for what seems like an eternity as we tickle playfully and feel the passion beginning to build yet again, like the embers of a fire that suddenly feel a burst of oxygen.

Howzat, ya horny bastard? I dare you to continue the story! Lets see if you can write a letter as well as you type an I.M.

Tag, you're it!

Breezy….. teee heee…….

It took me the better part of a week to recover from this note. To say the least, the woman I was seeing when I received this, was *quite pleased* that weekend as I lived out my fantasies through her…again and again and again!

I thought for a while about a good way to respond to this incredible note, yet the only way is, of course, to reciprocate.

Dear Breezy,

As I write this note you'll need to know that I'm just five minutes from your house. I will be handing it to you in person as I watch the look on your face as you realize that I am standing directly in front of you, ready and willing to call your amazing bluff!

However you asked me to continue the story so I will attempt at least to not only respond in kind, but to do it in a flowery girlie style that you'll no doubt appreciate! It ain't my style, but I do believe that you'll like it just the same.

As we lay there on the softness of your plush rug, slowly appreciating the wetness that seeped out of our bodies, we enjoy the smell of sex all around us. You realize now that you not only knocked over a lamp with your thrashing, but that we never did close the glass doors, now open for all the world to see our love making. You blush. I don't buy it! You touch my face so gently with your fingers that it sends a chill down my spine and a volume to my cock, which is ready for liftoff in round two. I turn you around and enter you from behind with a thrust that brings a deep growl to your lips, but then slowly, gently drive myself through your torso with ever deeper motions, ever wider, ever hotter, leaving you gleeful in the sweet light of the moon rising outside. I slap your ass with the fullness of my cupped right hand as I grab your left cheek so aggressively that you yelp "OUCH!" You laugh as I let myself slide from you and turn you once again to face me for the kill! I slowly glide my firm arms up your soft legs and pin them behind your golden tressed head, entering your dripping pussy so slowly as it seems I accomplished it all in one single gliding motion. You moan happily as I just leave my entire cock inside you, unmoving, until your body starts to rock back and forth in an aggravated attempt to convince me to give you more. As gently as I entered you, this is now how viciously I am violating the hollowed ground of your pleading but happy love triangle. I am pounding you with every ounce of energy in my body as you scream "OHHHHHH give it to me noooowwww!!!!! OHH-HHH....GODDDDDD.... OHHHHH!!!!!" and suddenly, amazingly, just as I had started, I suddenly stop, stare deeply into your stunning blue eyes and ask "well, are ya ready?" and you respond as you smile "ohhhhhh yesssss."

I begin to grind you slowly. You develop a smile as we move together as if choreographed by a champion dance instructor with a whip at the ready if we dared not move in exactly the right way. We are grinding each other into hamburger as we move together, up and down, left and right, breathing ever more labored as it is seems to be getting quite warm this fine summer evening. The glow begins to spread throughout our coupled bodies as we both realize that we are leading up to the utter joy of a spontaneous explosive orgasm, all the while retaining the splendor of each other's frozen gaze, open mouth's and labored breathing. We erupt together. It is as if the entire world has stopped just so we could have this moment in time, this utterly blissful moment that neither one of us may ever repeat with another lover as it is pure, unadulterated ecstasy.

We lay exhausted, content in each other's arms. We cannot speak for if we did speak any words they would assuredly pale in comparison to the perfect sexual moments we had just shared together. We kiss gently, so gently that we both shiver at the marvelous perfection of the human mouth, and the unbelievable bliss it can share with a mouth of similar design, similar thought, and similar skills. We kiss and kiss and kiss and then we kiss some more until a tiny, distant ember becomes a burning flame, and once again we are engaging in a frenzied effort to begin another session of lovemaking that will surely end the evening, as we could not survive another go-round after this one! I begin to mount you yet again but you push me away with a fury that belittles your petite frame. You then utter "no boy, you've been in control for a while, now it's MY turn to steer this machine."

You throw me onto my back and lick just the tip of my waiting, rock hard cock, and wink as you then crawl towards me slowly, painfully and lift your supple muscular thighs onto my waiting engorged rocket and slide them over me, enveloping me in the sheer exhilaration of a perfect moment. You do not move as you are paying me back for earlier disciplines of the flesh. You grin. It is an evil grin that has known many lovers, yet few as passionate as the evil we are sharing this twilight together. You lift up your ample bottom and initiate a sort of swirling, thrusting motion that rolls my eyes deeply into the recesses of my eye sockets, as you've no doubt nearly killed all who have cum before me! *grin*

I attempt to match the frenzy of your strokes but realize that my spine cannot possibly match the sheer exquisite passion that only a woman can endure as she rides her lover like a prized Montana Mustang. Suddenly, miraculously and after what seems like days, you thrust your torso onto me one seemingly final time, yet again, and yet again as if time is standing still between each stroke of your pussy on my cock.... and I realize that you are having an orgasm for the ages.

You lift up to stare into my eyes as I have not yet released my juices inside of your body and you wonder at this. You rise silently to leave the room and re-enter it with a tube of some foreign substance. I have no idea what you're up to but soon realize with a glint in your eye that you intend to please me in a way I've never attempted or been offered before. You cover my throbbing manhood with the silky substance, smile one final time, face away from me and mount me slowly, ever so slowly, as I feel tightness I have never experienced. You exhale deeply and let slip a deep sigh as I realize that I indeed am not inside your pussy, but instead you have brought the final tool in your arsenal to bear, your tight, perfect, ample, round ass is now lifting up slowly and sliding back down just as deliberately onto to my almost shell-shocked cock. You explain that I cannot move or I will hurt you badly as you have only tried this once, with mixed results. You glide yet again first up, then slowly back down as the fires of my soul begin to burn in a red hot frenzy to THRUST, VIOLENTLY......yet I dare not, so I stay awaiting the frenzied release that will not be long in coming. Three, four, five, six and seven more times you ride my cock which by now is glistening with a mix of juices and aromas never experienced before until finally, gratefully you allow the blissful release of my cum into your perfect ass cavity, as you scream one final time "aaaaaAAAAAGGGGHHHH!" as we are completely done for the night.

You lay your head on my stomach but I pick you up and carry you into bed, where we fall asleep cradled in each other's loving arms, for an evening, for a lifetime, for an eternity..... if only in our dreams.....

Howzat pookie??????

...D...just me!!! =)

Prepare yourself now. Earlier in the book I had mentioned a girl named Vixen and her propensity for eating a nice warm pussy rather than a rock hard cock. She does not like men, yet for some strange reason, she took a liking to me! Again, I would describe her as the penultimate dyke. She's large, overweight but muscular, brutally honest; extremely angry and pretty much despises anything that does not please her. Typical vegan, black-tressed, foul-mouthed, dressed in black, chain dangling from oversized carpenter pants New York woman! Yeah, she eats no meat of *any* kind except for that which is found in her obsessive search for that one perfect pussy to eat, and to eat her in return!

After sending several somewhat sedate yet suggestive notes to each other online, she sent off the following letter to me and both locked-in a friendship, of sorts, as well as forever engraining herself in my mind as the author of a story that needed to be told. There really *are* women out there like this so be afraid….. be *very* afraid!

> Dear shithead,
>   Just what kinda sick crap is it you're writing to me? Don't fuckin' tell me you're one a those cry baby assholes who buy dinner for their girl and then take them home, kiss them on the cheek and say goodnight? What a fuckin' wimp! *grin*…only kidding! I can tell based on your weak attempts at talking about oral sex that you indeed just MIGHT know what you're talking about. Do you KNOW how fuckin' rare that is for a man??? Shit I'm thinkin' that I might buy YOU a beer!!!!…….NOT! I actually (and I hate to admit this) used to like guys…. for like 5 minutes a loooong time ago, but then I came to my senses. You're really all just a big bag a shit wrapped up with occasional muscle tone to make the shit appear more amenable. What's totally fucked-up is the better the asshole usually looks, the bigger loser they usually are! I mean what the fuck??? Did you guys ALL miss the line for brains while you were off in the corner masturbating to some chick mag? OH< and what's the deal with your balls anyway? Aren't they supposed to be filled with juice so that you can go all night???? So why do you all poop out after we're just getting started??? *sheesh*….. lookit…. Now I'm even startin' ta write like you!!! What the fuck did you do to me anyway? Why AM I wasting my time writing to a cock bag anyway? I guess there might be hope fer yer race after all….. dickwad!
>   So I wanted to make you fuckin' nuts and tell you about last night. DAMN you shoulda' been a fly on my ass! There's a certain bar I go to in the Village, you know the sort, where all the people with brains, not balls hang out. So there's this chick and she is SOOOOOO fuckin' hot and I'm thinkin' "oh shit I've gotta be with her"…. so I walked over and attempted to be civil, but you know me! I asked if I could buy her a drink so she says that she's waiting for her boyfriend and could I just leave her alone? Her boyfriend? WTF? Guys almost never come to this joint and if they do they're almost always fags. So I kinda called her on it and she said that she was new. For you stupid ass males out there "new" means that she's never been with a woman but might

be open to it. Further for you cock bags it also elicits an excitement in us that is difficult to describe, it's like "OH SHIT, I can be her first!"

So she let me buy her a drink, and another, and another, and yet another until she could barely walk and was getting REALLY fuckin' friendly. We left together and walked to my apartment, which is just a couple blocks from the bar. Damn dude, when I laid her down on my bed I actually started to shake! This bitch was perfect! I ripped off her clothes and started to bite her ass as I wanted her to know what she had in store. I guess I bit a little too hard though because she was bleeding a little and wanted to leave. "No fuckin' way bitch, you ain't leavin'!" so I threw her ass back down on the bed and started to eat her sweet blonde pussy like she never felt a guy do! Man she really liked that and just started rockin' and shakin' and finally started to fuckin' scream her ass off so loud that my asshole neighbor was poundin' on the wall! Dude I was SO freakin' proud! So I figured that it was time for her to return the favor but she didn't seem too pleased with that idea. WTF? Like you got a choice bitch? So I threw her candy ass back on the bed and started to grind her face under my ass. She made a weak attempt at eating me, but I guess she just wasn't ready, or too tired, scared, or drunk.... Whatever!

I was fuckin' pissed! I mean if I wanted to be frustrated I'd have picked up a man! So she fell asleep and I sat there angry as a fuckin' bee who was just bitch slapped! I figured what the hell so I just crawled in next to her and got cozy. So believe it or not this seemed to warm her up and she starts to grab my tits and suck them better that I EVER thought she would. Just a little secret about me, I REALLY like my tits sucked...like a LOT!!! She was doing a great job too as her tongue seemed to be working in these awesome wet circles and getting wetter by the minute (how ya feelin' dude!? *smile*) and then she turns up the heat and slides her thumb into my pussy! OH FUCK, this was really fuckin' good now! My heads like spinnin' around between the alcohol and her fingers, which were now rubbing me really good! Well I get a little violent when I'm getting ready to cum so I grabbed her by the hair and rammed her face into my pussy, she surprised me again because with her fingers still inside me she ate me to heaven like I would have dreamed and just before I came she put her pinky up my ass pushing me over the edge! OH CRAP! I swear I thought of you at that point!........ yeah..... RIGHT!

So we played like this and she kept surprising me all night long and by the morning I think she was even crazier than me! AWESOME!!!! That's one more fem in New York for me to call when I need a good fucking!

I kicked her ass out the door in the morning and said I'd call her. Maybe I will and maybe I won't! If you buy me a few beers dude maybe I'll let you watch next time! HA!

In yer dreams!!!

Vixen...=I

Now do you see why I like this girl? We've never met and perhaps never will, but I do love getting her occasional letters and believe that she likes my dumb responses….. even if I am a "cockbag!"

I will give you one final story now from a friend who I will not identify. She is in a relationship now and will no doubt give me a fistful of crap if I give any indication of who she is, so I'll just let you guess who she might be.

> Do you have any idea girls what it's like to be with a man who knows your body better than you do? I can say that I do and that my sex life will never be quite the same! I'm not the type to kiss and tell but I have been asked to discuss a point so that's what I'll do.
>
> We had been dating for several weeks and the sex was amazing between David and I. He left me physically exhausted on many occasions, yet upon arrival at work the following day I'd always get looks from the staff as if something had changed in me. Perhaps it was the ear-to-ear grin and the fact that my feet barely touched the ground!
>
> I arrived at his apartment on a Friday evening and we decided to just remain home and watch a movie. We didn't quite get through the movie though as within 15 minutes we were kissing passionately and by the time David attacked my neck with that hungry mouth I grabbed him and RAN him up to the bedroom!
>
> He seemed even more passionate than usual (which is nearly impossible!) and within moments I had exploded in typical fashion into his waiting mouth. We always started our evenings this way but tonight would be slightly different, as I would shortly find out. I guess I'm like many women in the respect that once I cum I get very ticklish "down there" and push David away as I cannot take one more of his amazing licks! He would usually enter me deeply and then cum himself with a wondrously happy look while gazing deeply into my eyes, but tonight would be different.
>
> He held me down with his powerful arms and continued the onslaught on my nether regions. It's difficult to describe how it felt to me at that point as I was desperately attempting to get away, but he would not allow me to. It's sort of like ants crawling over you but dipped in warm honey first? Many of you realize that there is that one tiny spot we have that just BEGS to be caressed in just the right manner, by just the right tongue on just the right guy. Well, he WAS that guy! I could NOT get away from him! AAARRGHH! It tickled so much that tears were streaming down my face onto my neck, but at the same time it was becoming apparent to me that something else was indeed happening as a warm glow began to spread throughout my body. It started at my toes and slowly and precariously worked it's way up to the middle of my ravaged body. I realized now that I did NOT want to get away as my head was swimming in a sea of feelings that I could not comprehend, yet did not want to

cease as I needed to see where these feelings would take me. I began to unconsciously lift my torso beneath his mouth so he grabbed me by the ass and used his elbows like a tripod as he made a meal of me. Ohhhhh.... To get that complete and total attention from a man who knows, really really KNOWS what he's doing is..... indescribable! The warmth was now fast becoming a raging inferno as I came in an explosion of juices that left me shocked yet he was not yet through with me. His lovely tongue swirled faster and harder on the erection that my clitoris had provided for him as if it were saying "here I am, come get me again my love!" I came a third time, then a fourth as I finally lost count and just prayed that it would never end as I had never been able to achieve multiple orgasms before tonight.

True to form, David entered me with his hungry erection but I was incapable of doing anything but be compliant as I was too pooped to shoot! When he was done with me he laughed, got up to get a drink of water as I just lay there shaking like a leaf in a hurricane. My legs did not stop shaking for well over a half hour, funny though how that didn't bother me much! David seemed quite pleased with himself; especially the next day as I called in sick to work for fear that if I went in my legs would assuredly collapse beneath me!

We had many more evenings of that sort in the coming months so I'll leave you with one thought girls, if the guy you're with does not leave you exhausted and happy after sex, then you need to find someone who does!!!

Amen to *that* folks, Amen to that!

11

Success stories

Total bliss. The feeling you have after an amazingly perfect date comes to an end and you're in your car going home, glowing. You know it was an incredible date because you didn't feel *this* way after the last 10 dates ended. You didn't laugh this hard, feel this good, or float quite this high. You didn't feel this way when most of your dates kissed you goodnight, and by the way, most of your dates also didn't kiss you goodbye for 90 minutes like this one did. Perhaps that's why you're fantasizing about the house you'll live in together. The color the drapes will be, the size of your bedroom, the size of your BED! The names of your children, the town you'll live in, and what your friends will think of them.

You can live an entire lifetime with a person just on the drive home from a first date that went blissfully well. You can gather such extreme expectations of your prospective mate based on all those that have already been met, that they may never live up to them, so *chill out* and just enjoy the moment!

The purpose of this chapter is to discuss success stories, both great and small. Some are just beginning, some are well on their way, and some are nearing their completion, but they will all give you a warm glow because, dear reader, they can just as easily happen to you.

As usual, I will start with myself as the test dummy…um, what I meant was, I'll tell you about a young lady who e-mailed me recently and what happened from there. This is her basic profile on Match.com:

<u>How she describes Herself</u>
I am a fun single mom seeking a fun man who likes to go to dinner, movies, plays, dancing, etc. I have a great sense of humor and love to laugh. I am honest and want respect. I like taking vacations and love the beach. I enjoy walking/running and being outdoors. I am easy to talk to and can be a great friend. Friends first, then romance. Please reply if you are interested.

How she describes her ideal match

I am seeking a fun, good looking man, with a great sense of humor. I would like to meet someone who enjoys going on dates, visiting new places, likes the outdoors, and likes children. I am looking for a man who can be a true friend. Someone who is real and not a phony. Someone who really enjoys life, and is interested in spending time with me.

The following is the series of letters that pre-dated our first meeting. Read them if you dare!

Wow to both your picture and profile.

Double Wow to your ideal match. I love to kiss, cuddle on the couch and am so much looking for the right person to come home to and look in their eyes and have my belly do flip flops. It's been a while. I like to have fun, laugh, eat out, enjoy movies and the theater. I am looking for a best friend, who I can be myself around which includes being silly, goofy and romantic. I firmly believe in helping the man becoming everything he can be and would like the same in return. Have you ever dated a Jersey girl....we are lots of fun. I also enjoy music, writing poetry, dancing, watching movies and eating popcorn. I am very active and keep in shape. Please respond so we can get acquainted...you sound very interesting!

Charley...

Yup, that's right. This is my buddy Charley. I think you're going to like this story as told by us both.

Jersey Girls RULE!!!!!!

Well, wow back atcha! Not only do I PREFER Jersey girls, with kids (hey, mine gotta have someone to play with while we're busy doing, um, stuff! *giggle*) but I even know where Madd lake is! I lived in Pompton Lakes NJ for 2 years, and only moved back to the city 3 months ago, to be close to my kids. In fact Pompton would probably be a good midpoint between us to meet for coffee, assuming there's some chemistry on the phone, that is! I hope you love to laugh, and cuddle, and kiss, 'cause if you do, you're in for the ride of your life with me! I'd also love to see some more pics of you (that's just the photographer in me!) so if ya got some, send 'em to dosterczy@whatever.com...okee dokey smokey? Chat with ya soon! *hugs*...David...

◆   ◆   ◆

Hi David,

Glad to hear back from you so soon! You seem a lot like my type with your energy level, sense of humor and the romantic side to ya. Unfortunately I do not have more pictures I can send you but that should keep you curious and interested…there has to be some mystery about this match.com. I can assure you, you won't be disappointed. I keep myself in shape and do not weigh 300 pounds. I am 5'5" and weigh below 130. How old are your children? And I do love to laugh, cuddle and kiss. Where do you work? I work in Pittsfield, so Pompton would be a good point or somewhere near there. What about some more pictures of you???

Chat with you soon!

Charley…

◆   ◆   ◆

Your name is Charley?????? Hmmmmmmm,,,,,, how eeeenteresteeeeeng!!!! So, ya don't wanna send me more pics, eh? Well, to answer some of your Q's, Sammy is 7 and is a rock on the outside, like his dad! He is also a puppy dog on the inside, and as affectionate as they get…also like his dad!!! Sherry is 9, and is the clown of the family. She's also as moody as they get. She's gonna be that woman driving on the highway, and steering with her knee as she drinks her 32 oz. black coffee, and yells on her cell phone!!! Melanie is 19, and is the adult in the family (not me!!! I don't wanna grow up, I'm a Toys-r-us kid!!! LOL). She usually lives with me, but in her old age has decided to develop a closer relationship with her mom. She goes to SUPA Pittsburgh, and majors in computer science, with a graphic design minor…smarty pants!!!! She's the biggest tomboy going ('cause I raised her alone) but also has a girlie girl side to her as well. I work from home, as I'm a writer (starving artist syndrome!!) waiting for my first book to be published. Soooooooo,,,,, there ya go, now tell me a bunch about yourself, and your kids as well. Mystery is good, but I'll need to know a little more about you before I decide to meet…. okee dokey smokey?…. See ya soon!…*hugs*…D…

◆   ◆   ◆

Well, first off, why is my name so eeenteresteeeeeng? I have been a single mom for almost 4 years now and like having my own apartment, but would like to meet a partner, buy a house and settle down one day again. If it were the right person, I would marry again. I have an 8 year old daughter, Jeanette, her smile brightens up a room and she is a lot like her mom. Funny, sensitive, has beautiful green eyes and likes a lot of love. I really enjoy being with my kids. I also have a 6 year old son, Anatolle, we call him "Tony the terror" because he loves to tease his sister. He is funnier than ever though…a real character. It's hard to get mad a such a cute face. All of the women love him. I work for Platzxo and am in the Human Resources Department for the Sales Division. We are preparing for our acquisition with Peepeepants, so work has been pretty busy. As far as my personal life goes…I like to stay in shape which includes walking and running. I like to go out to eat, to the movies, like to see shows on broadway and would like to get some skiing in this winter. I love the beach and rent a house for a week in July every summer. I am a very easy person to talk to, have a great sense of humor and am "very real". Well enough from me for now. What else would you like to know? You may call me and we can talk this evening if you would like. 973-000-0000. I will be home after 7pm.

    Take care!

    Charley…

Well, since I had her number, I had to use it, right? So I called her that night, and we just spoke for hours. That's what happens when two people click really well. The time just passes and hours go by. You suddenly realize that you're yawning more that you're talking and it's time to go to sleep…you just don't want to yet!

We set a date to meet for coffee and a bite and the following ensued:

Good morning BeeBee, or is it BeBe?

    I am anxious to hear the Purple BeeBee stories…my daughter's favorite color is purple and like I said, my son calls his blanket BeeBee.

    It was nice talking with you last night….I had a hard time falling asleep….my brain was racing with all of the information you shared with me. You are a real unique guy with lots of interests, lots of feeling and a great sense of humor. I am definitely interested and am curious to see if the chemistry is as "electric" as the conversation. You have a very sensual side to you….that you reveal in small doses! I will talk to you later!!!

    Take Care and keep on writing….I actually have a poem I wrote about dating…maybe I will share it with you, if you would like, as well as my apple crisp…tomorrow night!

    Hugs to you!!

    Charley…

I was out early the morning of that letter, so when she didn't get a response, she sent this!

Good afternoon David!!!

What are you doing? What are you thinking about? Looking forward to meeting you in person tonight!!!

See ya later!

Charley…

◆   ◆   ◆

Whaddaya think I'm doing silly? I'm writing my book, and praying for some decent checks to arrive!!! Looking forward to seeing U 2!!!…D…

So we met at a small coffee shop, inside of a local supermarket in Pompton Lakes. I know, it doesn't sound too romantic, but it was the best I could do owing to my, er, finances! As I pulled into the parking lot, I was just hoping that she looked a *little* bit like her cute photo. Well, she far surpassed it, and I guess she felt the same way as the first reaction to me was a warm, friendly hug.

When you start a date with that kind of warmth, you just *know* it's going to be a nice evening. We talked for hours, and after several refills and her awesome lukewarm apple crisp, we decided to go sit by the lake and talk. Suffice it to say, there was a really big physical attraction for both of us and we didn't end up doing a whole lot of talking. Once we regained our senses though, we decided that a second date was definitely something we both wanted and discussed some of the details. We then drove back to the supermarket, said our goodbyes, and drove off, separately, into the dark night.

These are some of the discussions over the two days that followed.

Good morning to you!

I was up at 5:30 am….auto alarm clock in my head. Made coffee, wrote a poem about you and me, took a shower and sang "dradle, dradle, dradle" while drying my hair…..haven't thought about you a bit though!!! Ha-ha!! 4 hours of sleep…..it is going to be a long day…how is your day going so far? I am still thinking of a nickname for you…it won't be OZ, it needs to be more of a "pet" name. Looking forward to Friday….a day of exploring…..exploring Spring Lake that is!!!! LOL….You may call me at work toll free at 1-800-000-0000 Ext. 5678. Talk to ya later!!

XXXOOO

Charley…..

♦   ♦   ♦

Well, I just got in the door after hangin' with my 3 kiddies, and my aunt, who was in a pissy ass mood tonight! So, I'm tryin' to figure out if I should answer your mail or just call you. POEM? MOI? Y TU!!! (I know, I mixed there! LOL) Been not thinking about you too!!! Last night was….. near perfect, and I enjoyed your company immensely. I even told my kids about you and your kids. My little ones were excited about the similarity of ages! My eldest just rolled her eyes, "here goes another notch in daddy's belt" she said! Somehow, you don't seem the notch type to me…. whatever that is!! Oh, I like the dreidle song too!!! Even have a dreidel around here somewhere…Just got an e mail from my daughter so I'm gonna go read it, and then call my favorite green (I still say they look blue/grey!) eyed blonde! Okies?…….D…..just me…

♦   ♦   ♦

So nice to hear from you by phone and e-mail. I guess I spelled dreidel wrong in my e-mail….but you knew what I was talking about. I grew up with 2 neighboring Jewish families of which in one family there was my best friend Rebecca, who I hung out with all of the time. Loved eating matzha(?) with butter, bagels and lox, and hanging out in her house with all of her many toys in her cool room. And "no" we didn't have any lesbian experiences. We were best friends for years…I'd say 1st grade through 8th grade. I have to tell you I was also thinking about where we would live while I was driving home last night and also thought of living in Pompton Lakes, because I have heard it is a great town with great schools. I think we have made some kind of connec-tion….what do you think?
    Have a good night….pleasant dreams!!!
    Talk to ya tomorrow.
    XXOO
    Charley…

♦   ♦   ♦

Charlie, yeah, connection is a good word, as good as any I can come up with! Lets see how we connect on a second date, and perhaps, we'll see how our weekend together goes…. scary huh? Not too sure how either one of us is gonna feel by Sunday morning, but I've got a feeling……chat with ya tomor-row babe, I'm trashed….D…..

◆   ◆   ◆

Good morning "KOOLAID SMILE"!

I reread my poem this morning on my way to work that I wrote about us and had a tear in my eye. Now, this is a poem about us after our first date....without any kind of sexual words or ideas. So, I will let you read it when you come over tomorrow, so I can see your reaction. Yes, this weekend is a little scary, but I am quite excited. I have a feeling about this also...and NOOOOOOO I am not another "notch in your belt" type person. I will talk to ya later!! I like when you call me BABE!!

XXOO
Charley...

◆   ◆   ◆

OHHHHH...and PS.....

Hi it's me again!!

Let's stay over tomorrow night...I made reservations and we can check in at 2 pm and check out at noon on Saturday.... let's take it slow....I rather stay down there and drive back on Saturday. This way I can feed my cats Saturday morning and we can then head to your place. Does that sound OK?

Charley

Okay, bear with me here guys. I'm like, really digging this girl, and we're both deciding to take it slow, date other people, and keep our friends, all kinds of stuff that we talked about on the phone, right? So what does she say? We're going to get a hotel room on Friday night after dinner theatre down at the Jersey shore, sleep in the room together, and then feed her cats and head back to *my place*! Why, how casual...Nothing too heavy here at all...

Come on now! What message am I supposed to be receiving here? I already know that I like this girl a whole bunch. Besides being a very aggressive, wet kisser, (Oh my *God*, you have no *idea*!) she has an awesome personality to boot. Oh, and by the way, she booked the hotel room *before* she discussed it with me. How amazing is that? I *love* a woman who takes the initiative! Really! I *do*!

We had a nice chat on the phone that evening, including a few minutes with her 8-year-old daughter who *had* to talk to me. She is a *total* pisser, just like her mom! I figured I was going to be in for some *deep* trouble with these two pistols!

So, since Charley is one of my closest friends, I asked to her give her perspective on our little story.

The first time on the Internet can be very scary. After talking with friends and getting mixed feedback on their experiences, some good, some bad, I decided to do it anyway. Every Sunday evening I would do a search on the Internet, which would take me about one hour. As always, I would search for the most handsome guys, with a good sense of humor and between ages 35 and 48. I would e-mail the bachelors that popped up on my search and mention things we have in common and a special trait which I saw in his profile that sparked my interest. When I first saw David's picture I immediately thought, "What a cutie," and also thought he reminded me of the actor from "Full House."

So I sent him my first e-mail. After receiving and reading his first reply, I automatically got a warm, fuzzy yet tingling feeling. I thought, "This guy sounds great....fun, loving and witty."

Driving to our first date was very nerve racking. I was so nervous and was thinking, "Do I go...do I turn around and go home? I hope I don't get lost, I hope he is as cute as he sounds."

When I arrived at the supermarket, I wasn't sure if I should park on the right side or left side...so I parked in the middle. When he drove up in his Taurus wagon, I would normally say, "What a bore," but I thought, "Wow, this is the family man." Then I saw his handsome face and adorable smile. We greeted with a big hug, and boy did I need that bear hug, and I immediately felt better, more relaxed and definitely more attracted.

After the date I drove home thinking of a future with him. What kind of house, what town, would our kids get along, how would he be in bed...I already knew I liked the way he kissed...he was very sensual.

I made reservations for a comedy show in December in Spring Lake, NJ. Since it is one and a half hours driving time each way, I decided to book a room. At the time, I was planning on taking my girlfriend. After meeting David, and knowing that the chemistry and capability was there, I decided to ask him. What a risk, huh?

Friday morning, he picked me up at my apartment with a red bandana wrapped around his face. He is very allergic to cats...and I do have a few. I gave him a quick tour and we had to run out of there because of his allergies. At first I thought, "How dramatic," but when he started to get the sniffles, I realized he wasn't faking.

Driving down to Spring Lake, I was very nervous and apprehensive. I thought, "Am I nuts? This guy could be a murderer." But my girlfriend knew where I was going and so did my ex. Towards the end of our drive we started to rub each other a little and things started to get heated. We checked into the hotel, had the same "ideas" in our heads, and didn't like the first room. After arriving at the second room, we unpacked for two minutes and dove on top of each other, and in the bed we were. WOWEE KAZOWEEE!

"Wowee kazowee," indeed. I think that perhaps we unpacked for five minutes, but no longer! Charley called me her "afternoon delight." We were almost late for the show because we just could not get enough of each other in the three or four hours that we had to spare. Once we got there though, the show was amazing. It was a dinner theatre that was based on a comedy of organized crime and the entire audience participated. It was very interactive and fun!

Having sex for as long as we did due to the prolonged teasing in the car for almost 90 minutes, (rub each other?…Yeah, *right*!) followed by an evening of seeing each other in formal attire, produced several more, um, passionate moments together upon our return to the room.

We did sleep very well, cuddled up in each other's arms all night long. Upon awakening early in the morning, Charley ran the hot water in the hot tub, which was the *main* reason we liked this room, as opposed to the other one we had seen first! She then approached me, let her robe slip sexily to the floor, took me by the hand and led me to the water where we washed each other, several times, as it was necessary due to the other activities we were happily engaging in.

We had a wonderful breakfast with an elderly couple who were at our table the night before. We returned to our room, put on sweats, and proceeded to walk the freezing beach and engage each other in a game of football. She was almost as talented at throwing the pigskin as she was in other areas. She didn't complain about the subfreezing weather. Her only concern was for me and my lack of a hat as my ears were turning cherry red.

So we packed. We checked out. We drove the long drive back to her home and I left to return to mine. She followed me several hours later, but on her arrival to my apartment she seemed a bit distant and aloof. We ate a nice dinner and then Charley informed me that she was tired and truly needed to sleep. This was not the direction that I expected the evening to go, especially after the way the rest of the weekend went, but I jumped into bed with her and just held her close.

She asked if I had any pics of my kids and I immediately jumped up to get several bagfuls! I asked her to come over to the light across the room so that she could view them properly and she declined. I asked her why and she just seemed to get very agitated. She became very fidgety, and after a few more minutes just decided to get up and return home. I asked her to stay. I said that we were arguing over something very unimportant, yet she felt slighted and left anyway.

There was no fight, just a general feeling that our "friendship" had progressed all it would in the direction we were heading towards. We never spoke at length of the uncomfortable end of our physical relationship. We have become close friends and speak often. We discuss the lovers in our lives with a familiarity for each other that is both fun and refreshing. We meet for coffee, we meet for a meal, and we meet to chat, but that's it. I consider this a success story due to the fact that anytime you develop a friendship with a person, and can discuss anything with them, anytime, that's a very good thing, as well as a very rare thing indeed.

Swayne's up next with a cute story that will leave you all warm and fuzzy!

I walked in very late after a lengthy business trip and just crashed on my couch. When I awoke, it was the middle of the night, and since I had slept for over ten hours, (yeah I *was* tired!) I decided to just check my e-mail and play a few games online. I never did get to play the games though, as I received one of those "Match" select things and decided to open it up. Most of the women bored me, as usual, but one seemed interesting, as well as a bit familiar. So I opened up her profile and I was floored! It was my friend Mandy who I hadn't seen in over 20 years! We grew up together, went to school together, played baseball together, hell we even bathed together when we were babies! This was my *very* best friend all through childhood and through high school, but we had moved far from each other and lost contact quite some time ago.

So I sent her a cute message, but didn't say who I was, and since I had a beard and mustache at the time, I figured she wouldn't recognize me...I was correct! This was so cool! We chatted online for a week or so and booked a night to meet for dinner. There was an instant attraction the moment our eyes met. In fact it was *way* more of an attraction than I had anticipated since I was meeting her mostly to restart a very old friendship. We spoke over drinks before dinner arrived and she got very close to me very fast. I don't think she realized the reason for her apparent affection for me, at least not yet! I began to laugh during dinner and could not contain myself any longer, so I showed her a photo of us together when we played hockey in high school! She was the goalie and I was a left-winger! She looked at me and then looked at the photo. Then she looked at me and looked at the photo. She must have done this for five minutes in total denial, and suddenly smiled ear-to-ear and screamed *very* loudly, "You bastard! Cumeer!" We hugged and kissed and just had the most amazing evening together! We went to a club and danced all night, and then when we could not function any longer between exhaustion and alcohol, we decided to call it an evening.

I sent her home in a cab and myself as well, as we were way too inebriated to function behind the wheel of a car. We spent "the better part of a month" on the phone over the next week and laughed together, retelling old stupid stories of our youth. We decided to meet that Friday for a concert in Central Park as she had plans to be in the city for business. (She lived far out on Long Island at the time, which was over two hours from me.)

We had an awesome time at the concert acting like two 16-year-olds again and walked all the way to the Village to have some coffee and pastries afterwards. It was glorious, feeling like a kid again as we relived so much of our youth during our moments together. Then it happened. Neither one of us can explain, but we just looked at each other and knew that it was time to start acting like adults.

I took her to my apartment, and the moment the door closed the clothes began to fly in every direction conceivable. We kissed passionately, and then like in a movie we both started to laugh hysterically, as if it was in a script!

We just lay there on the couch with almost no clothing on, laughing like two idiots as we realized together that this was *not* going to go any further, at least not as lovers! We just knew *too much* about each other, and although we had a total blast together, this just was not meant to be.

We grabbed a bite from the fridge, cozied up on the couch with a bag of Doritos and some sodas, and watched TV for a bit until we fell asleep for an hour or so. When we awoke, we just sorta chuckled as we dressed, and I walked her to her car outside. We kissed like best friends do, on the cheek. Well, perhaps we let it slip a bit, but we laughed once again as she got in her car and drove away home.

In the months that followed we have caught up on all our stories as well as visiting each other's parents and renewing a childhood friendship that never should have ended to begin with. I adore Mandy and she feels the same way. I am thrilled to have my best bud back in my life, as she was meant to be!

I guess somewhere in the back of our minds we both wonder what might have transpired had we indeed had sex that evening in my apartment. It will never happen though, and we have never discussed it, but I'll leave you with this final piece of evidence. Although Mandy is very attractive, intelligent, and funny as hell, when I did finally kiss her it was like I was kissing my sister! That's all I needed to know and that's all there is!

The following story came to me secondhand, but I've known the girl my entire life and she never makes things up! It seems that one of her female friends posted an ad online after being divorced for the second time. She was so nervous that she put up the wrong location of her residence, as well as a very sketchy description with no photo at all. She didn't receive too many notes from men that she wanted to meet, until one day she received an adorable note, also with no photo, from a man that seemed just perfect. His profile described in detail exactly what she sought in a man. Their online chats went on for hours and since he was overseas, they didn't use the phone due to massive long distance charges. Neither had a dime to spare having both gone through recent horrific divorce proceedings. They agreed after several months that they should meet, as the burning desire to put a voice as well as a face to the text was undeniable.

She drove to Kennedy International Airport and awaited his arrival, scared to death! The flight was delayed due to inclement weather, so she was a total wreck by the time the airplane landed and he disembarked. She was so in love with the heart and words of this man that it was sheer agony wondering what he looked like, how he moved, kissed, touched, and smelled. Of course, fate placed him at the back of the plane so the wait was painfully longer than expected as nearly 250 people marched by her in single file to retrieve their baggage. Then, finally, there he was, standing alone with his carry-on bag and a huge bouquet of flowers that had seen better days. They moved closer, slowly at first, but then in a passionate frenzy to embrace when they suddenly realized that fate had dealt them an unexpectedly strange card.

Standing before her was the form of her first husband, whom she had not seen nor heard from in over twenty years! They had married very young, and the relationship, although passionate, had burned out quickly. They parted as friends, but had no true reason for a continuance as he had left and she had moved on to another.

Well, what was she to do now? They agreed that he would stay in her home since there were no other arrangements that could be made on such short notice. They drove to her home together with large lumps in their throats, as neither knew what to expect from this odd quirk of fate. They had dinner together cooked in tandem as they had discussed online. The conversation was light but friendly, and as the evening went by they both realized that the feelings for each other that had developed over the Internet were just as real in person, even given the odd circumstances.

They slept in separate rooms that evening thinking about the possibility of more. Neither slept very well, and upon awakening in the morning they greeted each other with a warm hug...which turned into a tender kiss...which turned into looks of surprise...which turned into two days and nights of passion that can not be contained in this chapter!

They wed three months later and are still happily married three years hence. They do not wonder what might have been had they remained together all those many years ago, preferring to believe that the timing was wrong, even though the people were right.

Man, I love that story!

There are dozens more stories I could share with you. However, I'd prefer to dedicate the remaining space to one that is near and dear to my heart, Anna's story. I will be narrating the story, because she was unable to sit down to an interview with me due to her schedule. However, I lived through this period with her and had everything *graphically* described to me as it happened, with several details fleshed out on different occasions over lunch or coffee in the city.

When Anna and I parted ways, she was pissed to say the least. She drove to my apartment in Jersey and removed every single indication that she had ever been there. She did not do this in a pleasant manner. I guess that after the initial anger had faded and she realized that she was indeed alone, the shock set in and she sank into a deep depression that took her nearly three months to come out of. I was dating other women at the time and Anna would not disappear. But though my heart was elsewhere, I didn't want her to disappear either. I loved her deeply, but just not the way she desired me to. At about this point we began to correspond again and see each other on a casual friendly basis. No, nothing else was going on between us. She helped me through some difficult times, always my savior, just as she has also called me, and we shared an office together for almost three months.

During this period, I took photos of her, per her request, so she could put her profile onto Udate, which I was also a member of. It was cute sitting five feet away from her and IMing each other while comparing notes about the opposite sex. Silly, but still cute. She found several possible suitors and even double dated with Linda and I. It turned out to be a hysterical evening when her date showed up with a fractured ankle, but didn't want to cancel because he was so excited to meet her. He dragged his leg around all evening, and after he left, the three of us were so smashed that we started to make fun of him as we nearly passed out from laughter! She had that horrible date in Chicago and several other sedate meanderings here in NYC, but nothing much to write home about.

Then it happened. She began to correspond with two gentlemen from Europe and after the first one (who she originally thought was the cute one) disappeared, all her attention was taken by "Nigel" from the North Country! They chatted incessantly online as she showed me photo after photo of Nigel and his "manly bare chest."

"Daaaviiid, look at how *gorgeous* he isss!" she'd say as I viewed photo after photo of this guy who looked sort of like a terrorist to me, and I told her so.

"He does *not!*" she'd spew at me. She was totally nuts over this Limey and when it went to the phone after several weeks online, I can tell you that she just went off the deep end. He became her entire focus from the moment she walked in the door until her bedtime, cooing like a pigeon in heat!

This went on for over seven weeks, until neither could stand it anymore and he flew to New York on a Friday to spend three days with Anna. As he walked towards her in the airport, she described to me that her knees felt like they were just going to collapse, and her heart felt as if it would explode when he held her in his arms for the very first time. It was perfect. It was the way she always wanted to be held by a man. They drove to the hotel and spent three glorious days there. Oh, yeah, they saw a bit of the city as well, but considering Anna's level of, um, anticipation after going without for almost six months, they didn't leave the room very much. It was the most glorious three days…and nights…of her life, she stated.

So Nigel returned home, as did Anna. Her daughter picked her up from the airport, and when she returned home, I was waiting for her with a huge smile. We didn't hear a *word* from her for the entire three days so I was *dying* to hear the entire story! I was greeted with a coy smile, shuffled feet, and one simple sentence, "I'm engaged!"

"*What???*" I said.

"I'm engaged. You got a problem with that?"

I was beyond floored. I was happy and confused at the same time. I mean, she'd known this guy in the flesh for *three days* and now she's engaged? Sheesh! You know what though? He was the right one. They were both ready. It was the right time. It was the right place…well, er, they *made* it the right place. Three weeks later, Anna traveled to Europe to meet his family for nine days and lock in a relationship that will last forever!

They married on Valentines Day of last year and have been blissfully happy since then. Nigel has worked on the very old house she lived in and has made it something of a palace! I adore them both more than I can express. Where I am boisterous, he is quiet. Where I am tall, er, he is not! We are opposites in so many ways, yet when we are together there is a warmth that he exudes that is undeniable. Anna is a lucky woman indeed. No one deserves it more than she who is a beacon of light and joy, even though her life before Nigel has been less than happy to say the least.

And I can't think of a better way to end this chapter.

12

The writers.

These letters need no introduction as their very brilliance speaks for themselves.

It was actually the keyword search for "writer" that pulled you up, not the search for "nonchalant pose with rippling striated forearm strategically draped across sofa back", though that might have found you, as well. Or perhaps the search for "guys who look congenitally predestined to have been firefighters but were apparently too smart to pursue it." Then again, I'll try my third and last search: "guys who are ridiculously inaccessible due to geography."

You WOULD have to live directly across the continental U.S. So selfish. I mean really; it's always you, you, YOU!

So I thought you were a likable looking sort—you stood out from the panels of mulletards, frat boys, militia dorks, possible ex-cons, new age back-rub-freakos and guys exactly one eighth of an eyelash away from being totally goddamn gay (or at least one would think so by reading the things they write, no doubt convinced that quote unquote sensitivity, beach hand holding, rose petal bubble baths with Barry White undertones is What Women Ostensibly Want.) Not that we don't want sensitivity, of course, but that doesn't mean you have to write a bio that reads like a transcribed freaking Air Supply song.

My needs are simple: imagination. Along with about fourteen hundred other tiny things but imagination's the biggie.

I've always been the sorta girl where to get into the lacey parts you pretty much have to traverse the brain. One time I let someone enter through the heart first but that, sweet as it was, fermented and I was afterwards left with someone who didn't get my jokes, couldn't make me laugh, and of course never truly understood the quivering depth of my genius (I was kidding there. I just hate smiley emoticons so don't hold your breath). That riveting melodrama (entitled "Shitty Marriage, Rocking Kids") should be coming soon via satellite to Lifetime, Television for Those Doomed to Live One Dimensionally.

I'm not sure exactly why I'm writing you, a dude who had the audacity to live on an opposite coast when I'm living in the beige-est part of the country I've ever had the dubious privilege of living in. Ever wonder what happened to that big "salad bar" trend of the early 90's? I think all of them packed up and moved to Oregon, where they became part of this disturbing restaurant chain called "sweet tomatoes," where there are like eleven thousand salads, all of which taste alarmingly like packing peanuts. I crave the multidimensional flavors of a good Vietnamese place, would kill for tapas that didn't taste like mayonnaise, dim sum that doesn't have a faint disconcerting sub-flavor of...this is for real here...chicken mcnuggets.

But all of that is neither here (Portland) nor there (the Bronx). People are happy here as long as they have their few liberal and vocal lesbians, their green spaces and studiously hip shopping districts festooned with Gap outlets, Shoe Pavilions and Chili's...all wrapped up around the edges by a red-faced phalanx of mulleted gun-rack sporting bible fundamentalists with dual flags waving out their windows. People are placated by trips to Costco, where the grim-faced shoppers throng behind heat-seeking maxi-carts wielded like battering rams against all of mankind (the Asian grannies can feel like they're once again back in the old country, knocking the weak and slow-moving off the sidewalk to get at the last $45 watermelon), lest you interfere with their quest to fetch five-metric-ton-toilet paper packages large enough to fend off wayward meteorites, horrific 5-lb spools of splashily marketed blue fruit leather strings, or nine-hundred-dollar google-packs of ergonomic rubberized ballpoint pens encapsulated by a pound of intricately shaped/molded plastic packaging so sophisticated and impenetrable they could be sent into space unharmed—all to be precariously shoveled into their hulking Ford Excursions, the cars whose very shadow can flatten a poodle.

<sigh> but I digress. Actually, digressing is all I ever do.

More to the point, I'm a pretty hot ex-salsa singer with two toddler boys who makes plenty of money and wants someone to tickle my brain-pan. If you liked hearing my unhinged rant, send me words; it's really what I'm hungriest for. If you can wrangle words, send em my way, cowboy. I know how to handle 'em on this end.

Shakira...

Oh, yeah: 5'9" 150# (quite muscular: think a prepubescent competitive male swimmer—sans dick and plus the usual femme acoutrements; it's just that I'm slim-hipped and broad-shouldered; that's where I'm going there). Ah frack now I sound like a Russian shotputter. Well, tell ya what. If you e-mail me back I'll send pictures.

Oh my God! Wow! What *can* you say in response to such an incredible dissertation? I mean really? Would most guys even read through that entire letter? If they actually *did* read through it, would they have the guts to respond? I laughed sooo hard in several different spots, well, she just capped a really awesome evening. An evening which was discussed in the "Success" chapter!

By the way, this was my response several days later.

HOLYJUMPINJEHOSEFAT BATMAN!!!!! This girl can WRITE!!! So, like after I picked myself off the floor from reading the BOOK that you generously typed to me yesterday, I realized that I needed to respond with something witty and urbane...but since I had company, I decided to wait until a CALMER moment to respond to your incredulous dissertation.

Well, lemme tell ya, that was SOME rant-n-rave girl!!! What the hell are you doing on the wrong coast? You need to move to NYC and kick some SERIOUS bootayyyy!!!

So what IS IT really like in Oregon. It must be very peaceful there, kinda like New Jersey, but drier? So what exactly IS a "papito" anyway? and does "Ay" connotate something like "ay caramba"????? or is it some mid western sexual phrase I'm not familiar with? Ya know, the kind of phrase...that explodes from your mouth just before you RELEASE with your lover? AAAYYYYYYYYYYYEEEEEEEEEE!!!!!!! PAPITO!!!!! :)

sorry, I AM into the silly emoticon type personages.. leaves less room for cyber misunderstandings!

Anyhooooooo..sooooo.. um, howz the weather in Portland today> No no no, that's not what I wanted to ask you! Grrrrrrrr.. I've been writing all day between planning events in the city (y'know, the REAL city! hehehehe!) so I'm a wee bit spent here, but I guess after reading your mail, I can't say that I have TOO many questions, as you covered most of the bases! Killer personality, sharp as a tack, sarcasm that could cut through titanium plating, and VERY vocal and outspoken! Is there a man alive who could even BEGIN to contain your passionate outbursts??? Hmmmm. I wonder? I look forward to seeing your "pre pubescent competitive male swimmer" photos, as well as another amazingly well written dissertation of the trials and tribulations that are your life, living in Portland.

Lemme ask ya though, are there REALLY lots of ports there? What kinda ports ARE they? Little ports, or big ones? Happy ports or sad? We have ports in New York too but we call them piers and slips. I guess you guys just needed to be different, and call your land after your ports or something. VERY original!

Well, I'm starting to get silly now, so I'm gonna go, but my personal e-mail is dosterczy@whatever.com. I hope to hear back from ya! I am totally psyched to get another one of your kewl rants!!!!!. TTFN!.*hugs*.David.

And she came right back to me with her genius!

A rich, sweet, fortified wine...

Or at least, that's one kinda port, but less favored. Portland, what it has in spades—aside from hand-holding college students, sheltered untraveled folks who believe themselves to be terribly urbane, a few neighborhoods so unrelentingly tame it would make your eyes tear up but which, still, people fear irrationally because you can sometimes See Black People!—is bridges. Lots of bridges. I will never understand the why's of the how many's but jeezus they are bridge happy. There's a bridge like 1/4 mile away from the last. WTF?! Uh, just walk it, ya know?

The weather was cottony mild today, soft diffuse and feathery gray, as opposed to dark and turbulent grey, or soupy grungy gray or fetid miserable gray like Cruela's crotch, as I described it a few days ago.

Oregon knows gray. That's fer dang sure. I have been purchasing lots of boots. I do like boots. I got some sleek eggplant-colored high-heeled, based-on-the-cowboy-boot-template but hold the garth brooks kinda boots yesterday, and some extremely weird ones which seemed to have vague S and M over tints but it was very subtle. They're black and made out of some sleek funky material that clings to your leg up to the knee, and the heel is high, and kind of like a skinny wedge heel—but it's lucite, so it's perfectly clear. From a distance, it's a trip—looks like your levitating with your feet in this trippy cantilevered position. I couldn't decide if they were weird/cool or weird/disturbing. I really couldn't. Usually I'm very decisive.

So I finally used the trustworthy brand name to rationalize to myself they were edgy and cool rather than merely freakish. I could still be wrong, but they're a conversation piece, if nothing else. Now if I could just make myself LEAVE THE HOUSE I could start wearing these things. It's sad, but these days my ass is like hermetically fused to my office chair, then it's chitlin time, salsa-dancing abandon with my two little tots, dinner and clearing out the wreckage, books upon books capped off with a new improvised story every night (you should hear some of the winners that come out of that magical hour—not all of it is my best work, let's just say), then down they go, trundling off, brushing of teeth, and into the arms of Morpheus. Then back I go to the computer to animate and illustrate until blood comes out of my eyes. Yes, I know I'm on the wrong coast. Certainly at least the wrong latitude of this coast. I have never been to New York, but I am afraid to because I know with certainty that I will want to live there. I understand my depth of adoration for San Francisco, which I instinctively feel is merely a pocket-sized replica of New York, with a bit more somnolence, complacency, and softness.

I may make a pilgrimage soon, to visit my friend Carmen Webster, a writer for Salon.com whose web site I built and who is the Next Coming. But that's a ways off, I'm sure. Okay, without further ado, I will cast to you the random pattern of my puzzling pixels, and you can decide if they create symmetry in your esteem. Then we can talk more. An avuncular kiss on the forehead, Shakira...

◆   ◆   ◆

Hiya cutie. Ya probably thought I didn't like your pics, so I didn't answer you. NOPE! WRONG! I actually think you're quite cute, but I've actually been quite busy, and have not had too many opportunities to even sit down! Fall down, yes, sit???? Uh uh. Normally, after receiving such AMAZING letters from a person, I'd leave my phone number, but in your case, considering the distance between us, and the fact that I LOVE to read through your incredible thought process, I figured I'd just keep on writing, thereby receiving. The only problem with this line of reasoning is that you have peaked my interest, and I feel the NEED to speak to someone INTELLIGENT once in a blue cheese moon.. so here is mine, and if ya give me a yell, I'll call ya right back 'cause I've got unlimited! (ain't it great!) 718-000-0000.

David. In case you forgot, with time! hehehehehe..:)

◆   ◆   ◆

I had so gone flaccid on match.com. Never have I pulled up such a motley crew of mullets, trolls, bald guys with chernobyl ponytails, and walk-on-the-beach, sad-sack wussballs. When I "narrowed" my search to the word "writer," the shit got even more treacherous.

Headlines like "writer seeks _____" where blank is
*muse
*inspiration
*a happy ending
*a romantic plot

And all of these people, as if their cliches didn't already render them facially handicapped, looked like a cross between WC Fields and the unabomber.

Today I am suffering through a tumultuous cleaning frenzy. My son's birthday is tomorrow and I've got to vacuum all the fruit leather out of the houseplants, make the piñatas, create a robot cake and then later tonight deal with my by-turns-weepy-and-accusatory ex (don't worry; no knife-wielding, however; crimes of passion would require more initiative than he's capable of. Also they require passion!)

Anyway, it would be most agreeable to clean out the foxhole while talking. My phone number is 503.000-0000. Give a holler

Shakira

Suffice to say that we've spoken a few times, and she is just as intelligent on the phone as she is online. Too bad she lives on the left coast. Oh well!

The next letters sort of explain themselves. The only one missing is the first one she sent to me, which I cannot retrieve because the 7-day free membership to the site we were using expired. Doh!

Thanks for the lovely note, but I decided just last night to never date women without kids again. You all say that you love kids, but when the relationship begins to get serious, and you start to think (as all women do) you all run like hell because you cannot fathom loving that many more people. Just my luck, you'd be the exception to the rule, but last night was strike three for me, so I guess I should wish you luck, as you seem very nice…. sorry, just been hurt one time too many……. David…

◆　　◆　　◆

Hello David-

While I can completely understand your position—for me to say that not only do I believe I am the exception to the rule (in regards to what women do)—which ultimately means nothing without you experiencing who I am—but I am the exception to many rules. Once again, moot point, however I do appreciate your honest response.

Take Good Care.

Debbie

The following letter was sent before the previous one she had written was received.

why the hell couldn't you have sent me that AMAZING, perfect profile 24 hours ago……ya just caught me on a REALLY bad day, my love…gimme a wee bit of time, and maybe, just maybe, send me a pic, and after my heart heals…we shall see……D…just me…

David-

◆　　◆　　◆

Reading your profile certainly gave me a sense about who you are and that is why I contacted you. Your e-mails clearly demonstrate a rare ability to self reflect and express. I appreciate that so I took some time to write back to you.

My experience of the week online showed me that my profile only attracts certain individuals who think outside the norm—as I do—and sending a visual generally adds to the allure. I would rather you let me know when you feel you have sufficiently healed as I prefer for you to not prematurely contact me because your curiosity is piqued. Additionally, while most of us go online because we are curious—ultimately, the desire to find a mate exists. However, my approach has been somewhat different as I would rather discover a friend who I feel a nice connection to, than do a somewhat more 'refined' meat (mate) market search. I only communicate with those I feel I could want as a friend.

I suppose that is why I am taking the time to write to you now. Although it is not my desire to have an e-mail buddy—it is far too time consuming writing back and forth—I find you endearing and charming and I am compassionate to the fact that you are clearly challenged by your most recent relationship.

I also wanted to propose a thought to you in regards to this. I have observed that generally when a person feels sincerely cared for they are not threatened by their mate expressing love towards family members and friends. However, those who lack self-confidence and esteem often interpret their partner's attention to others as taking something away from them. Of course it does not—as long as the partner knows how to make time to focus on them and balance the many relationships—together and apart—all can be well. Perhaps this observation will have meaning to you.

With all this said, I will leave it up to you to contact me when you know you it is appropriate, then I will be happy to send a photo and we can go from there.

Take good care of your self.
Debbie

What a bright young lady! It is amazing to me how someone could be so understanding and wise, without even knowing the person they're chatting with! Our e-mail exchange continues…

Life can be so very strange. Just when you think you have it all figured out, you miss a down and away curve for strike ONE…. then, after you brush yourself off, you get the heater down the middle, catching you unaware, for strike TWO…now, on your guard for something off the plate, low and outside, comes a little chin music, throwing you to the ground violently, one ball two strikes. Now you're PISSED! You brush the mud from your uniform, stand as tall as you can, and get back in the box for another try…heater down the middle, foul ball…uncle Charley low and outside, two balls two strikes. She looks at you with disdain, but respect, as you glare back at her, twirling your 34 oz. bat around like it were a toothpick. She goes into the stretch, the sign, the delivery, as you swing with everything you've got…IT'S A LONG FLY BALL, DEEP TO LEFT, IT'S LONG ENOUGH, IT'S HIGH ENOUGH, IT'S, IT'S, IT'S……..; FOUL……. You wince, as another awesome effort is wasted. Hard to return to the batters box after that last one. You've should've had it, ya jumped all over it, leaving her gasping for breath, and afraid to give you another one down the middle, as you wore her out on the last go round. She steadies herself as the manager pats her on the butt. She studies your every move now, thinking, debating every tiny movement and sound you make. You smile at her, and step back up to the plate, as you know that you own her. Low and inside, high and outside, fastball, slider, curve, it does not matter. You can handle anything she can throw at you. She sets, you brace, here it comes, right down the middle, but dropping rapidly, and slowing, falling.... you back off, ball three in the dirt, full count. Now it's on, as there will be only one winner here. Bases loaded, two outs, three balls, two strikes. The crowd is out of their minds. The sweat is trickling down her nose, onto her neck, glistening in the sun, but you cannot lose focus now, this is the real deal.

She heaves a deep sigh, takes in a full breath. Her chest rises, and falls, as she climbs the hill back to the mound from which she will deliver her final pitch. She sets, gets the sign from the catcher, and you call time and step out of the box, just to shake her up even more, just to get her thinking, "what IS he gonna do next?"

You put some pine tar on your bat handle, as you wipe the sweat from your brow. Kicking the mud from your spikes, you glance out at the mound. There she stands, proud, defiant, amazing, talented. Exactly the type of pitcher you'd like to go to war with. Unbowed, undaunted, but you HAVE put an ounce of fear into her, just by being who you are, nothing more, nothing less. You flash a sudden smile in her direction, and she gives one back that cuts into the very fiber of your soul. You stagger, and she knows she has you.

You enter the box with a confidence level, just slightly bowed by a tiny doubt, due to the glint in her eye. The first baseman had said something to her. You have played with this first baseman before, and had success, but she knows you. All the good and all the bad, and you wonder, just what it was that she shared with the pitcher that has her smirking? You are unbowed though, and prepare to give her best pitch the ride of it's life. So she sets, and you dig in. The delivery is swift and sure, but you are prepared. You connect on the sweet spot, solid, strong directly back at the pitcher a blistering line drive that will surely go for a bases clearing double. If only life were so simple. If only we got what we deserved, what we worked for. She raises her glove in self-defense as her eyes close. The ball sticks, the glove closes, three outs. You gasp! You did your best. There was nothing more you could possibly have done! You may never have hit a ball this sweetly before, yet you come away empty, game over, and on to the next one......oh well......

We ended up meeting later that day at a small botanical garden here in Riverdale. We had a nice time together, but there just wasn't that "chemistry" we all seek, and it was mutual, so I guess it really was "on to the next one" after all!

Are you reading between the lines of my humor? Yeah, there was a lot of pain, and a multitude of relationship messages in my baseball letter. I'm sure that any good psychiatrist could read *volumes* of content there. The letter was partially based, obviously, on my relationships with two girls who knew each other and who, in their innocent conversations with one another, may have screwed it up for all of us. We do the silliest things at times, and are so busy looking for the one negative thing that we tend to ignore a thousand positive things about a person or a situation. I tend to take the opposite tack in my relationships and seem to put blinders on once I've decided that I want to pursue a relationship with a young lady. This, unfortunately, can often backfire, for as soon as you put the blinders on, you may find that when you *do* allow your eyes to open fully, the person you're with is not genuinely who you seek as a mate. By then it's too late, because you are in a relationship where someone is *bound* to get hurt. So folks, keep your eyes *open,* and if something bothers you, talk about it. If that doesn't make it better, then perhaps it's time to move on. Wounds tend to get deeper with time if the boo-boo isn't kissed by our mates, increasing the chance of a scar.

The next note was written by Doreen, who has been mentioned several times in this book. We don't really speak much anymore, because when two candles burn very brightly, they tend to cancel each other out. At the time this was written however, we were speaking regularly. She was going through some very difficult times, and as we were close, I tended to be her shoulder from afar, as we live several hundred miles apart. Several nights before she wrote this, she exploded at me for no good reason, and I hung up the phone. This amazing letter was her response to that occurrence.

In my own words…
David,
I am deeply sorry for any pain that I have caused you. I am sorry that you feel that you no longer want to know me. I am sorry that you are so angry at me. I will understand if you do not want to ever talk with me again. I will be very sad, but I will understand. I also want you to know that I wanted to call you Friday night (I did not go out because I was too upset) but I felt that it wouldn't be the best thing to do. I thought that we both needed some time to cool off and collect ourselves. So, I didn't call. Perhaps I should have. I know in the past that you have gotten upset with me if I didn't "stop" when you needed me to "stop" and I viewed your hanging up on me as one of those times. I didn't want to make things worse but I also didn't want you to think that I didn't care. I do care. I care about you and our friendship. You have been a friend to me and I appreciate that and perhaps I haven't honored our friendship in the way that I should have, this I regret. Sometimes I am so busy protecting myself that I lose sight of the emotions of others. I was insensitive and yes, self absorbed. It is never pleasant to come face to face with your own imperfections and it seems I have been inundated with facing such recently. I have not handled it with the grace one would hope for. But, as you have so

eloquently stated on several occasions, I am human. And I AM trying. Perhaps not at a comfortable pace. Perhaps not according to everyone else's agenda. But I am trying. I think you are a wonderful man. I think you are deserving of all the love you have to offer. I hope you find it. And I hope you accept my apology.

I am not perfect. I am becoming and I will continue to become. Sometimes slowly, other times, quickly. These are my tools..if you care to know. Sometimes, I misplace them. Sometimes, I forget that I have them and struggle thru without them. Sometimes, I am stubborn and think that I don't need them...Always, I am wrong.........Right Knowledge, to supply me with the tools necessary for my voyage. Wisdom, to assure me that I am using the accumulated knowledge of the past in a manner that will serve the discovery of my presence, my "now." Compassion, to help me accept others whose ways may be different from mine, with gentleness and understanding, as I move with them or through them or around them on my own way. Harmony, to be able to accept the natural flow of life. Creativity, to help me to realize and recognize new alternatives and uncharted paths along the way. Strength, to stand up against fear and move forward in spite of uncertainty, without guarantee or payment. Peace, to keep me centered. Joy, to keep me song-full and laughing and dancing all along the way. Love, to be my continual guide toward the highest level of consciousness which is humanly possible. Unity, which brings me back to where I started, the place where I am at one with myself and with all things.

You have told me that you love me. You have also told me that you don't know me. Perhaps you know me a little better now. For what it is worth…

Love, Doreen

The following message was written to a very interesting young lady that I had a very short date with due to time constraints. She is quite cute, and very intelligent, but our date was so rushed, (we were both in a hurry,) that we just sort of missed each other. Happens to the best of us. I think the e-mail from this guy is creative, playful, and adorable. She thought otherwise. Well, to each their own! She opens with her insight into his prose to her.

Here's one for your book…This guy has way too much time on his hands…
:-) Lydia

WHOA!!!!!!!—!!!!!!

SCREECHING of tires and brakes locking with tires smoking.......Whew.... Sorry about the skid marks on your profile :) 49 Explorer (Eddie Bauer edition) lQQking for an experienced driver!

NO Right-hand lane drivers puhlease!!!!

Original paint job...really...NEW TIRES...top is most of the way down.....grrrrrrh

Frame in good shape (warranty expired), 50,000 miles, reliable good commuter vehicle with class, shines up well for weekend excursions (fill me up—premium—and I will take you places you have always wanted to go)

Owner's manual available with some coffee stains and dogged eared pages. I hope you prefer hands-on, trial and error..... just play with it until you figure it out

Used but dependable and with all accessories; needs to be warmed up before starting...I trust you know the buttons to push....

Handles bumps and curves in the road well..sturdy shocks with power to spare....so why don't you just see what I can do?

Generally takes the low road, not the high road....gets me to the ocean faster. Anyway the view I want is driving me (wink)...wherever we go, I promise it to be the best road. Heater works well (can warm you on a cold evening—may need the defrost by morning) Tow package (can pull most things and bags you wish to bring along.....mine fits in any overhead) 4x4 with traction; Goes off-road for camping and other excursions, such as moon light sparking.... where does your imagination take you). Loves the road less traveled, hence the frequent washings! Are you handy with a sponge and soap? Has been known to make spontaneous trips at the drop of a hat, so keep a bag handy! Does moving to Kauai in September of last year sight unseen qualify?!

Good fuel economy, but likes to get parked in a nice restaurant for refueling once in a while....credit card is in the glove compartment. You are my guest. Good for hauling home improvement and gardening supplies. Very handy and flexible, a car for all seasons and occasions. Can go from the beach to the theatre in an easy day. Radio preset to jazz, classical, and news stations and more recently only the local aloha channel....NOT Don Ho......(spitting tiny bubbles....excuse me I'm better now)

Garaged for a while from bad experience with previous driver, but willing to try the road again. No clean driving record required...just valid. Unable to find driver the conventional ways due to busy schedule...with work and being relocated to honeymoon island where one gets the impression that you are going stag on Noah's Ark. Shy or quiet drivers need not apply. Must know how to make a pass! Both hands firmly gripping the wheel unless shifting the stick for full performance (wink)

I am looking for a 1-owner kind of girl, who doesn't keep her eyes out constantly for the newest models and can stay out of the used car lot.

Lease option available! Title available.......don't hesitate....well...what are you waiting for....you are leaving the engine idling here....... tap tap tap......

Check under hood and take me for a test drive…is most encouraged. Step on it! err I mean take me out. (Please don't kick the tires) thank you All (un)reasonable offers will be considered! BeepBeep

ps..in human form I am told I look like "Billy Bob Thornton" The agents guarding me in the federal witness protection program will give me a good reference. Bring donuts and coffee for cooperation.

Michael

NB A man's reach should exceed his grasp or what is heaven for! soooooOOOOOOOOOO

…. "it does not serve the world to play small".

Nelson Mandela

disclaimer: You just had a racy ride, I confess, but KNOW FOR CERTAIN this vehicle is a class model that will perform the way you want and better than you have experienced with any previous models.

Can you believe that she didn't like this guy's personality? In a cyber world of one-liners, I'd think that most women would *love* to get such a well thought out message. I would be proud to have written it myself, but cannot take such credit. Maybe someday I can meet this guy and buy him a beer!

Funny thing is, the guy wasn't half bad looking. Sort of looked like an older version of Mark Messier, so I guess he has kind of a tough-guy look which was, unfortunately, totally not the look this girl was into. But I digress…

I have so many detailed messages from the next young lady that I could easily fill a chapter. I picked the next one because it was both silly *and* serious, and also leads into another subject. It leads into a subject that's going to get me in a wee bit of trouble with some of the ladies, but not the ones who know the validity of the statements I'm going to make.

Dear David,

I'm certainly glad we're in agreement about CatDog!! However, although you watch "manly" cartoons, let's see how you feel about my all-time DUMBEST program! It is partly cartoon, which I can handle, but it's the "human" in the show that makes me want to just strangle! I'm referring to Blues Clues!

I know children love that show, but could the adult in the show get any dorkier????

I agree with your take on shooting weddings, that's EXACTLY why I DESPISE them! No matter how you look at it, they are "SNAPSHOTS" not portraits! Creativity is what I'm all about. What I put my children through year after year was torment for them, but they made such beautiful subjects! BUT, I believe they tired of me saying "JUST ONE MORE!"…. after a while, they knew that was not going to happen!" You know I had a "link" with samples of my photography, but when my system crashed (!^%#@^@$!!), I lost it all! I'll find it somewhere! That is "my specialty.... children's portraits!" BUT, I go a weeeeeeee bit overboard with the props to create the illusion or feeling I want!

About your statement, David "43 is no problem, as long as you look 33, and act 13!" First, you tell me! You've seen my photos! Do I look 43? I was sitting at a bar the other day with a friend when one "young teeny bopper...OK, so he was 21, he's still a baby" wanted to know how old I was! Of coarse, I love FFCs (hmmm, sounds a litttle perverted!)...FFC's stands for Fishing For Compliments! No one has ever guessed it correctly, so I was hoping he wouldn't break the record! He said "34".... well I was elated that I reached over, held his face in my hands, and kissed him, then THANKED HIM! I then proceed to tell his friend and he thought his friend insulted me because he said I looked much younger! I couldn't kiss him though.... his fiance was the bartender and I didn't want cianide in my drinks! I also act so much like 13 that my girls claim I embarrass them.... ask me if that has stopped me? NOT! They just don't think it's KEWL for mom to have more than one piercing in her ear and a tattoo (can't tell you where) and wants another one! I think it's a bit more tolerable with fathers! (discrimination of the sexes!!! NOT FAIR!)

OK, David, time for "confession".... as long as you don't send me to church to say 100 Hail Mary's and 200 Our Father's (lol)! I'm sorry to tell you that I do "not" live in Tarrytown! I lived there my ENTIRE life until I had my first child and couldn't afford a one-family home! Being a woman and a mother, and VERY VERY new to this "internet dating" thingy, I was so fearful of it that I told a "little" fib! Forgive me? I actually live in what's considered "upstate!" IT'S NOT! It's 50 minutes to an hour from Tarrytown! I live in Orange County! OK, Phew, that's off my shoulders

.... SIGH!

There! I've said it! I will probably not hear from you again, and don't worry that I am very sensitive and bruise very easily! Truly, don't even give it a second thought! I have plenty of Prozac (JOKE!)

As my last statement (because I think I've written a novel by now!) let me say thank you for calling me "cute!" Heck, if that didn't make me feel like a high school kid, I don't know what would! If you haven't "caught on" that was an FFC! Cute is good! Yeah, I think my dog is cute, and my girls, and even their little friends! Cute is good (boooooo hooooooo!)

Well, David, the ball is yours <devilish smirk>! I still frequent Tarrytown, so if you'd still like to meet for "a slice of pizza" that would be cute and KEWL! I'm bust'n on you aren't I? Have a wonderful day, David!!!! Ya se que no me vas a escrevir-me, pero te tuve que decir la verdad!

ADIOS!

Carmen....

P.S. NOW FOR THE BAD NEWS! Now, I didn't "lie" about this, but I just didn't reveal myself (roflmao)! Sadly, I am in the process of a sad, hurtful, but much-needed divorce! NOW, don't hit "DELETE" yet! It's been over for years, we just haven't "finalized it!" for the good of the girls! If you're still speaking to me after my "come clean" honesty, I'd love to know how "you survived it!" I do pride myself on my honesty and integrity and have always been a "good girl!" WELLLLL, something happens when a woman reaches that explosive age of "40".... it's all true (yee-hawe!) ALL OF IT (oh dear!) Do you blush?

Did she say "Yee hawe?" Yes she did! Do you know *why* she said "Yee Hawe?" Well, let me tell you a little story…

As teenagers, when we guys get aroused because a girl even gives us a *hint* of a smile, *they* are in *complete* control of *any* sexual situation. Well, like Carmen said, around the time women hit their 40th birthday, they somehow magically become 17-year-old boys. What do I mean? Well, simply put, (and don't go getting all uppity on me here girls, 'cause this here be the gospel) something magical happens to women at this age. It's as if God just flipped a switch and made women into sex maniacs at the age of forty plus. I can tell you this from *major* experience, and have been the beneficiary of multiple sleepless nights and ear-to-ear smiles the following morning, afternoon, or evening. And although not all of these encounters have turned into relationships, I have some *really* close female friends who have a very interesting perspective on me…and me on them!

Now what I do *not* know is if this same phenomenon happens to women who stay married. I would tend to believe that it most definitely *does*! Why you say? Well, why do you think so many men in their 40's and 50's suddenly need Viagra?

The next letter came from a girl who I thought could be "the one," if you know what I mean. We had gone back and forth with extremely cute e-mails and telephone conversations for several weeks. This letter was sent to me just days before we met and touched me very deeply, as did almost everything she wrote or spoke to me of.

> David,
> Your children are angels……and my response was just as you had imagined it to be. They are so adorable!! Thank you for taking the time to send them to me. Last nights' conversation was pretty intense.....we have really been covering so many deep issues, but in reality they are not "deep…scarey", they are intimate topics that two people that are on the same cosmic plain would normally discuss. In reality, i feel that we are bonding naturally, because we are in the exact same place, and maybe this is one of those miracu-

lous meetings of the minds that one wishes for, or reads about in books, or maybe just like an old black and white movie from the 40's'. It all seems so innocent in a very special way, speaking with you and relating 100% to what you are about. I think that we could both learn much about the joys of life from one another. What more could one wish for? I do look forward to meeting you this next weekend, and investigating how it will be when we meet face to face. I am not nervous or tense about our first meeting because i feel like you are already an old friend that is near and dear to my heart. I will welcome and embrace your friendship on any level that works for us. Of course, our first choice being something that encompasses equal amounts of the physical attraction for a potential lover, to equal amounts of the friendship of a dear friend. And the best of both, ultimately, just melting togeather to form one great feeling of harmony. Of course, this is hard to find....but i feel as if we have a great chemistry on the telephone, and we have formed something solid! I know that you said last night that my photos were not as striking to you as some of the other gals that you have seen.....which is a bit scarey to me, for i would like you to be very very attracted to me. but much of it is all in the mind anyway, and i look better in person than those pieces of paper with an image attached by lots of micro-mini dots connected to form a face, so i don't really have any major worries. And as far as my bod goes, each person has their own type to be turned on by, and i will have to take my chances on that one too. I myself, am not really concerning myself with how your butt looks or how big your pecks are, because you have swept me away with all that you are in reality. You are one big bundle of love. As for my reaction to the sweetie that sent you the photo of her BREASTS, i feel that a gesture such as that is not very classy, and actually quite vulgar. I need not feel so small, as to advertise myself like some add in the back of a magazine. You will find that all of my wisdom and global experiences, have created a worldly self-esteem that speaks for itself....in every breathe i take, in how i carry myself, and how the world outside of myself sees me with their eyes. I know i am a beautiful girl physically, and i turn heads. But, my mind and feelings are also an extension of my physical attributes, and i am a modest person, and seem to rely on my inner energies as the test of my beauty to the outside world. I am just different in my approach to luring a man in.......I know that you have been seeing many many woman for the last 6 months on a physical basis, as well, and that surely did not float your boat in the long run. This was also, as i feel it to be, a test from the universe for you. Maybe it was much of your anger and hurt manifested in a physical way of acting out your pain. I have listened to your heart, and understand the pain that you have incurred in the last number of months. And In your heart of hearts the boat you were sailing never quite reached paradise......you just visited lots and lots of ports, like an explorer does, in search of his private island of peace and happiness. I would love for you to have that peace and happiness. Maybe my ship can take you to the place that you need to be! The rest is up to fate!
    Samantha....

So we met. I ran up to her and threw my arms around her since we had gotten very close over the phone and through the Internet chats back and forth. Imagine my surprise at her black business suit, her arms remaining at their sides, and an attitude so aloof it seemed to be able to chill the heat right off the hottest Mexican food.

"Who *was* this imposter?" I thought. This could not possibly be the same amazing woman I had conversed with passionately for weeks on end. She decided that she wanted to go to a local fancy-schmancy lounge and just talk. We did. She ordered her favorite $15.00 drink and I ordered a $2.00 cup of tea with honey for my sore throat. Can you spell "high maintenance?" We talked. I paid. We departed after only a short time together.

The date went badly as she seemed distant and not very pleased with me at all. I attempted to hold her hand to get close, to no avail. We crossed the street to head back to her home and as I sat on a car to stop to talk, she thrust her torso into mine, glared at me with a look of total and complete disdain and said, "Is *this* what you want?" I was floored. For a woman who professed such class and worldly knowledge, it was one of the rudest, classless things I have ever endured from the fairer sex.

I drove home to my empty room in New Jersey with a tear in my eye, a lump in my throat, and a total lack of understanding as to what had changed between her last passionate e-mails and the failed meeting. We never did speak again, so I will never know.

13

Interknot Knotes

Relationships. Why do they have to be so very difficult? Well, I guess there are two sides to the coin. There are those who will tell you that if it is meant to be for two people to be together, then it will all go swimmingly and smoothly as God intended it to be. Then there is the camp that will say that anything worth having does not come easy and is worth fighting for. So which is it? Does a relationship only work if everything goes well from the beginning until the inevitable first disagreement? Will you even get through that first fight without ripping each others guts out and will you survive it and learn from it, or is having controversy and pain from past relationships a good thing as a barometer for what to steel your self against?

There are many other difficult and painful sides to the coin in new relationships. There are those who will drag their past experiences kicking and screaming into every new situation. This can sabotage a wonderful relationship before it ever gets off the ground because as soon as this person sees behavior from their new mate that resembles behavior from their old mate, they run away, and often with no explanation. This leaves one partner extremely confused, hurt, and bitter, because they don't know what they did wrong, and often didn't *do* anything wrong. It was just misperception on the part of another that broke up another budding love affair. This leaves both partners with a bad taste in their mouths, and extra wary the next time a similar situation occurs.

The flipside to this scenario is perhaps the most painful and horrible of all. You meet someone that you seem to have been waiting for your entire life. Their hair, their laughter, their mouth, their smile, the age of their children, their personality, everything seems perfect for you and yours. They feel exactly the same way and you hug yourselves at how lucky you are to have found each other. You talk for hours on the phone every night. The dates go so smoothly that you almost forget the rest of the world exists and when you kiss, the breath leaves your body, your head swims, your mind races, and you just wish that it would never end.

They tell you that you are the person they have always hoped would come into their life but never met. They have always been with unfeeling people before, who could not express their feelings or share the love that you have already shown them. They seem so *very* happy when they are with you and you feel the same. And then it happens. They run, because the reality dawns on them that they have finally gotten exactly what they've always asked for, but they're not ready for it, can't discuss it, and just leave you and your feelings in a pile of ashes to recover alone.

I wish that I could tell you that this scenario is a rare one, but it's not. It's happened to many of my friends and it's happened to me. It sucks more than I can relate and leaves you feeling miserable. What follows are two e-mails picked from many that were sent from the very girl who did this to me and, in effect, hurt me, confused me, and damaged me in ways she will never understand nor ever admit to. These were sent a mere *five* days apart. We had barely known each other two weeks.

David:
Will everything be ok....hmmmm, I wish I could tell you for sure. I have never wished more for that proverbial crystal ball. What I can tell you is that I hope with all my heart that it will be. It is not a lack of trust in what I think is possibly the most amazing relationship I have experienced yet in my life, but out of protecting myself from possible hurt and pain should it disappear that makes me say that it is my hope and not my belief. I believe that we potentially have an amazing thing here. I have wanted for so long to have someone who would "get" me and that I would be able rely on and truly let myself go with. Someone who I could talk to for hours on end and have it feel like mere minutes, just aching to pick up the phone and see how they are doing when they aren't with me, hear their voice, feel them in my heart. It scares me now that it could be happening...mostly because I am afraid of it disappearing. I think from our conversations thus far, we will both have to just talk about those things in order to work on it and not let it ruin things. I am still in that dream state and I DON'T WANT TO WAKE UP *smiles* You are right in saying that we need to be patient, smart, and hope for all the luck in the world. I think it will help us save those many hearts that we love so dearly from getting hurt. I think this is the first time in my life that I have been so happy and so incredibly scared at the same time. I want to do things the RIGHT way this time. And I hope to do those things with you....ok, so now who is the silly one?! You or me? How about....just you-n-me!
Stacey

◆   ◆   ◆

David:

You gave me a lot to think about. I promised you one thing last week, which I haven't gone back on….that I would be honest if I felt something, that I would talk about what scares me. I do understand what you are saying, but I have so much on my plate right now (as do you) and I just need to take a step back from it all! I am giving myself the proverbial break I need to clear my head. I am so sorry that you can't understand this. I told you I might need patience or time. I am sorry that you feel so hurt. I had no intention of doing that. I will call you later on. I am going to talk with one of my best friends after I drop off the kids.

Stacey

She didn't call later on. In fact, she didn't call at all. Four days later I received an "e-card" just saying hello from her, after which I never heard from her again. She would not return messages of any sort. There was no fight or disagreement, just a horrifying fear on her part of losing something that she desperately wanted and was indeed getting. So sad. So damn sad.

Freeda went through something similar with one of her guys and became so bitter and resentful, (which is not her way) at the lack of closure or explanation that she decided to set him up for a terrible letdown. (This was discussed in Chapter Seven.) I can't begin to tell you how *nuts* a lack of closure can make people like me. I happen to lay my cards on the table. I happen to be very honest and straightforward. I happen to give my affection very easily to a woman I *feel* something for, and therefore I happen to get hurt pretty easily when she isn't on the same page.

"*Ohhh,*" you say. "You sound *sooo* needy!" Izatafact? I said affection. I didn't say love. There is a *huge* difference between the two. Affection is a required piece of the puzzle in love. Love is not necessarily required to give or receive affection.

My friend Cody is a girl I had just one date with. It was an odd date, (just as she's an odd sort of girl) but she is beautiful and has a personality with the wit to match. We remained friends after the date and e-mail each other with our "relationship stuff" pretty regularly. She is dating a guy right now that she is really nuts about, but he's just beginning the divorce process…so it's dicey. She sent me the following message in response to a note from me.

Hi. Thanks for sending. You're a trip, and I am not ODD!!

Things are a bit better. He signed the retainer and sent it in, so the ball is rolling. We'll see how it goes. I am scared to death. Maybe you're right....maybe I'm afraid to be happy. Talking to my therapist about that very subject today! I think I can handle the happiness…it's this absolute and total fear of losing the happiness that makes me want to avoid it in the first place! Uugggh

So it sounds like you are crazy-busy. I guess that's a good thing. Glad to hear the roommate from hell is gone too. LOL

Talk soon—

Codey

"Absolute and total fear," she said. How the hell do we let ourselves get so screwed up in our relationships that we become so afraid of the loss and thus avoid the happiness? That makes about as much sense as freezing to death in the middle of the forest because you're afraid of getting burned if you build a fire, or rather, being afraid of losing the warmth when the fire dies out. Funny thing though, as I know exactly what she means.

So I'd like to share a bit of wisdom with some of you folks out there, who think they're sooo ready to find the love of their life. Close your eyes and picture the perfect person for you, the person who makes you melt when you're in their arms, the person who makes your knees weak when they kiss you passionately, the person who is giving, caring, loving, and everything you've always sought in a mate but could never find, a person who turns you to jelly when they make love to you. Picture this person and the amazingly strong feelings you'll develop for them over time and ask yourself the most important question in the world. Will you be ready if you meet this person tomorrow? Be honest with yourself and think about this long and hard, because if the answer is not an honest one and they do suddenly appear, you may just lose that one perfect person because the timing was wrong.

What you also need to understand is the tremendous damage you can cause to this wonderful "other" by not being ready and flipping out on them after a week or two, or even worse, a month or more. If they have developed the same feelings for you and you suddenly fall silent, needing "time away," you are being extremely unfair to someone who genuinely cared deeply for you and whom you are now chasing away with your fear.

So my friends, if you're not *completely* sure that you are ready to find the love of your life, then date casually and keep it honest, or you'll hurt some really nice people, most of all yourself.

So you're all upset because you've been dating online for six months now, have made lots of friends, had a few close calls, but no love interest to date. So you're thinking to yourself, "I didn't get into this to make friends! I have enough friends!" And then it happens. You meet "the one." It's perfect. Every moment, every move, every word, look, glance, caress, kiss, hug….possibility…is amazing. For two weeks you are inseparable, insatiable, incorrigible, and then…nothing. No calls, no e-mails, no contact, no closure. You are going out of your mind. You can't think, can't eat, can't work or function in any way. Suddenly, one of those "friends" you thought you didn't care about calls you, listens to you, does not judge you, and literally saves your life.

Never, ever, ever underestimate the power of a caring heart, and pray there is one, or two, or a zillion out there for you when you desperately need them. Linda called me every day for two weeks after the "Stacey" fiasco. She e-mailed me silly messages to cheer me up. She is a dear friend who I cherish more than words can relate, but I think she knows that.

In fact, I'm sure that she does.

Here's a little talk with the boys.

Okay, you guys read that last section. Has the same thing ever happened to you, or have *you* ever done that to a woman?

Swayne:	No, I can't say it has. But if it ever did I'm sure I'd be pretty hurt. I've had some great relationships that went sour for one reason or another, but there was always a closure. A disappearance of that sort would have me climbing the walls.
Brando:	Yes, it has. I suppose you're asking about short term romances that just up and disappear, but I'll have to put Nina into the mix here. I had no clue. I thought we were happy and for her to just do what she did….. don't get me started. On the opposite tack, I have done that to several women. Things started to crop up in their personalities or maybe they just sucked in bed…whatever. I just find it easier to disappear then to try and hash it out and really hurt someone's feelings. It's better this way, easier. Besides, most of them deserve it. They're all manipulative, conniving bitches. If you can't provide the financial status that they expect of you, then they just spit you out and seek their next meal ticket. It's also my experience

that when people are letting go of a relationship, often time they seek to avoid specifics. That is why, well, my personal philosophy is that a good number of us wish to avoid accountability. So if you can just sort of like, let things peter off, or not, or, or, "I just can't be in a relationship anymore." They've made a decision. One or the other person usually makes a decision. They made that decision to themselves, how they take action is…by that individual…for a variety of reasons and they don't always wanna give the reasons. So how do ya say…yeah, usually I would say it's because they're not getting all of their needs and desires fulfilled. People want more.

That was harsh dude!

Brando: I speak the gospel.

Next is a question for the ages. Should you sleep with a person on the first date, and if you do, how will they feel about it the next day? First the guys respond back and forth and then a lengthy conversation with the girls.

Well, how do you feel about sex on the first date?

Brando: If the body is willing, then I'm right there. Why not get the tension outta the way so that you can find out who the person really is? I'm not one to kiss and tell though, and I think the women I've been with would appreciate that.

Swayne: Oh, no way. I've been there too many times and it gets old.

Only if there's no major interest in seeing them again.

Swayne: That's different. If this is a girl who's only into me for one reason…what am I saying…scratch that…I go with my first answer! Call me what you like, but I've done it too often in the past and I'm so done.

Brando: I guess I haven't arrived at your place yet, but Dave's right. I'd be more inclined to be aggressive with a woman who I don't particularly care to see again than one I'd truly like to know more about. On the other hand, if a woman is that aggressive and really pushes me, there's no way I can say no if there's any attraction.

I guess, but I haven't done that in a long time and my last one night stand turned into six months with the same girl. We just really fit sexually and in other ways, but not in all the ways I needed. She was amazing but disappeared as soon as her feelings got deeper for me as she knew it wasn't reciprocated.

Brando:	I've been there.
Swayne:	Me too, just ended something good because the timing was off. I wish I didn't have to travel so damn much.

So do we all agree that you'd be more prone to sleep with someone immediately that you didn't ever see yourself being with long term? I mean, as opposed to someone really cute, smart and nice?

Brando:	Definitely, especially at this point in my life, I need all the strokes I can get! *laughter*
Swayne:	In the past, yes, but something changed recently. I guess what you're *really* asking me is if I want to see a girl again, will I push for sex early? Absolutely not! I would not respect a woman who had sex with me before she even has a clue about who I am.

Me too, Swayne. Something changed this year. In the past...same answer as yours. I just guess I need to feel respect for the girl and a *real* affection before moving on to deeper waters.

Now on to the same conversation with the girls, and lo and behold, check out the answers!

Charley:	I met another guy one night at a cocktail lounge, cuter than cute! He was so handsome, Italian, *really* cute. I wasn't quite sure what he did for a living. He gambled, loved the racetrack, yada yada yada. So we had a few drinks and I walked around the hotel with him. He joked around and said, "Let's go upstairs and get a room," and I said "No waaayy!" Y'know, after the last experience I had with the pool table guy! So he kinda knocked me up against the wall and we started kissing and stuff and things got a little passionate. So we went back to the car to say goodbye as it was getting late, and he kept pushing my hand down on his...his you know what! So I said, "Will you knock it off!" And he's like, "What, what, what? I'm not doin' anything." And he did it again! And I'm like, "I'm not doing this on a first date. There's

just no way!" So he starts with, "Oh, lookit Miss High and Mighty, Self-Respect, Independence here!" Sheesh!

Linda: Wasn't he too pushy though? If he wasn't pushy, you might have been more...

Charley: He was pushy, but then from that point on he took off!

Linda: Then that's all he was looking for.

It *is* all he was looking for.

Linda: When a guy is pushy like that from the beginning for me, that's all they're looking for. You just have to know that going in.

I suppose this was less an interview, and more of a taped chat between three good friends. At this point, the conversation was jumping all over the place, so I intervened since I hadn't gotten the chance to answer their question to me, which was what my feelings were about sex on the first date.

Okay lemme answer...lemme answer...Shaddup! Lemme answer your question first! Um, um, I've had, I dunno maybe five or six one night stands. Um...

Charley: You're sick, SICK!

Stop it! The vast majority, I never saw the girl again, never talked to the girl again.

Linda: Why?

No respect on either side because basically you knew that is was what both of you were looking for and that was it. However, um my last...I wouldn't call her a girlfriend, but I'll say six-month relationship, was with a girl named Racy who my kids still really like, and I do miss. On the first date there was this absolutely mad sexual attraction and we were in bed in my house within maybe two hours of first meeting and it was very interesting and it continued for six months. That's a rarity, and the only reason it continued with her was because there was so much about her personality and her physicality that I liked. That, and the fact that she was getting into me very quickly, that it kind of induced me to find out more about her.

Linda: Right, because you were interested in her, so whether she had sex with you or not on that first night, would that have made a difference? You still would have been interested in her!

Yeah. Yeah, it really, it wouldn't have made a difference to me, but in all the others...and it's funny and this is very, very true. I would be more prone to have sex with a woman on a first date that I like less and that I'm less attracted to than a woman that I'm very attracted to, who I like a lot because I'll probably give her more respect...

Linda: And that's why you and I never had sex, never actually had intercourse.

Because I liked you a lot.

Linda: Right.

Okay.

Charley: Never have!?

Linda: No, we never had sex.

Everything short of, but...no...literally everything short of.

Charley: Why don't you two just get it over with!

Both: SHUT UP!

laughter

We'd probably kill each other, we already know, but, um, it's true that, and I've discussed this with the guys, if it's a girl that's pretty attractive, who you absolutely don't ever see yourself being with long term, but she's open to screwing on a first date? You're gonna do it! You're absolutely gonna do it with her because you don't care how she feels about you...

Linda: But you'll know that by the way they react, if that's all. If they're pushing, touching, y'know, if they're that forward and you can see that it's what they really want. Then you know that. If you're up for that, fine, but if you're not up for that then you need to say no.

Like my first date with both of you was very...It was touchy-feely. It was cute, it was fun, it was something where you knew there was gonna be a continuance and I would never have tried to induce either one of you to go to bed with me on the first date.

Linda: Well David, the kids were there! Hahahahaha!

Well besides that! But with Charley they weren't and I was close to home, but I wouldn't have either way because there was enough of a physical attraction and there was enough of an "I like this girl" that it just wasn't something that just jumped right into my mind.

Charley: So the answer to the question is don't ever have sex on a first date with a guy?

No. I would say, and most of my male friends would say never, never have sex on the first date because a man will not respect you, because if he respected you he wouldn't be asking you for sex on a first date...at all...I know I wouldn't. If a woman put across every kinda vibe...I have pulled back from women on first dates who were more aggressive than me, believe it or not...

Both girls: NOT!

No, really! Sometimes it ended up being in a relationship. You would not have believed how aggressive Anna was on our first date! She was straddling me in my truck.

Linda: David, I have neighbors you know.

We were outside during this interview.

In the middle of the night...The windows were so fogged up, okay, and this was a *very* successful, almost unapproachable woman that had millionaires chasing after her, and here she was humping me in my truck! Okay, and although we were together shortly thereafter, on the first date it was just cutesy, cutesy heavy petting. Because I liked her and I respected her and I knew that I wanted a continuance, so I wasn't gonna disrespect her with sex.

Linda: So you can play a little but you can't have inter-course.

You can play a lot but you can't have intercourse. And it's funny too, because girls that I have liked, where we just let it go too far on a first or second date, um, especially second dates where it's just gone *waayy* too far, and maybe it wasn't as good as you thought it was gonna be...it ended right there, because maybe you're nervous and if it's the second date and you kinda like somebody and the sex sucks? It's over. That's it. There's no more, you don't even wanna talk to them. It's just not gonna happen again. Maybe they're just nervous and maybe they're just not ready, and y'know for a guy, maybe he just won't get it up as hard as normal. For a girl, maybe she just won't get as wet, she's over-reacting or over-compensating orally 'cause that can happen too, and hurts you, y'know, and there's a million things...and maybe something that could've been good...and I've been very guilty of this. I have pushed it too well because I've got certain skills, y'know, that women like and y'know.... STOP IT!!!

laughter, snickers, coy female faces

Come on, I don't have to pat myself on the back, you both know. Shut up! But when you can convince somebody to go a direction that maybe

they were thinking of, but they kinda wanted to be "pulled" that way a little bit, and it's too soon, you can screw it up really quickly with sex, especially when it's not where you thought it was gonna go. I don't know if this has ever happened to either one of you, where you've been with somebody and it's just been horrible and it's over for you?

Linda: Uh huh. See now, I had a date though, an Internet date with a guy I dated a few times. This guy really raked me over the coals! Not that I fell in love with him, but I really thought we were connecting. We had gone out on one or two dates and we started out with having a drink, but we decided we got along, so we'd go shoot some pool or something.

Charley: Ohhh, *pooolll* *laughter*

Linda: Y'know, and that's always like a good way to have a date. You sit and you can converse, but you're *doing* something, so if you can do something simple like that, that's not terribly physical, you can talk and you can goof up and it doesn't matter!

Charley: I had a pool date once!

Both: Shut up!

Linda: So we had a couple of dates and they went really well and…we kissed…that was as far as it went, and we kissed. I mean we kissed for like *two hours* we kissed! I guess maybe the third time we went out I went over to his apartment, but now that night nothing was gonna happen because…Mother Nature had given me the whammy! So I knew I wasn't going there…

Didn't stop us.

Charley: Ewwww!

Linda: *blushing* Well yeah, but that was the end of it anyway! So um, he knew that going in and like, y'know, I know that you're home alone tonight and your roommate's not in and that's cool but I gotta tell you…because we had *talked* about it, about finally getting together and doing something and um, it's not gonna happen because I can't! So we wound up in bed that night doing all kinds of fun things! It was the most passionate night I'd had in such a long time because we were in bed and we were both totally naked and…touching, kissing, being very like, affectionate and passionate, but he wouldn't even let me finish him off! "I, I won't! If I can't bring you there then I don't want you to bring me there." We spent *hours* like that, which was unbelievable! I mean, I walked outta there and I was like, "Huh-huh-uh-uh-uh,"…trembling! And then the next date he was at my house and we were watching a movie and we wound up in the bedroom and, y'know, we actually initiated it and actually had sex, but he, um, he had this thing where it happened very quickly for him…. It happened *twice* in an hour! But very quickly for him, and I never heard from him after that.

He was embarrassed

Linda: I think so too.

Very disappointing for both of you. He was very embarrassed because he came so quick, and you know what? It's happened to me.

Both girls: Nooo, not *yoouuu*! **hysterical laughter**

Not a lot, but it has happened to me. Sometimes it's just emotional and you really never know exactly why it happens. I think it happens to a lot of guys.

Linda: Yeah, and I didn't even make a big deal out of it. I was like…

You didn't have to because he did.

Linda: Yeah, he did, and that was that! We went out on a date maybe six months later. Just went out, played pool, kissed, and that was that. I never ever heard from him again. I don't know if it was his embarrassment about it or, I dunno. It must have been? And that was it. That was done.

How very complicated we all make it for each other. We're searching, chasing, catching and running away all at the same time! Why don't we seem to be able to make up our minds? We have such advanced technological tools at our disposal, which should make finding love as easy as picking a flower in a garden. So why is it so difficult? Why are there so many unfulfilled people out there looking year after year, jumping from dating site to dating site, from bed to bed, relationship to relationship, and in all their haste missing time and again what they so desperately desire?

Brando touches on a bit of what I think the answer might be. Well, one possible answer anyway.

I've met a few nice people in this cyber thing, but they haven't been lasting relationships. I think there's a downside. If someone were to do a really scientific study of online dating and meeting and how long those relationships last, as opposed to how long relationships last for people that were more local or already of a community, y'know the traditional way? I don't think they last as long! And I think that people are restless and they're just saying, "Well, this isn't so great. I think I can get better. Lemme see what else is out there. Uh, all right, he's an okay guy, but I think I can get better."

So everybody's doing this business of "How high can I trade up? What am I really worth on the market? Gee, if I can get that guy maybe I can get a different guy. Who else can I get?" And guys are always like, "Well, I wanna get a more beautiful girl, or one that doesn't nag me as much, or one that gives me better head." I dunno. So there's a lot of...restlessness, this mobility in short term, and I dunno where it's leading to, but it seems to spell trouble for the integrity of families and communities.

Used to be the idea that with computer dating and stuff, they were looking for spouses. They're looking for people that have the right qualifications to be the type of person you'd marry. You're looking for marriageable qualities. I think there's still some of that, but a lot less. I think that most of these dating sites...isn't about people looking for marriageable partners, just looking for someone with enough acceptable, and a minimum of unacceptable qualities that they can say, "I agree to be seen with you." How mercenary can you get?

So, as far as Internet dating is concerned, even though it's less than perfect, there's always something you can learn. We learn about ourselves. We learn from the conversations that are going on in our lives. We learn about what's going on for other people because all in all, every encounter is another human being. It's another potential person that has interest. We all have our story. We all have certain qualities, unique aspects that we bring to the table, and I contend that there is something to be learned, everywhere.

If you're a hopeful or optimistic person, as I hope anyone is who says, "I'm gonna go online. I'm gonna put my thing out there, because I'm hoping someone's gonna go, 'Oh! That's an interesting person. I think that I should talk to them.'" So there has to be hope or optimism for the future, and a great sense of "I don't know. I don't know if this is gonna work, I don't know what this chemistry is, I don't know how it's gonna be if we ever do get in bed, if it's gonna be any good. But I will continue to play along until it's clear that either this is a dead end path, or, or, or, something else comes along."

We go along, we take risks. You risk spending time, money, energy and it's not predictable, it's not a predictable outcome, how it's gonna go. You can't force things to go a certain way because you would prefer or like or want it that way. It becomes an exercise of going with the flow, being in conversations, directing things towards either knowing a person better, or saying, "Been good getting to know you, but I really just don't feel there's anything for us here. Y'know, stay in touch if you'd like but I'm staying in Connecticut, have a good time wherever you are!"

So guys, you want to know what women want? You want to see how their little wonderful minds work? You want get some perspective into their inner workings? You want the secret to the age-old question, "What did I do anyway?" You want to see how they answer the same questions? Read this next chat and you'll better understand why we'll *never* figure them out!

The two of them cut each other off in conversation so often that, well, this is as close to everything that was actually said as I can get. Man, get two girls talking about men and…well, you'll see.

What was your mindset when you went online for the first time?

Charley: I was in a relationship that was going sour and I just wanted to wait through the holidays before I broke up with him. I know that's dumb, but timing is everything and I'm polite! So we got through the holidays and I put my profile online thinking, "What the heck, let me try." I'd heard good and bad, but mostly good, so I went online and started e-mailing back and forth and, um, it's definitely a lot easier to e-mail. After a few e-mails you know if you're gonna hit it off or not with a person. Actually, after the first phone call you kinda know.

Linda: If he has a bad voice, forget it!

Charley: I mean, seeing a picture is one thing, that helps, y'know? But, um, and that's why I guess meeting him for the first date for coffee or for drinks and not for dinner…because an hour is a long time to sit with someone that you don't wanna sit with! The phone is definitely the ice breaker 'cause you're more relaxed when you finally do meet them in person…

Linda: Because it's not as scary.

Charley: Because you know the person already, a little background. At least you can ask more questions, y'know, like, "So how're your kids, what'd ya do with your kids this weekend."…ya know.

Linda: You know a little bit about them because you've read about them and you've had some conversation, but when you meet somebody in a bar or meet anywhere else ya know…how do you strike up a conversation? Waddaya say? "Hey, what are you drinking?" I mean, how interesting is that? But if you have something else to talk about, the conversation will flow a little bit and then you can see if you're compatible.

How important is information in the profile to you? I mean, if they write next to nothing? 'Cause I know that even if a girl is drop dead gorgeous, but she writes two sentences in her profile and there's four misspellings in there, I'm moving on! Y'know, I'm just not gonna contact her because I know I'm not compatible with this woman no matter what she looks like. So how important is the written word in their profile to you?

Charley: Very important. I mean that's what they are, and if they write very little…I mean, what really gets me mad is the good looking guys that'll have the profile that they just kinda type any key on the keyboard, just go, "Blah blah blah," and they really don't say anything to just kinda keep themselves a mystery…which I hate!

Linda: There are some people that just don't know how to write. I can accept that too, but what I do is look at their preferences. Y'know, like, I'm not a skinny person and guys who want like, slender, I'm not gonna respond to them. What, to get shot down? Although that's what *you* wrote ya big mouth! *chuckles* He was all about, "They have to look like this, and they have to have this, and they have to have that," and I'm like, "David, I am not the one for you!" I mean, if we get along, fine, but I'm not the one for you because I am not that little statue that you're painting, I am *not* that!

But we agreed on that pretty much going in, and y'know, we played a little and we had our fun and now we're buddies. And remember, you BS artist, that *you* contacted *me* first!

Linda: Right!

And that's a success story to me.

Linda: Right. But normally I won't respond to somebody who specifically puts those kinda things in, because I'm not about the physical things. I mean you have to have some kind of an attraction, but a guy doesn't have to be good looking for me to dig his personality and see beneath the surface into the parts I might wanna spend a lifetime with.

Then you're rare because women are not that way, not anymore, not nowadays.

Charley:	After their looks? I'm *mostly* after their looks! First (pause) they have to be a good looking guy. I've always been after the good looks. Always been after the good looks and that's where I've gotten myself in a lot of trouble, because the good-looking ones are always the assholes.

HEY!

Charley:	Now I'm going for good-looking, but not like *sooo* good-looking, because they end up being all stuck up and…
Linda:	You see, to me that doesn't matter. I mean, in my profile I always say a guy is from "skinny" to y'know, "average." I don't want a huge guy, y'know, I don't wanna have him *die* when we're having sex! *laughter*I mean, I don't want that, but the physical thing does not matter as much to me, and that's another thing, when you finally meet that person and you get to see them, when they talk and you watch the expressions on their face, y'know, like see them smile. That's when you get to know what somebody's about. I mean they can talk great on the phone and they can type real great on the Internet, but when you meet somebody and you can look in their eyes and they can have conversation with you and their face isn't all distorted in a weird way looking like they're lying, y'know? Then ya know that, y'know, that they're like okay, and maybe you'll have a second date with them if you guys hit it off.
Charley:	You said if the guy looks into your eyes and talks to you?
Linda:	If his eyes are that expressive and tells you something, then *that's* the attraction.
Charley:	I think their personality makes them better looking, if it ever comes out. If they're a nice and funny person…they might not be gorgeous, but after the first date and after spending that first amount of time, they get better looking as you talk to them. Their mannerisms, their cuteness, just the way they present themselves, the way they carry themselves. Y'know, they become cuter as the time passes. You've done pretty well for yourself! *laughing* and it's not just because you look okay. I mean, you sweep a girl away

with all that you are, that so many don't have about them, y'know?

Was that supposed to be a compliment?

Linda: You know what she means David.

Charley: Yeah, get over yourself!

Two against one is not fair!

Linda: You should be so lucky! Yeah, you start talking to some of these guys and you get totally turned off. I had a 34 year old sitting at a bar one night with me, and we were talking and stuff and he was all fine and we were, "Yack yack yack," and this guy was like *so* into me, and the more he talked, the uglier he got! I mean, he was adorable, he was 34 and it'd be great for my ego to have you on my arm, but you're a schmuck! Y'know? I don't care how good-looking you are, it doesn't matter.

Charley: I talked to some guy the other day that, um, we started seeing each other when he was separated from his wife, and then he went back to her and we talk once in a while and that's it. We still get kinda a little worked up when we talk to each other because we were together when they were separated. So he was stuttering the other day on the phone, which I thought was the cutest thing, and he got so embarrassed, he's like "Oh my God, what an asshole I am!" He's like "I'm stuttering, I'm so embarrassed" and I think that was so cute because he was getting so nervous.

Linda: Because that's honesty. When a guy can be honest, that's very attractive. When a guy has all the lines and knows exactly what to say to you, it's not, y'know…

Charley: "Oh, I'm stuttering right now. I need coffee; I can't even drive and talk to you."

Linda: No, when they have to cover their ass then that's not attractive. I almost like them when they're a little more vulnerable. Not because I wanna take advantage of that, but because that shows me that they're real. A guy that's like, so plastic, ugh! You could be an Adonis, I don't care! I know I don't wanna date a guy that's prettier than I am!

So this went on and on for quite a while. The thing that I find interesting is that early on, Charley was all about the looks, but when Linda took the high ground, Charley seemed to cave in and agree with her. And women wonder why we don't understand them! Sheesh!

So here I sit after listening to the last words spoken on the last interview tape from the last of my friends, agonizing about a wondrous way to end this book. Linda and Charley are both in relationships that I can only describe as "biding their time," which is a shame, as I know the depths of passion that both these women are capable of, depths that are not being met presently.

Swayne is dating, but only casually, and so is Brando, who is really screwed up right now and describes himself as "toxic relationship material." Freeda has all but given up and seems at peace with the total love of her life, that being her new puppy! Anna is Anna, and seems happy in her new marriage, although getting her to discuss it is like pulling teeth. I wonder why? I hope it's nothing…. I really do, as few deserve happiness more than she.

It's Fathers Day, 2004. I spent a glorious day running all over Rockland County, New York with my kids. Their mom and I seem to be getting along swimmingly for some time now, and although this was not my weekend with them, it was perfectly fine with her for them to spend today with me. She delivered them to me about 11:15 this morning and I made them a quick breakfast. The phone rang and I went into the bedroom, wondering who could be calling me on a Sunday morning. Well, I'm a storyteller, so how better to end this book that with another one of my tales?

Three weeks ago, I resigned my membership at Match.com. My research was long over and, not having met the girl of my dreams, I just decided to go on hiatus since I really wasn't dating much anyway this year. I received two final e-mails from women, both from New York.

The first was a 47-year-old cutie from Brooklyn, who after several one-sided conversations, I just decided was not for me. She was not pleased. The second was a 41-year-old brunette from the Bronx! A local girl! Her photos were not that attractive to me, but her e-mails were wonderful, and after speaking to her on the phone the first time, (for four and a half hours) I was hooked.

We had so much in common that it was almost uncanny. We talked for two more nights and met for coffee this past Thursday. She kept me waiting for almost thirty minutes, but when she walked in it was well worth the wait. She was perhaps only the third girl in three years of dating that totally and completely blew away her photos online. This was her first date, so she was very nervous. She was so adorable that I became very nervous. We seemed to get through it though, and became comfortable and slightly snuggly by the end of two and a half hours together. She needed to go tuck in her child by 10:00 pm at her mom's, so I walked her to her car. I gave her a tiny kiss on the mouth and then pulled away. Not the passionate sort of date that I'd had with Anna, or Charley, or a plethora of other women, but I had a feeling about this one and did not want to rush anything.

So the phone rings and I pick it up, and it's her. She's just calling to wish me a happy Father's Day and to have a blast with my kids...and I'm floored. We just had the one date, like she had nothing better to do? I thanked her sincerely, spoke pleasantly for a few minutes as her daughter whacked herself in the eye with a toy she was swinging and hung up the phone. I have not stopped thinking about her since.

Will she be the one? Will this be my final success story in another book? I don't know, but that's the point. That's why we're all here, for the hope, the dream, and the fantasy of everlasting happiness with that one person whom you cannot possibly live without.

This is what I wish for every dear person reading my words. I wish it for myself, and my children, and all those who have crossed my path in the past years who are now friends, confidantes and acquaintances. I wish it for a world that seems to be teetering towards a precipice that may engulf us all. I wish, I envision, I embark, I conquer, and I win.

May you all win your inner battles, and in so doing win your war. I love you all.

...me...just me...=)

0-595-66629-9

www.ingramcontent.com/pod-product-compliance
Lightning Source LLC
LaVergne TN
LVHW091942060326
832903LV00049B/276/J